四川外国语大学教材建设基金资助项目
（2025年资助）

Chinese Classics:
Selected Readings (Second Edition)

中国文化经典选读（第二版）

张婷 夏歆东 主编

北京大学出版社
PEKING UNIVERSITY PRESS

图书在版编目(CIP)数据

中国文化经典选读：英、汉 / 张婷，夏歆东主编. -- 2版. -- 北京：北京大学出版社，2025.8. -- ISBN 978-7-301-36561-8

Ⅰ.K203

中国国家版本馆CIP数据核字第2025M4II086号

书　　　名	中国文化经典选读（第二版）
	ZHONGGUO WENHUA JINGDIAN XUANDU (DI-ER BAN)
著作责任者	张　婷　夏歆东　主编
责任编辑	李　娜
标准书号	ISBN 978-7-301-36561-8
出版发行	北京大学出版社
地　　　址	北京市海淀区成府路205号　100871
网　　　址	http://www.pup.cn　　新浪微博：@北京大学出版社
电子邮箱	编辑部 zpupwaiwen@pup.cn　　总编室 zpup@pup.cn
电　　　话	邮购部 010-62752015　发行部 010-62750672　编辑部 010-62759634
印　刷　者	河北滦县鑫华书刊印刷厂
经　销　者	新华书店
	787毫米×1092毫米　16开本　16印张　430千字
	2017年10月第1版
	2025年8月第2版　2025年8月第1次印刷
定　　　价	48.00元

未经许可，不得以任何方式复制或抄袭本书之部分或全部内容。
版权所有，侵权必究
举报电话：010-62752024　电子邮箱：fd@pup.cn
图书如有印装质量问题，请与出版部联系，电话：010-62756370

第二版前言

在全球化的广阔浪潮中，文化的交流与融合已成为一股不可阻挡的时代洪流。面对这一历史性的趋势，我国提出的"中国文化走出去"战略，为英语专业的人才培养设立了新的标杆。新时代的英语专业人才，不仅要精通英语语言的艺术，更要深刻理解和把握中国文化的精髓，以便在国际舞台上精准、生动地讲述中国故事，传播中国声音，展现中国风采。正是基于这样的需求与愿景，我们精心编撰了《中国文化经典选读（第二版）》，旨在培养一批批具有国际视野、文化自信以及卓越跨文化沟通能力的英语专业精英。

本教材的编纂紧密围绕当前国际文化交流的新趋势与国内人才培养的实际需求展开。我们的目标是通过这本书，使学生在掌握扎实的英语语言技能的同时，能够深入钻研并理解中国的思想传统，洞悉中国传统经典文化如何对西方现代化进程及当今全球化格局产生深远影响。进而，我们致力于培养学生的跨文化沟通能力与国际传播素养，为他们成为未来文化交流的桥梁奠定坚实基础。

这本教材不仅原汁原味地展示了中国文化经典的原典文本，还精心搜集并编撰了现当代学者对中国文化的深刻解读与品鉴材料，旨在凸显中国文化在漫长历史中对世界文化发展所留下的独特印记。特别值得一提的是，中国近现代著名的民主革命家与国学大师章太炎先生（1869—1936）。他生前坚持将严谨的考据与深邃的哲思相结合，致力于重新发掘中国传统思想文化之"特别的长处"，坚决反对简单以西方哲学框架来解读和评判中国思想。章太炎先生的这一深刻见解，对于当今我们思考"英语专业"学生应秉持的学术追求、面对"多元化价值"在全球动荡中面临的挑战，以及如何在百年未有之大变局中充分发挥传统学术与文化优势，都具有极为宝贵的启示作用。

正是基于挖掘和突出中国传统思想之"特别的长处"，《中国文化经典选读（第二版）》在原有基础上，进一步扩展并精选了《易经》《论语》《孟子》《道德经》《庄子》《心经》《金刚经》和《坛经》等中国传统文化经典中的核心篇章，确保学生能够准确把握经典文本的原意和精神。

同时，为了拓宽学生的国际视野，教材特别引入了多位国内外知名学者的研究成果与评论。在第一章中，英国汉学家理查德·拉特对《周易》独特魅力进行了深刻剖析，20世纪瑞士心理学家卡尔·古斯塔夫·荣格在其为《易经》撰写的序言中挖掘了这本经典于现代心理学的价值，此外，当代《易经》翻译家杰弗里·雷德蒙关于《易经》与西方战后早期反文化运动关联的独特见解，展现了这部中国古老经典对现代性的影响。第二章选编了由中西比较哲学家安乐哲撰写的《儒家自然宇宙论》，以及美国儒学研究者艾文荷为伊莱娜·布鲁姆译《孟子》所作的序言，这些材料为学生提供了深入理解儒家思想及其全球影响力的宝贵资源。此外，教材还拓展了丰富的跨文化视角：D篇《人类与社会》选自约翰·诺布洛克编译的《荀子》，为我们呈现了儒家关于社会伦理与治理的深刻见解。而E篇《孔子——良善治者》，由美国当代学者威廉·阿普尔顿撰写，从现代视角出发，探讨了孔子思想对于良善治理的启示。此外，F篇《儒家思想与英国浪漫主义时期的政治思想》由英国当今学者克里斯·默里撰写，进一步揭示了儒家思想如何跨越国界，对西方浪漫主义时期的政治思想产生深远影响。第三章首先选编了美国汉学家安乐哲与郝大维合著的《哲学导论：关联宇宙学——一个解释性背景》，该篇深入探讨了道家哲学特别是庄子思想的"创造性"，为我们提供了一个理解宇宙万物相互关联的新视角。此外，当今学者伊丽莎白·哈珀在《早期现代欧洲对〈庄子〉文本的（不）接受》中，细致分析了庄子思想在欧洲早期现代社会的传播与接受情况，揭示了东西方文化碰撞下的思想火花。C篇《一位中国圣人》则以19世纪爱尔兰著名作家奥斯卡·王尔德的独特视角，高度赞誉了庄子思想的深邃与智慧，展现了这位中国古代哲人对浪漫主义运动的吸引力，彰显中国古代思想跨越时空的魅力与影响力。第四章拓展性材料包括赤松所著的《〈心经〉的历史背景》、现象学学者长友繁法对《金刚经》逻辑的独到分析、马克瑞对禅宗法脉的新视角审视。这些材料不仅揭示了佛教经典的深厚底蕴，也展现了其在现代社会的价值与意义。最后一章则从中国文化的总体特质方面选编了学者们的经典篇目，包括：普林斯顿大学东亚系奠基人牟复礼所撰的《中国认识论的内涵》；辜鸿铭的《中国人的精神》，该文深刻揭示了中华文化的精神内核；英国当代汉学家苏立文对中国绘画与书法等艺术遗产的精妙论述；奥利弗·哥德史密斯对中国园林艺术的赞美，这些篇目都从世界文化的广阔视野为学生提供了重新认识中国文化的契机，不仅为教学内容增添了深度，也为学生提供了多角度的思考和讨论空间。

  本教材采用中英文平行呈现的编排方式，这不仅方便学生对照学习，更有助于他们在语言对比中发现文化差异，理解文化意涵，提高语言运用的灵活性和准确性。在练习部分，我们设立了大量思辨性问题，鼓励学生主动解读古代文本，探索其在当代社会的应用价值，培养他们的批判性思维和创新能力。通过引入不同文化背景下的学者观点，本教材拓宽了学生的国际视野，增进了他们对多元文化的理解和尊重。此外，教材还深入挖掘文本的哲学和伦理内涵，激发学生的思考与探索，促进他们道德情操和智慧思维的培养。

  在编撰本教材两版的过程中，我们深感荣幸地获得了四川外国语大学英语学院及北京大学出版社的鼎力支持。特别值得一提的是四川外国语大学深耕比较文学领域的张旭春教授。他不仅是本项目启动的灵感源泉，更在编写过程中担任了启发者、引导者与核心指导者的角色。英语学院的赵永峰院长始终给予教材编写以热情鼓励与坚定支持，他的关怀与指导为团队注入了持续的动力。北京大学出版社外语编辑部刘文静主任为本教材提供了专业而细致的指导，编辑李娜女士更是以严谨的态度和精益求精的精神为本书的完善付出了巨大努力。在此，我们衷心地向所有为此付出辛勤努力与无私奉献的同仁表达最诚挚的感谢。

我们深知，尽管编者已竭尽全力，教材中仍可能存在不足之处。因此，我们恳请各位同行和广大读者提出宝贵的意见和建议，共同为提高英语专业人才培养质量，推动中国文化的国际传播而努力。这是一次大胆的尝试，也是一次深入的探索，我们期待与各位一起，为促进文化交流与理解，为构建人类命运共同体贡献力量。

Preface to the Second Edition

In the vast tide of globalization, cultural exchange and integration have become an unstoppable historical trend. Faced with this trend, the "Chinese Culture Going Global" strategy proposed by our country has set a new benchmark for the training of English majors. English professionals in the new era must not only master the art of the English language but also deeply understand and grasp the essence of Chinese culture, so as to accurately and vividly narrate Chinese stories, spread the voice of China, and showcase Chinese elegance on the international stage. It is based on such needs and visions that we have carefully compiled *Selected Readings of Chinese Cultural Classics* (Second Edition), aiming to cultivate a group of English professionals with an international perspective, cultural confidence, and excellent cross-cultural communication skills.

The compilation of this teaching material closely revolves around the new trends of international cultural exchange and the actual needs of domestic talent training. Our goal is to enable students to not only master solid English language skills but also to delve into and understand the intellectual traditions of China, and to understand how traditional Chinese culture has had a profound impact on the modernization process of the West and today's globalized world. Subsequently, we are committed to cultivating students' cross-cultural communication skills and international communication literacy, laying a solid foundation for them to become bridges for future cultural exchanges.

This teaching material not only presents the original texts of Chinese cultural classics in their original flavor but also carefully collects and compiles in-depth interpretations and appreciations of Chinese culture by modern scholars, highlighting the unique mark that Chinese culture has left in the development of world modern culture throughout its long history. It is particularly worth mentioning that Mr. Zhang Taiyan (1869—1936), a famous modern Chinese democratic revolutionary and master of Chinese studies, insisted on combining rigorous textual research with profound philosophy to re-explore the "special strengths" of traditional Chinese thought and culture, and was firmly opposed to simply using Western philosophical frameworks to interpret and judge Chinese thought. Mr. Zhang Taiyan's profound insights offer valuable guidance for us today as we consider the academic aspirations that "English majors" should uphold. They provide insight into addressing the challenges that "diversified values" encounter amidst global instability, and suggest ways to leverage the strengths of traditional scholarship and culture during unprecedented times of change.

Based on the exploration and highlighting of the "special strengths" of traditional Chinese thought, *Selected Readings of Chinese Cultural Classics* (Second Edition) has further expanded and carefully selected core chapters from traditional Chinese cultural classics such as the *Book of Changes*, the *Analects*, the *Mencius*, *Dao De Jing*, *Zhuangzi*, *Heart Sutra*, *Diamond Sutra*, and *Sutra Spoken by the Sixth Patriarch*, ensuring that students can accurately grasp the original meaning and spirit of the classic texts.

At the same time, in order to broaden the international perspective of students, the teaching material specially introduces research results and comments by well-known Chinese and Western scholars. In the first chapter, the British sinologist Richard Rutt deeply analyzes the unique charm of *Zhouyi*, the 20th-century Swiss psychologist Carl Gustav Jung explores the value of this classic in modern psychology in the preface he wrote for the classic. In addition, the contemporary translator of the *Yijing*, Geoffrey Redmond's unique insights on the connection between the *Yijing* and the post-war counter-culture movement in the West show the influence of this ancient Chinese classic on modernity.

The second chapter selects "Confucian Natural Cosmology: An Interpretive Context" written by Roger T. Ames, the comparative philosopher of China and the West, and the preface written by the contemporary American Confucian scholar Ivanhoe for the translation of *Mencius* by Elena Blum, which provides students with valuable resources for in-depth understanding of Confucian thought and its global influence. In addition, the teaching material also expands a rich cross-cultural perspective; "Man and Society" is selected from *Xunzi——A Translation and Study of the Complete Works* compiled by John Knoblock, presenting the profound insights of Confucianism on social ethics and governance. And "Confucius, The Good Governor," written by the contemporary American scholar William Appleton, starts from a modern perspective to explore the inspiration of Confucius's thought for good governance. In addition, "Confucianism and the Politics of Romantic Britain," written by the contemporary British scholar Chris Murray, further reveals how Confucian thought has crossed borders and had a profound impact on the political thought of the Western Romantic period.

The third chapter selects "Philosophical Introduction: Correlative Cosmology—An Interpretive Context" co-authored by the American sinologist Roger T. Ames and David L. Hall, which deeply explores the "creativity" of Taoist philosophy, especially Zhuangzi's thought, providing us with a new perspective for understanding the interconnection of all things in the universe. In addition, the contemporary scholar Elizabeth Harper in "The Early Modern European (Non) Reception of the Zhuangzi Text" carefully analyzes the dissemination and acceptance of

Preface to the Second Edition

Zhuangzi's thought in early modern European society, revealing the ideological sparks under the collision of Eastern and Western cultures. "A Chinese Sage" praises the profound and wise Zhuangzi's thought from the unique perspective of the famous 19th-century Irish writer Oscar Wilde, showing the attractiveness of this ancient Chinese philosopher to the Romantic movement and highlighting the charm and influence of ancient Chinese thought across time and space.

The fourth chapter's extensive readings include "Historical Background of the *Heart Sutra*" by Red Pine, the unique analysis of the logic of the *Diamond Sutra* by phenomenological scholar Shigenori Nagatomo, and John R. McRae's new perspective on the examination of Chan Buddhism, which not only reveals the profound heritage of Buddhist classics but also shows their value and significance in modern society.

The last chapter compiles classic articles from scholars on the overall characteristics of Chinese culture, including "Implications of Chinese Epistemololgy" by Frederick W. Mote; *The Spirit of the Chinese People* by Gu Hongming, which profoundly reveals the spiritual core of Chinese culture; the British contemporary sinologist Michael Sullivan's exquisite discussion on the Chinese art heritage, such as painting and calligraphy; Oliver Goldsmith's praise for Chinese garden art. These articles all provide students with the opportunity to re-understand Chinese culture from the broad perspective of world culture, adding depth to the teaching content and providing students with a multi-angle space for thinking and discussion.

This textbook uses a parallel presentation of Chinese and English, which not only facilitates students' comparative learning but also helps them to discover cultural differences in language comparison, understand cultural meanings, and improve the flexibility and accuracy of language use. In the exercise part, we have set up a large number of speculative problems to encourage students to actively interpret ancient texts, explore their application value in contemporary society, and cultivate their critical thinking and innovative abilities. By introducing the views of scholars from different cultural backgrounds, this teaching material broadens the international perspective of students and enhances their understanding and respect for multiculturalism. In addition, the teaching material deeply explores the philosophical and ethical connotations of the texts, stimulating students' thinking and exploration, and promoting the cultivation of their moral sentiments and intellectual thinking.

In the process of compiling the two editions of this textbook, we are deeply honored to have received the strong support from the School of English at Sichuan International Studies University and Peking University Press. A special mention must be made of Professor Zhang Xuchun from Sichuan International Studies University, a distinguished scholar in the field of comparative literature. He not only served as the inspiration for the initiation of this project but also played the roles of mentor, guide, and core advisor throughout the compilation process.

Professor Zhao Yongfeng, Dean of the School of English, provided unwavering encouragement and steadfast support for the textbook's development, and his care and guidance infused the team with sustained motivation. Ms. Liu Wenjing, Director of the Foreign Language Editorial Department at Peking University Press, offered professional and meticulous guidance for this textbook. Ms. Li Na, the editor, demonstrated rigorous attention to detail and a commitment to excellence, contributing immensely to the refinement of this work. Here, we would like to extend our sincerest gratitude to all colleagues who have dedicated their hard work and selfless efforts to this endeavor.

We are well aware that although the editors have done their best, there may still be shortcomings in the teaching material. Therefore, we sincerely ask for valuable opinions and suggestions from colleagues and readers to jointly improve the quality of English major talent training and promote the international dissemination of Chinese culture. This is a bold attempt and a deep exploration, and we look forward to working with you to promote cultural exchange and understanding, and contribute to the construction of a community with a shared future for mankind.

Contents

Chinese Culture and Thoughts: A Historical Overview 1

Timeline of Chinese Culture and Thought 8

Chapter One　The *Book of Changes*: A Treasure of Chinese Intellectual History and Its Impact on 20th-Century Western World 9

　　Selections from the *Book of Changes*《易经》选篇 14

　　Extensive Readings 47

　　　A. The Fascination of *Zhouyi*《周易》的魅力 47

　　　B. Foreword to *I Ching*《易经》序言 51

　　　C. The *Yijing* in Early Postwar Counterculture in the West
　　　　《易经》与西方战后早期反文化运动 53

　　Exercises 60

Chapter Two　Confucianism: Historical Context, Core Tenets, and Global Influences ... 63

　　Selections from the *Analects*《论语》选篇 66

　　Selections from the *Mencius*《孟子》选篇 73

　　Extensive Readings 79

　　　A. Confucius《史记·孔子世家》选段 79

　　　B. Confucian Natural Cosmology: An Interpretive Context 儒家自然宇宙论 84

　　　C. Introduction to the *Mencius*《孟子》序言 90

　　　D. Man and Society 人类与社会 95

　　　E. Confucius, The Good Governor 孔子——良善治者 101

　　　F. Confucianism and the Politics of Romantic Britain
　　　　儒家思想与英国浪漫主义时期的政治思想 107

　　Exercises 113

Chapter Three Philosophical Daoism: Its Enduring Legacy and Contemporary Relevance 116

Selections from *Dao De Jing*《道德经》选篇 118
Selections from *Chuang Tzu*《庄子》选篇 125
Extensive Readings 144
   A. Daoist Correlative Cosmology 道家关联宇宙学 144
   B. The Early Modern European (Non) Reception of the Zhuangzi Text
      早期现代欧洲对《庄子》文本的（不）接受 152
   C. A Chinese Sage 一位中国圣人 161
Exercises 166

Chapter Four Essential Sutras and Chan Teachings—Exploring the Heart of Buddhist Wisdom 168

The Heart Sutra《心经》 170
Selections from *The Diamond Sutra*《金刚经》选篇 171
Selections from *Sutra Spoken by the Sixth Patriarch*《坛经》选篇 175
Extensive Readings 186
   A. Historical Background of the *Heart Sutra*《心经》的历史背景 186
   B. The Logic of the *Diamond Sutra*: A is not A, therefore it is A
      《金刚经》的逻辑：A 则非 A 190
   C. Looking at Lineage: A Fresh Perspective on Chan Buddhism 201
      审视法脉：理解禅宗的新视角 201
Exercises 213

Chapter Five The Diverse Intellectual Landscapes of Ancient China—Beyond the Mainstream 215

Selections from the *Mohist Canons*《墨经》选篇 218
Selections from *Han Fei Tzu*《韩非子》选段 221
Selections from *The Kung-sun Lung Tzu*《公孙龙子》选篇 223
Selections from *The Art of War*《孙子兵法》选篇 225
Extensive Readings 227

A. Implications of Chinese Epistemology 中国认识论的内涵 227
B. Selections from *The Spirit of the Chinese People* 中国人的精神 229
C. Chinese Painting and Calligraphy 中国的绘画与书法 233
D. The Perfection of the Chinese in the Art of Gardening 中国园林艺术的完善 ... 238
Exercises 240

Chinese Culture and Thoughts: A Historical Overview

The Prehistory

Chinese culture is formed throughout a continuous encountering and integration of varied and diverse regional cultures across the land of China. During the Middle Neolithic period (c.4000 BC–3000 BC), distinct regional cultures had emerged in China, which laid the foundation for later Bronze Age civilizations: the Yangshao and Henan Longshan cultures in the Central Plains (associated with later Huaxia identity), the Shandong Longshan culture (considered a precursor to Eastern Yi groups), and complex Yangtze societies like Liangzhu (possibly ancestral to some Baiyue peoples). Archaeological evidence since the 1970s reveals both regional distinctiveness and interregional exchanges. This diversity may have inspired later mythological narratives of the Three Sovereigns (三皇), while the subsequent Five Emperors (五帝) — particularly figures like the Yan Di and Huang Di — could reflect actual interactions between late Neolithic chiefdoms, as suggested by their archaeological correlates in the Yellow River valley (c.3000 BC–2000 BC).

Though vague and without reliable evidence, the legendary sage rulers represented the ancient Chinese's imagination of their ancestors, especially their early struggling, self-preserving and developing in different regions. Their varied cultural origins might have also contributed to the different accounts of the groupings of these mythological rulers and deities. One account is from the *Records of the Grand Historian*, which identified Heavenly Sovereign, Earthly Sovereign, Tai Sovereign (or Fuxi, Nüwa, Shennong) as the Three Sovereigns, and Huangdi, Zhuanxu, Diku, Yao, and Shun as the Five Early Rulers. Other primitive cultural heroes included Chiyou, who fought against Yellow Emperor and was later subdued by him, and Houyi the divine archer, both of whom came from the Eastern Yi.

These cultural heroes, though existed only legendarily in historical texts, became symbols of historical transitions from primitive groups to matriarchal and patriarchal clans, then to tribal groups. The Three Sovereigns were accredited in the early tales as having created mankind or imparted essential knowledge and skills for survival, hence being regarded as god-kings or demigods in Chinese prehistory.

Philosophical interrogations and explorations of the human-heaven relationship also started during this age, as suggested by the creation of the eight trigrams, legendarily attributed to Fuxi. The Five Early Rulers, who were known by their supreme morals and leading powers, were demigods, with their stories marking the establishment of a patriarchal ruling in the development from family clans to the establishment of the Three Dynasties. Besides, their identities as demigods also suggested the historical continuity from the worship of deities to the worship of human ancestors.

The Three Dynasties

A prevalent worship of deities characterized Shang Dynasty when state-sponsored ceremonies were frequently held to offer sacrifices to ancestors and natural powers for their divine protection. At the same time, Chinese written language developed with the divinational use of inscriptions on oracle bones and bronze vessels, which were necessities for these religious ceremonies. The rulers during this period were called kings and regarded as speakers and mediators for deities. They became the highest oracle of the state and led the people in state worships, which were done with diviners working with the oracle-bone inscriptions. The dates and locations, the diviners' names, and sometimes the topics were inscribed on the bones made of bovine shoulder bones and turtle plastrons. The divination charges were often directed at ancestors as well as natural powers and the legendary rulers. The charges represented the divine wills on which the royal house based its actions, concerning issues from illness, birth, and death, to weather, warfare, agriculture, and so on. After the diviner learned about the cracks on the bones made from a heating process and gave interpretations, the king occasionally added his readings of the cracks to define the nature of the omen. The mediating role of the king as a communicator with the deities and ancestors was gradually strengthened when the king became the sole interpreter of the cracks on the bones in later Shang. The monopolized reading of the oracles by the king implied a diminishing role of the natural power and deities in deciding politics and state affairs when Shang gradually came to an end.

The divination tradition changed after Shang was replaced by Zhou Dynasty, which, though still acknowledged the power of spiritual beings and highly respected "the Mandate of Heaven," kept the deities at a distance. As claimed by Zhou's historical documents, the heavenly power was not shown in any other ways but through its moral aspect and only the king who served people's needs could preserve his mandate and the rightful ruling that came with it. The shift of responsibility from heavenly beings to humans called for the Zhou kings to consolidate their governance, and they did so by establishing the Zongfa system of patrilineal primogeniture. The term "de" (moral and virtue), which was not found in the oracle bones of Shang, was a key term in many documents of Zhou. And the divination no longer came from mythical revelation from the heavenly being through cracked bones, but from "words of wisdom" as systematized in the form of numbers, yin-and-yang graphs, and prognostic texts in the *Book of Changes*. The elusive yet inclusive message of this divination text has fascinated thinkers throughout Chinese history and has also shaped the Chinese mind through its variations in different schools of thoughts.

The Spring and Autumn and Warring States Periods

The cultural legacy of Zhou had such a great impact that the Confucian classics were mostly passed down from it. The *Book of Poetry*, the *Book of Documents*, the *Book of Rites*, and the *Book of Music* were traditionally attributed to Confucius' compilation based on materials from Zhou's official schools, though historical evidence suggests these works underwent collective and prolonged editing. For instance, the *Book of Poetry*'s formation likely involved multiple contributors over time, with Confucius possibly only standardizing its musical arrangements. The *Book of Changes* was expanded with commentaries, called the *Ten Wings*, by Confucians, reflecting its intellectual alignment with Confucian philosophy. Preserved as bound bamboo-slips, these Zhou texts were canonized as jing (cultural classics) in Chinese history.

One of the causes that drove the Confucian ambition to form the Zhou texts into cultural canons is the fact that the society, after Zhou had been brought down by wars between the lords, fell into a chaos with battlefields of separatist regimes. No trace of order and harmony could be found. Confucius and other pre-Qin thinkers tried to devise a rationale for something to replace the bankrupted political institutions. And this gave rise to a grand opportunity for different strata of the society to speak for their political ideals and propositions, hence the contention of the Hundred Schools of Thought. By criticizing, complementing, counter-arguing each other, the various schools crystallized the myriad voices representing different social status, academic traditions, and ways of thinking during the Spring and Autumn and Warring States periods.

It is observed that while Confucianism emphasized social order and active involvement in the society, Daoism concentrated on individual life and spiritual transcendence, giving inspiration to the development of Chinese Buddhism and Confucianism in Ming. And different from Confucius who took the Western Zhou as the model and emphasized humanity and love based on a gradation in human relations, Mozi looked to Xia and insisted on righteousness with a preference for universal love without any distinction among familial relations and social rankings. The privately-run school as initiated by Confucius was groundbreaking considering that education had only been accessible to the family of aristocratic officials. It is the flourishing of thoughts that has characterized the periods as the Axial Age in China, bringing into form the

Chinese civilization that integrates the various regional cultures across the land.

Qin and Han Dynasties

The Qin Dynasty got its name for its origin in the state of Qin, a fief of the confederal Zhou Dynasty. It was formally established after the conquests in 221 BC, when Ying Zheng, who had become king of the Qin state in 246, declared himself to be "Shi Huangdi," the first emperor. The emperor's power was gathered through the extension of the administration system of prefectures and counties and the appointment and dispatch of officials by the central government, the establishment of a network of roads and the defense system, and the standardization of measurements. Along with these reforms was the further unification of different fields of culture, including the standardization of the written language and the controlling of varied schools of thoughts.

The short-lived Qin was succeeded by the Han Dynasty (206 BC–220 AD). In the reign of Emperor Wudi, more-intensive political organization and stronger authority of the government were in critical need of the peace and prosperity of the expanding empire. Confucianism, with Dong Zhongshu's interpretive emphasis on its ideas about regulating relationships between people assumed to be positioned in degrees of social rankings, had been gradually adopted as official norms, morals, and ritual and social behavior. Hence Confucian classics were sought-after, reinterpreted, debated over, and widely used in the civil service. This most immediately led to Confucianism's canonical status in Chinese culture. Another change that painted the picture of traditional intellectual culture of China was the Han system of recruiting eligible and meritorious men to staff the civil service of the empire, which laid the foundation for the formation of the regular system of national exam and appointment based upon an education of Confucian classics in Sui and Tang dynasties.

Wei-Jin Period and Southern and Northern Periods

When Confucianism exerted its influence mostly in politics and academia in Han, Daoism developed in the mundane and was turned into the native Daoist religion, by combining the Huang-Lao cult, the teachings of the *Book of Changes*, the School of Yin-Yang, astrology, and divination. Daoism, with its teaching of spiritual freedom and enlightenment in nature, lent much inspiration to the development of Chinese art. Meanwhile, with the opening of trade route between China and the West, i.e. the Silk Road, cultural exchanges were more frequent. And this also caused the influx of Buddhism through travelers who had taken the Silk Road from northern India. Chinese Buddhism developed from Han and flourished in the Wei-Jin period, through the translation of Buddhist scriptures and its blending with popular religious beliefs and practices.

The spirit of free intellectual criticism and interrogation, devoid of political vulgarism as in the Confucian scholasticism during Han, characterized the "qingtan" or pure conversation concerning metaphysics and philosophy in the form of informal gatherings for discourse and debate. The most famous of those indulged in the pure conversations, the Seven Worthies of the Bamboo Grove, engaged in elegant, carefree, and witty talks and poetry.

This period also saw the emergence of the School of Xuanxue, bringing together Daoist and Confucian beliefs through revision and discussion. The major thinkers of the school include Wang Bi (226–249), He Yan (d. 249), and Guo Xiang (d. 312), who synthesized and extended Confucian and Daoist ideas, applying the mysterious truth of Dao with the intention to review the social and moral philosophy of Confucianism.

Sui, Tang, Song, and Yuan Dynasties

The Sui Dynasty (581–618), short-lived yet significant in unifying the country after over three hundred years of division, set the stage for the succeeding Tang Dynasty (618–907). The general prosperity of Tang and its extensive ties with the world, accompanied by the state patronage, contributed to the development of Chinese thoughts in full bloom. Philosophical Daoism was canonized. Religious Daoism enjoyed imperial favor and ended up being a state cult through its doctrinal and organizational development, and even when it lost its state patronage in the following dynasties, it still enjoyed popularity among the masses.

The famous pilgrim Xuanzang spoke for the continued imperial favor for Buddhism for most of the dynasty. Most importantly, the development of Buddhist sects during this period raised the subject of consciousness to prominence in Chinese philosophy. Apart from the great project of Buddhist translation led by Xuanzang, the indigenous Buddhist schools of Tiantai, Chan, and Pure Land came into being.

If early Buddhist translation could not have won its popularity without its use of Daoist concepts and terms, then the Chinese Buddhist schools would not have rooted in this land without its embracing diverse elements of Chinese culture. The southern Chan gained its anti-textual and anti-metaphysical revelation influenced by Daoist dialectics. And the salvationist preaching of the Pure Land incorporated classical ideas to its doctrines.

The tide of Confucian decline during early and mid-Tang was reversed by Han Yu, one of the greatest literary masters who highlighted the Golden Age of culture in Tang and Song, together with Li Ao. They started a Confucian revival, strengthening the Confucian concentration on human nature and social morality against the dominance of Daoism and Buddhism, which became another force that invigorated Confucianism in the Song and Ming dynasties.

The gem of Tang culture were undoubtedly its poetry and visual arts, the brilliance of which was carried on into the Song Dynasty (960–1279), despite Song's delicate ruling and weak national power. The fighting with the "barbarian" tribes in the north, say Dangxiang or Tangut, Qidan or Khitan and Nüzhen or Jurchen ended up beefing up the cultural integration of Chinese culture that went all the way into the Yuan Dynasty. A wider readership was witnessed with the development of commerce and printing technology, which naturally expanded the education of Confucian classics, based on which the civil service examination continued to sway the bureaucratic staffing. The intellectual center had now shifted from Buddhist temples to regional schools and noted scholars with many followers. One of such scholars was Hu Yuan, whose ideas singled out substance, function and literary expression as the Three Treasures of Confucianism and had a great impact on the Song Confucian classicists as Wang Anshi, Sima Guang, Ouyang Xiu, Fan Zhongyan and Su Dongpo. These classicists were engaged in political applications of Confucian principles to state reforming programs.

The most preeminent aspect of the Confucian revival during Song was in metaphysics, known as the School of Principle and the School of the Mind or Intuition. With inspirations from the Daoist cosmogony and Buddhist quietism and subjectivism, the School of Principle reaffirmed a Confucian tradition that stressed on human values and ethical principles and built them into a universal principle consummated by Zhu Xi (1130–1200). Despite many disputes, Zhu Xi's thoughts have been well acknowledged by the Far East countries as the most complete expositions of Confucianism.

Ming and Qing Dynasties

After the Cheng-Zhu school of Confucianism had been canonized through the civil service examination system in the Yuan Dynasty for over 200 years, it started to lose its vigor in the Ming Dynasty (1368–1644), giving way to Wang Yangming's philosophical ideas representing the School of the Mind. Wang Yangming's intuitionism attracted many thinkers in late Ming, but also anticipated, together with Cheng-Zhu school, a reaction against speculative philosophy and a resuming of the practical side of Confucianism, especially its use in political affairs. The Donglin Academy was such a group that directed its contention against the corrupt Ming governance and called for a moral regeneration of the ruling class by going back to Confucian ethics.

Huang Zongxi and Gu Yanwu, two of the three great Confucians, attempted to reverse the trend of empty speculation and rigid formality and scholasticism as developed in late Ming intelligentsia. In a certain sense, the leaning toward practicality and objective truth in the Confucian studies came under the influence of western knowledge introduced by the Jesuits, who brought with them the scientific revolution. The third one of the three great Confucians was Wang Fuzhi, whose earlier failure in resisting the Manchu rule had most probably formed his strong sense of racial consciousness and culture preservation in his reapplication of Confucian ideas. He rejected the transcendental principle (*li*) upheld by the Confucianism in the Ming Dynasty and took on a more materialistic approach by emphasizing the integrated existence of the material force (*qi*) and the concrete object with its specific principle inherent. From a cyclical view of material force as being involved in constant fusion and intermingling and thus of principles kept being renewed, Wang Fuzhi rejected the Confucian look-back upon the past as the model for today.

Despite the early signs of enlightenment as shown in the practical Confucianism, the possibility of a more open and unbarred intellectual engagement was stifled by the centralized despotism and literary censorship during the Ming and Qing dynasties. This turned many scholars in the Qing Dynasty from politics to the Qian-jia school which focused on verifying the authenticity of classical texts, questioning the canonized ones, and challenging the Confucian orthodoxy. Influence of European mathematics and mathematical astrology should be credited in this trend of study. During both Ming and Qing dynasties, the pride that the imperial authorities enjoyed from a stable, prosperous society and far-reaching international impact fueled the national project of compiling cultural heritage in huge anthologies and encyclopedias. This also set an example for the private endeavor of book publishing and library building in the literati. The most famous among the great works that have preserved the legacy of Chinese intellectual culture were the *Yongle Encyclopedia*, the *Index of Native Herbs*, the *Treatise on Military Preparedness*, the *Creations of Heaven and Human Labor*, and the *Kangxi Dictionary*.

Timeline of Chinese Culture and Thought

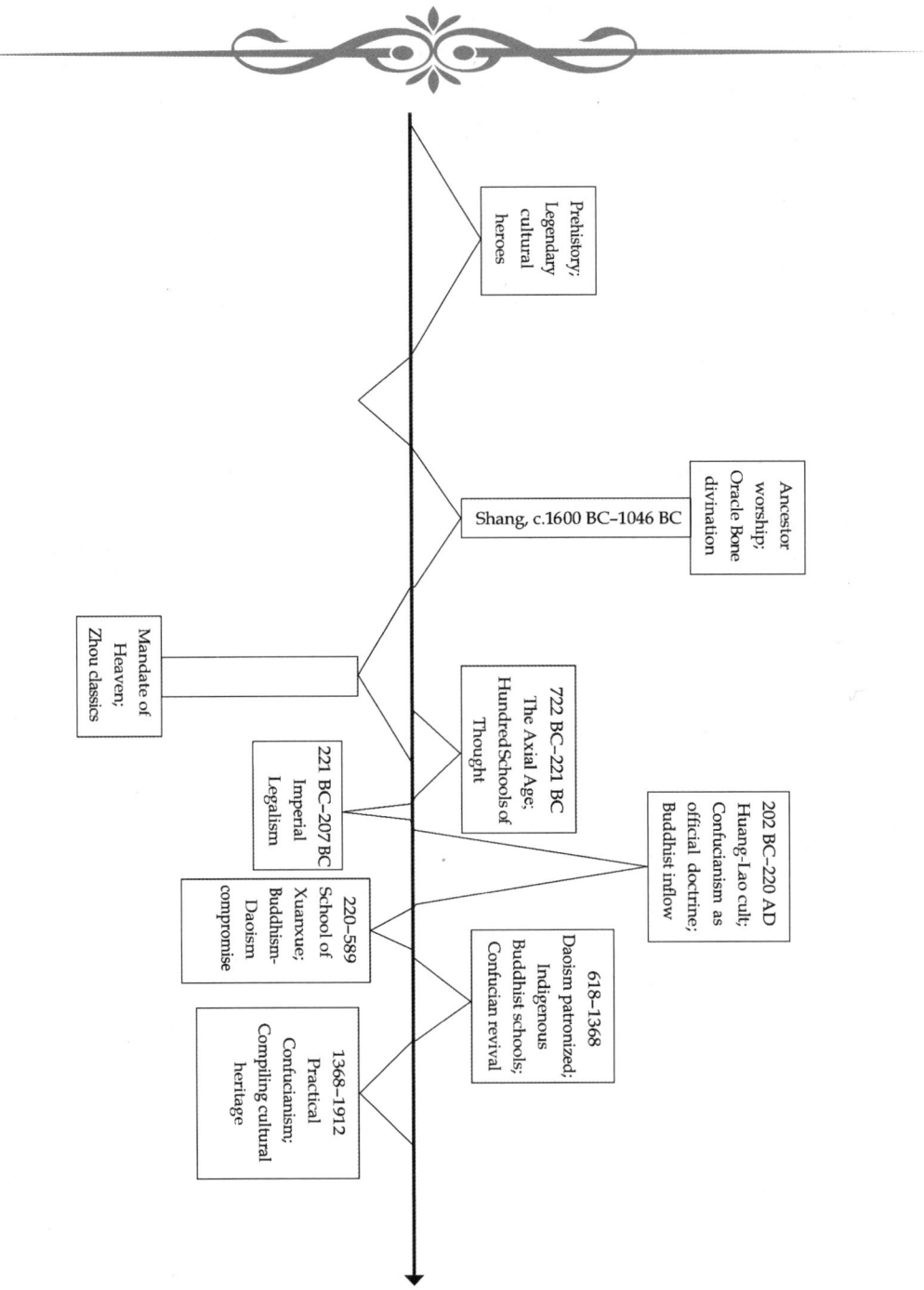

Timeline of Chinese Culture and Thought

Chapter One

The *Book of Changes*: A Treasure of Chinese Intellectual History and Its Impact on 20th-Century Western World

> 导读
>
> 本章课文节选《易经》"乾""坤""屯""泰""同人"等五卦卦辞和爻辞，以及《易传》对此五卦的相关解释。拓展性阅读材料包括当代英国汉学家理查德·拉特所著《〈周易〉的魅力》、20世纪瑞士心理学家卡尔·古斯塔夫·荣格的《〈易经〉序言》，以及当代《易经》翻译者杰弗里·雷德蒙的《〈易经〉与西方战后早期反文化运动》。

Introduction

1. The Eminence of the *Book of Changes*[①] in the Annals of Chinese Thought

The *I Ching*'s eminence in the annals of Chinese thought is a testament to its multifaceted nature, serving not only as a guide for divination but also as a profound philosophical text that has shaped the Chinese worldview for millennia. Known as the *Book of Changes*, it delves into the intricate dance of Yin and Yang, the primal forces that underlie the universe's harmony and discord. This foundational concept is reflected in the *I Ching*'s 64 hexagrams (which originate from the combinations of Fuxi's eight trigrams), each a unique combination of six lines that can be either solid (Yang), indicative of strength and action, or broken (Yin), signifying flexibility and receptivity.

The *I Ching*'s hexagrams are not mere symbols; they are dynamic representations of life's complexities. Each hexagram is composed of two trigrams, which are primary gua representing

---

① For convenience, "the *Book of Changes*" is frequently referred to as "the *I Ching*" in this chapter.

the fundamental aspects of existence such as heaven, earth, water, fire, wind, thunder, lake, and mountain. These elements interact to form a rich tapestry of meanings that can be applied to various situations, offering guidance for decision-making and self-reflection.

The *I Ching*'s influence extends beyond the metaphysical. It has been instrumental in shaping Chinese ethics and governance, providing a framework for understanding the natural order and human conduct within it. The text emphasizes the importance of aligning one's actions with the Tao, or the Way, which is the path of harmony with the universe. This alignment is achieved by recognizing and responding to the changing cycles of Yin and Yang, as well as the positions and relationships within the hexagrams.

The *I Ching*'s approach to divination is rooted in its philosophical underpinnings. Divination in the *I Ching* is not about predicting the future with certainty but rather about gaining insight into the present and the potential outcomes of various courses of action. The judgments and messages derived from the hexagrams are not absolute; they are conditional, reflecting the *I Ching*'s belief in the power of human agency and the transformative potential of moral rectitude.

The *I Ching*'s philosophical depth is further illuminated by its emphasis on key concepts such as the centrality of the middle path, the importance of timing, and the interdependence of all things. It encourages a balanced approach to life, recognizing that extremes can lead to instability and that adaptability is essential for navigating the ever-changing landscape of existence.

2. The Divination Content of the *I Ching* and Its Historical Context

The divination content of the *I Ching* is deeply enmeshed with the historical tapestry of the Western Zhou Dynasty. The Zhou people, an agricultural tribe from Shaanxi province, were led by King Millet, who is not only credited with imparting agricultural knowledge but also revered as a deity of farming. This agrarian heritage laid the foundation for the Zhou's prosperity and is symbolically reflected in the *I Ching*'s emphasis on the harmony between humans and the natural world.

The narrative of the Zhou Dynasty is one of transformation and resilience. Following invasions by other tribes, Lord Dan Fu spearheaded the tribe's relocation to a new land, which came to be known as Zhou. His visionary leadership, which included the abolition of the slave system and the reinstatement of the ancient commune system, set the stage for a society that valued communal living and collective prosperity. This period of growth and the establishment of a city-state under the aegis of Tribe Zhou is mirrored in the *I Ching*'s exploration of societal structures and the dynamics of power.

Ji Li's formidable leadership, which provoked the Shang Dynasty's king to execute him, is a pivotal moment in the Zhou's history. His son, King Wen, who is posthumously honored as a paragon of magnanimity, continued to expand the Zhou's influence through diplomacy and the establishment of a feudal system. King Wen's reign is emblematic of the *I Ching*'s principles of wise governance and the importance of moral leadership.

King Wu, building upon his father's legacy, meticulously prepared for an expedition against the Tyrant of Shang. His strategic acumen and the support of over eight hundred lords in his campaign reflect the *I Ching*'s teachings on the art of leadership and the necessity of aligning with the collective will. The successful overthrow of the Shang Dynasty and the establishment of the Zhou Dynasty under King Wu is a historical milestone that underscores the *I Ching*'s belief in the cyclical nature of power and the inevitability of change.

The *I Ching*'s divination content is not merely a reflection of the Zhou's history but also a philosophical interpretation of it. The text's emphasis on the interplay between lines (Yao), the centrality of certain positions within the hexagrams, and the concept of "host" (Host) as the principal element of a hexagram, all echo the social hierarchy and the importance of positioning during the Zhou Dynasty. The *I Ching*'s guidance on navigating adversity, correcting faults, and embracing good fortune aligns with the Zhou's leaders' approach to governance and their response to the challenges they faced.

Furthermore, the *I Ching*'s integration of the five elements during the Han Dynasty, which correlates with the natural world's energetic balances, provides a deeper understanding of the Zhou's connection to the land and their agricultural roots. The text's emphasis on the cyclical nature of time and the importance of adapting to change (Solar Terms) resonates with the Zhou's historical journey from a tribe to a unified state.

3. Key Concepts Essential for the *I Ching* Textual Reading

The *I Ching*, with its rich lexicon of terms, provides a complex and nuanced system for divination and philosophical reflection. Let's delve deeper into the specific terms mentioned, using the information provided in the documents:

Carry: The concept of "carry" in the *I Ching* refers to the supportive relationship between lines in a hexagram. When a yin (broken or yielding) line is positioned above a yang (solid or firm) line, it is said to "carry" the yang line, much like a horse carries a rider. This is considered auspicious as it symbolizes support and nurturing from a supportive yin to a dynamic yang.

Central: A line is considered "central" when it occupies the middle position of either the lower (second place) or upper (fifth place) trigram. Central positions are auspicious as they represent balance and harmony within the structure of the hexagram.

Correct: The term "correct" in the *I Ching* pertains to the appropriateness of a line's position within the hexagram. A yang line is correct in the odd positions (initial, third, or fifth), while a yin line is correct in the even positions (second, fourth, or top). Being in the correct position signifies that the element is well-placed to exert its influence effectively.

Correspond: "Correspond" describes the relationship between complementary yin and yang lines in corresponding positions within a hexagram. These lines are said to "respond" to each other, creating a dynamic and harmonious interaction. The correspondence is particularly significant between the second and fifth lines, which represent the relationship between a leader and their followers.

Host: The "host" in a hexagram is the principal yao (line) that the divination focuses on. It is the line that embodies the central theme of the hexagram and should be virtuous and well-positioned to represent the essence of the situation. The host is often found in the second or fifth place, with the fifth place being superior and thus more frequently the host.

Judgment: The *I Ching* provides judgments that are the outcomes of divination, reflecting good fortune and misfortune based on one's subjective intention and objective action. The judgments are not arbitrary but are the result of one's actions and decisions. The principal judgments include:

Adversity: A difficult situation that can be overcome with alertness and self-improvement.

Fault: A state of hardship that can be rectified by correcting mistakes.

Good Fortune: A positive outlook that signifies favorable circumstances.

Humility: Suffering and distress that can lead to misfortune if not addressed.

Misfortune: Sudden and unexpected negative events that may stem from carelessness.

Regret: A fault that is salvageable if recognized and corrected.

Place: Each line in a hexagram has a specific "place" that ranges from the initial (bottom) to the top. The placement of a line carries significance, with the fifth place being the position of a king or ruler, the fourth for a minister or adviser, the third as a place of transition, the second for an official or general, and the initial for someone new or with little power.

Yao: A "yao" is a single line within a hexagram, which can be either yin or yang. The nature of the yao (yielding or firm) and its position within the hexagram contribute to the overall meaning and interpretation of the hexagram.

These terms[①], when considered together, form the intricate language of the *I Ching*, allowing for a profound understanding of the dynamics at play within any given situation. The *I Ching*'s divinatory system is not merely about predicting the future but about providing insights into the present, guiding individuals towards actions that are in harmony with the natural order of the universe.

---

① These terms are referenced from Alfred Huang, *The Complete I Ching: The Definitive Translation*, Inner Traditions, 2010.

4. The Wisdom of Ancient Chinese Philosophy and Its 20th-Century Western Influence

The *I Ching*'s profound philosophical insights have resonated far beyond the borders of ancient China, penetrating the intellectual and cultural fabric of the 20th-century West. The document provided, "The Making of the Global *Yijing* in the Modern World," underscores the *I Ching*'s transformation from a revered Eastern text to a globally recognized source of wisdom.

The *I Ching*'s influence on Western popular culture is particularly evident in its adoption by the postwar generation in the United States. Geoffrey Redmond's introduction highlights how the *I Ching* served as a wellspring of dreams, comfort, wisdom, and inspiration for baby boomers and the countercultural movement. It became a spiritual mainstay for a generation grappling with societal upheaval and seeking a deeper understanding of life's complexities. The Beat Generation, in particular, found in the *I Ching* a philosophical ally, interpreting the hexagram arrays as representations of psychedelic experiences.

The *I Ching*'s conceptualization of time is deeply rooted in the cyclical and dynamic balance between yin and yang. This view has significantly challenged the cause-and-effect logic of linear progression inherent in modern Western ideas of time. This difference is particularly highlighted through the work of Carl G. Jung, the Swiss psychiatrist, who bridged Eastern wisdom with Western psychology. Jung's interpretation of the *I Ching* as a tool to access the unconscious mind resonated with the counterculture of the 1960s and 1970s, characterized by a quest for personal truth and self-discovery. Central to Jung's fascination with the *I Ching* was its alignment with his concept of synchronicity, which posits meaningful coincidences between external events and mental states without causal connections. This idea provided a psychological framework for understanding the *I Ching*'s divinatory process, which often involves random actions like tossing coins or sorting yarrow sticks to select a hexagram, thereby revealing insights that transcend conventional notions of cause and effect.

All in all, the *I Ching*'s ancient wisdom continues to offer a unique perspective on time, change, and personal growth that resonates with modern people. Its conceptualization of time as cyclical and its emphasis on balance and harmony provide a framework for understanding life's complexities and navigating the ever-shifting landscape of human experience. The *I Ching*'s impact on modern culture, both in the East and the West, is a testament to its timeless wisdom and its ability to inspire and guide individuals on their journeys of self-discovery and spiritual growth.

《易经》选篇[1] Selections from the *Book of Changes*[2]

一、乾卦第一 1. Qian • Initiating

Qian·Heaven
Qian·Heaven

乾：

元、亨、利、贞。[3]

Decision

Initiating.

Sublime and initiative.

Prosperous and smooth.

Favorable and beneficial.

Steadfast and upright.

《象》：

大哉乾"元"，

万物资始，

乃统天。

云行雨施，

品物流形。

大明始终，

六位时成。

时乘六龙以御天。

乾道变化，

各正性命。

保合大和，

乃"利贞"。

首出庶物，

万国咸宁。

Commentary on the Decision

Vast indeed is the greatness of the Initiating.

It is the source of all beings.

And regulates all creations under Heaven.

Clouds flow and rain falls.

All beings complete their forms.

Greatly luminous, from beginning to end.

Each of the six stages completes itself in its own time,

As mounting on six dragons soaring the sky.

The way of the Initiating is change and transformation,

So that each being obtains its true nature and destiny.

And the union of great harmony is preserved.

This is what is favorable and upright.

The initiating is high above all beings.

And thus all countries are united in peace.

---

① 选自陈德述：《周易正本解》. 成都：四川出版集团巴蜀书社，2012 年。

② Excerpted from Alfred Huang, *The Complete I Ching: The Definitive Translation, Inner Traditions*, Inner Traditions, 2010. The name of the classic is also known as *I Ching* in the western world.

③ Key passages throughout this textbook have been intentionally underlined to serve two primary purposes:

a. Emphasis for Close Reading: Underlined sections highlight essential concepts, critical analyses, or foundational theories. These are strongly recommended for focused study and classroom discussion.

b. Connection to Exercises: Each underlined passage directly correlates with questions in the chapter-end exercises. Engaging deeply with these sections will enhance your ability to critically apply concepts and succeed in practice tasks.

Teachers may use underlined content to structure lessons; students are encouraged to treat them as active learning anchors.

Chapter One
The *Book of Changes*: A Treasure of Chinese Intellectual History and Its Impact on 20th-Century Western World

Commentary on the Symbol 《象》：

    Heaven acts with vitality and persistence. 天行健，

    In correspondence with this 君子以自强不息。

    The superior person keeps himself vital without ceasing.

Yao Text 爻辞：

    Initial Nine 初九：

      Dragon lying low. 潜龙勿用。

      Do not use.

    Second Nine 九二：

      Dragon arising in the field. 见龙在田，

      Favorable to see a great person. 利见大人。

    Third Nine 九三：

      The superior person— 君子终日乾乾，

      All day long, initiating, initiating. 夕惕若。

      At night, keeping alert. 厉无咎。

      Adversity, no fault.

    Fourth Nine 九四：

      Probably leaping from an abyss. 或跃在渊，

      No fault. 无咎。

    Fifth Nine 九五：

      Dragon flying in the sky. 飞龙在天，

      Favorable to see a great person. 利见大人。

    Top Nine 上九：

      Haughty dragon. 亢龙有悔。

      There is regret.

    All Nines 用九：

      There appears a group of dragons without a chief. 见群龙无首，

      Good fortune. 吉。

Wen Yen 《文言》：

(Confucius's Commentary on the Words of the Text)

    Yuan, the sublime and initiative, "元"者，

    Is the first and chief quality of goodness. 善之长也；

    Heng, the prosperous and smooth, "亨"者，

    Is the accumulation of excellence. 嘉之会也；

    Li, the favorable and beneficial, "利"者，

义之和也；	Is the harmony of all that is just.
"贞"者，	Zhen, the steadfast and upright,
事之干也。	Is the core of action.
君子体仁足以长人	Because the superior person embodies all that is human,
	He is able to be the head of men.
嘉会足以合礼，	Because he presents the assemblage of excellences,
	He is able to unite people through courtesy.
利物足以合义，	Because he is favorable and beneficial to all beings,
	He is able to bring them into harmony with justice.
贞固足以干事。	Because he is steadfast and upright,
	He is able to carry out all kinds of achievements.
君子行此四德者，	The superior person applies these four virtues in actions,
故曰："乾：元、亨、利、贞。"	Therefore, it is said: Qian is yuan, heng, li, and zhen.
初九曰：	Initial Nine says:
"潜龙勿用"，	"Dragon lying low. Do not use."
何谓也？	What does it mean?
子曰：	The Master says:
"龙德而隐者也。不易乎世，	The dragon holds virtue but conceals his light.
不成乎名，	He makes no change with the influence of the world.
遁世无闷，	He acts on nothing to secure his fame.
不见是而无闷，	Withdrawing from the world, he bears no regret.
乐则行之，	Experiencing disapproval, he embraces no sadness.
忧则违之，	Acts with joy if he is able to carry his principles into action.
确乎其不可拔，	Casts off sorrow if his time has not come.
潜龙也。"	Truly, no one can tear him from his roots.
	This is the hidden dragon.
九二曰：	Second Nine says:
"见龙在田，	"Dragon arising in the field.
利见大人"，	Favorable to see a great person."
何谓也？	What does it mean?
子曰：	The master says:
"龙德而正中者也。	The dragon shows his virtue,
庸言之信，	He is properly in the central place.
庸行之谨，	Truthful in his ordinary words,
闲邪存其诚，	And cautious in his usual conduct.

Chapter One
The *Book of Changes*: A Treasure of Chinese Intellectual History and Its Impact on 20th-Century Western World

Guarding against degeneracy 善世而不伐，
And maintaining in his sincerity. 德博而化。
He dedicates himself to the world but without the least boasting,
And his virtue is extensively displayed, having great influence.
Thus the *I* says, 易曰：
"Dragon arising in the field. '见龙在田，
Favorable to see a great person." 利见大人'，
This refers to the qualities of a superior person. 君德也。"
Third Nine says: 九三曰：
"The superior person— "君子终日乾乾，
All day long, initiating, initiating. 夕惕，若厉无咎"，
At night, keeping alert.
Adversity, no fault."
What does it mean? 何谓也？
The Master says: 子曰：
The sage advances in virtue "君子进德修业。
And improves his deeds.
With true heart and good faith 忠信所以进德。
He advances in virtue.
With attention to his words and stable sincerity 修辞立其诚，
He improves in deeds. 所以居业也。
Knowing the utmost point to be reached and reaching it, 知至至之，
He is able to grasp opportunity. 可与言几也。
Knowing the end to be rested in, and resting in it, 知终终之，
He is able to comprehend appropriateness. 可与存义也。
<u>For this reason, he is able to not be proud in a superior position</u> 是故居上位而不骄，
And not distressed in a lowly one. 在下位而不忧。
Thus, being active and creative as circumstances demand, and watchful, 故乾乾因其时而惕，
In this way, even in a situation of adversity, 虽危无咎矣。"
He will not make any mistake.
Fourth Nine says: 九四曰：
"Probably leaping from an abyss. "或跃在渊，

无咎",	No fault."
何谓也?	What does it mean?
子曰:	The Master says:
"上下无常,	Ascending or descending,
非为邪也。	There is no constant rule
进退无恒,	But not to commit evil.
非离群也。	Advancing or retreating,
	There is no permanent measure
	But not to desert others.
君子进德修业,	The superior person advances his virtue and improves his deeds
欲及时也,	In order to seize the opportune time.
故无咎。"	Thus no fault can be made.
九五曰:	Fifth Nine says:
"飞龙在天,	"Dragon flying in the sky.
利见大人",	Favorable to see a great person."
何谓也?	What does it mean?
子曰:	The Master says:
"同声相应,	Notes of the same key respond to one another;
同气相求,	Odors of the same nature merge together.
水流湿,	Water flows toward what is wet,
火就燥。	Fire rises toward what is dry.
云从龙,	Clouds follow dragons;
风从虎。	Winds follow tigers.
圣人作而万物睹。	Whatever the superior person does, it can be perceived by all beings.
本乎天者亲上,	Those who draw their origin from Heaven move toward what is above;
本乎地者亲下,	Those who draw their origin from Earth cleave to what is below.
则各从其类也。"	All beings follow their own kind.
上九曰:	Top Nine says:
"亢龙有悔",	"Haughty dragon.
何谓也?	There is regret."
	What does it mean?

Chapter One
The *Book of Changes*: A Treasure of Chinese Intellectual History and Its Impact on 20th-Century Western World

The Master says:

Being noble, yet no corresponding position;

Dwelling high, yet no following of people.

A talented and virtuous person in the position below gives no support,

Should be move in such a situation, there will be no excuse for regret.

子曰：

"贵而无位，

高而无民，

贤人在下位而无辅，

是以动而有悔也。"

The Significance of Qian

This accomplished gua is one of the eight that is constructed by doubling one of the primary gua. Here the accomplished gua is Qian, Initiating; the primary gua is Heaven. Qian expounds the nature of Nature, the principle of Creation. Qian, the Initiating, is the most sublime, the most firm, the most central, and the most upright. It possesses the attributes of initiation, prosperity, harmony, and steadfastness. It moves forward endlessly and inexhaustibly. It is an ideal model of human conduct. For this reason, Confucius did not tire of explaining it in minute detail. According to him, Qian and Kun are the gate of *I*, which means that if one intends to understand the *I Ching* one should first understand Qian and Kun; then the gate of *I* opens for understanding the rest of the gua.

King Wen's Decision gives yuan, heng, li, and zhen—the four attributes of Heaven. Translated into English, they also encompass the meanings of sprouting, growing, blooming, and bearing fruit. Each of these four attributes gives way to one another according to the change of the seasons, cycling around and starting again. The ancient Chinese believed that humans should follow the way of Heaven, understanding the nature of change and adjusting to the situation, knowing when to advance and when to retreat. When it is not favorable to advance, it is time to gather one's strength, hold one's faith, and stand steadfast waiting for the right time and proper situation. When the time is right to progress, one still should guard against arrogance and rashness, making no move without careful thought and always keeping in mind that things that go beyond their extremes will alternate to their opposites.

The significance of the gua is to explore the healthiest movement of Heaven. In ancient times, the Chinese believed that the Tao of Heaven was also the Tao of Humanity, especially for an emperor, who was regarded as the Son of Heaven and whose duty was to lead and educate his people to practice the Tao of Heaven. King Wen's father, Ji Li, was a nobleman of the Shang Dynasty. He was granted the title of the West Lord and ruled the territory on the west side of the Shang empire. Ji Li manifested the Tao of Heaven; people from all around were drawn to him. The emperor of Shang felt threatened and killed Ji Li. King Wen carried on his father's magnanimous administration with great humility and circumspection for fifty years. He still could not escape the Tyrant of Shang's suspicion and jealousy, and eventually he was imprisoned. During his seven years of imprisonment King Wen worked with the *I* and pondered his future duties. He realized that every undertaking or revolutionary cause needed to pass through the four stages of yuan, heng, li, and zhen, or sprouting, growing, blooming, and bearing fruit. He visualized that his sublime initiation (yuan) would be prosperous and smooth (heng), favorable to the people and successful (li), and should be kept steadfast and upright (zhen). At that time he had already worked out an overall plan of how to rescue the people from the Tyrant of Shang's brutality. He was deeply attached to the Tao of Heaven and the law of natural development. He rearranged the sixty-four gua and put Qian at the very beginning to serve as the general guideline of the Upper Canon and as the polestar of his revolutionary course.

Heaven's movement is constant, persistent, and stable; it follows its orbit without deviation, still maintaining its equilibrium. (According to ancient Chinese cosmology, Earth was the center of the universe.)

Confucius said that "with vitality and endurance Heaven acts without ceasing! Heaven's motion is the healthiest." Greatly influenced by the significance of this gua, Confucius explored its truth in his Doctrine of the Golden Mean. The nature of Heaven is to follow the central path with no excess and no insufficiency. Applied to human lives, all our actions should follow the way of Heaven, maintaining an equilibrium. In other words, every action should be in accord with the proper time and circumstances. When the time and situation are not suitable for one to move, one should have patience. On the other hand, when the time and circumstances are favorable for one to advance, one should not lose the opportunity. This is what the ancient sage meant: following the way of Nature. It is as simple as putting on more clothing when the weather gets cold. When your stomach feels empty, take something to eat. Likewise, the ancient sage encourages the diviner to follow the way of a superior person, always vitalizing and advancing oneself. In this way, one will obtain the four attributes of Heaven: initiation, prosperity, favorableness, and steadfastness.

Following the steps of his father, the Duke of Zhou used the image of six dragons to expound upon the six stages of change represented by the six yao. The dragon was the most revered animal in ancient China. It was believed that the dragon was able to swim in the ocean, walk on the ground, and fly in the sky. Its constantly changing actions were unpredictable, like changes in the weather.

The host of this gua is the solid line at the fifth place. Qian represents the Tao of Heaven; thus, the fifth place is the symbolic seat of Heaven. Qian also illustrates the Tao of an emperor, and in that regard the fifth place is also the symbolic seat for an emperor. This place possesses the four virtues of the yang aspect—firm, strong, central, and correct—and is thus the most suitable place for the host of this gua. Confucius's Commentary on the Decision says, "As mounting on six dragons soaring in the sky.... The Initiating is high above all beings." This is the Tao of the Initiating, the perfect time and position. Beyond this position, things begin to alternate to their opposites. In this yao, a yang element is at a yang place, indicating a perfect situation for a ruler or a leader. One in this position requires the qualities of a superior person: firm, strong, magnanimous, and energetic.

Qian is one of the twelve tidal gua, representing the fourth month of the Chinese lunar calendar. In the solar calendar, this month is May.

(1) Initial Nine. Qian alternates to Encountering (The 44th Hexagram, Gou)

This line is represented by a dragon lying low. The dragon is in the lowest of the six lines, indicating an initial stage. The time is not suitable and the circumstances are not favorable for action. However, it is a time for preparation. This was exactly King Wen's situation when he was imprisoned by the tyrant of the Shang Dynasty for seven years, but he conducted himself with remarkable patience and self-restraint.

(2) Second Nine. Qian alternates to Seeking Harmony (The 13th Hexagram, Tongren)

The second line is symbolized by a dragon arising in the field. This line is in the central place of the lower gua. It means that a great person is on the central path. The time is coming, and the situation is suitable; he is ready to take action, and his virtuous influence will spread extensively. But before a definite goal and direction have been established, it is advisable to seek guidance from someone who is great in virtue or experience. This was King Wen's situation when he was released after seven years of confinement.

(3) Third Nine. Qian alternates to Fulfillment (The 10th Hexagram, Lv)

The third line represents a situation in which one has gone beyond the central place and reaches the top of the lower gua. This line is a yang element at a yang place—it is not good to become too yang, meaning self-willed and arrogant. One who is at this place should be watchful of not straying too far from the central path and thus creating an unfavorable situation. King Wen found himself in this position when he returned from prison to his own state and made determined efforts to prepare himself and influence his people to reestablish his kingdom. The Yao Text says, "The superior person—All day long, initiating, initiating. At night, keeping alert. Adversity, no fault." This describes King Wen's actions precisely.

(4) Fourth Nine. Qian alternates to Little Accumulation (The 9th Hexagram, Xiaoxu)

The fourth line symbolizes a dragon getting ready to leap out of the abyss and fly into the sky. Since this is the first line of the upper gua, the time and the circumstances have reached a new level, but only at the initial stage. Before taking action, one should wait for the best timing. In both advancing and retreating, it is important to wait for favorable timing. It is worth mentioning that in this yao, the Duke of Zhou uses the word huo, meaning "if" or "probably." The dragon can either leap or take no action. One should be extremely cautious. The Duke of Zhou reminds us that in a difficult or dangerous situation one should act cautiously; then there will be "no fault." This yao is exemplified by the actions of King Wu, son of King Wen, who, under the instruction of King Wen, sent troops against Shang Dynasty and then retreated, making only an exploratory attack. He was testing his capability for success.

(5) Fifth Nine. Qian alternates to Great Harvest (The 14th Hexagram, Dayou)

The fifth line is the central line of the upper gua. It is a yang element at a yang place-central, correct, and most auspicious. It indicates that the time and situation are ripe for taking action. The dragon is already flying—a man of great virtue is ready to be a leader. Everything is in its proper place. However, even in this context a wise leader still needs to seek assistance from worthy people. It is said that this gua represents how King Wu, under the instruction of his father, sent armed forces to suppress the tyrant of the Shang Dynasty, gaining the love and esteem of the people.

(6) Top Nine. Qian alternates to Eliminating (The 43rd Hexagram, Guai)

The sixth line is in the uppermost place. The haughty dragon reaches its limit. One in this place should be cautious of not going too far and afterward having regrets. The *I Ching* always reminds us that extreme joy begets sorrow. How can one expect a state of abundance to be everlasting? Always remember that one loses by pride and gains by modesty. The Yao Text says, "Haughty dragon. There is regret." The haughty dragon represents the Tyrant of Shang. He had committed countless evil deeds and was heading for his doom.

(7) All Nines. Qian alternates to Responding (The 2nd Hexagram, Kun)

All nines indicates that all yang lines alternate to yin lines. Among the sixty-four gua, only this one and Responding have an extra Yao Text applied to the situation when all six lines move. When all six lines change, one should read the Decision on the approached gua. The ancient Chinese believed that, although dragons were the strongest and most powerful creatures, they never fought for leadership. Only the most magnanimous and humble, the one who is able to manifest the will of Heaven and represent Heaven, would be selected by Heaven. Thus Confucius says in his commentary, ("Following the virtue of Heaven, one should not appear as a chief."[①]) An emperor or a leader is an initiator, but at the same time he is responsive. He is responsive to the will of Heaven. Thus, the next gua, Responding, expounds the Tao of the Subordinate. In this way, Initiating and Responding, the yang and the yin, merge into one. This yao indicates that the subordinates of the Shang Dynasty did not regard the tyrant as their leader. It was time for a true leader to be ordained by Heaven. Thus good fortune follows.

---

① The bracketed statement is a re-interpretation of the Yao Text by the translator. Similar cases in the following text will not be annotated.

Chapter One
The *Book of Changes*: A Treasure of Chinese Intellectual History and Its Impact on 20th-Century Western World

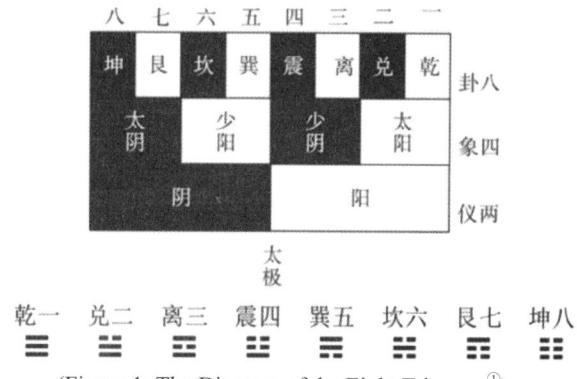

(Figure 1: The Diagram of the Eight Trigrams[①])

2. Kun • Responding   二、坤卦第二

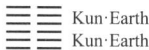
Kun·Earth
Kun·Earth

Decision

    Responding.

    Sublimely prosperous and smooth.

    Favorable with a mare's steadfastness.

    Superior person has somewhere to go.

    Predetermining loses.

    Following obtains a master.

    Favorable in the southwest:

    Finds friends.

    In the northeast:

    Loses friends.

    Be composed and content.

    Being steadfast and upright: good fortune.

Commentary on the Decision

    Perfect is Responding's greatness;

    It brings birth to all beings

    And accepts the source from Heaven.

    Responding in its richness sustains all beings;

    Its virtue is in harmony without limit.

坤：

元亨，

利牝马之贞。

君子有攸往，

先迷后得主，

利。

西南得朋，

东北丧朋。

安贞吉。

《彖》：

至哉坤"元"，

万物资生，

乃顺承天。

坤厚载物，

德合无疆。

---

① From Chen, Deshu, *The Comprehensive Interpretation of the Authentic I Ching by Renowned Scholars over a Century*, Bashu Publishing House, 2013, p. 45.

含弘光大，	Its capacity is wide, its brightness is great.
品物咸"亨"。	Through it, all beings attain their full development.
"牝马"地类，	A mare is a creature of earthly kind.
行地无疆，	Its moving on Earth is boundless,
柔顺"利贞"。	Yielding and submissive, advantageous and steadfast.
"君子"攸行，	The superior person comprehends her way of life:
"先迷"失道，	Taking the lead brings confusion,
	She loses the way.
"后"顺，	Following and responsive,
"得"常。	She finds the normal course.
"西南得朋"，	Find friends in the southwest,
乃与类行；	Proceed with people of the same kind.
"东北丧朋"，	Lose friends in the northeast,
乃终有庆。	In the end congratulations will arrive.
"安贞"之"吉"，	Good fortune comes from resting in steadfastness.
应地无疆。	It corresponds with the boundless capacity of Earth.
《象》：	**Commentary on the Symbol**
地势坤，	Earth's nature is to extend and respond.
君子以厚德载物。	In correspondence with this,
	The superior person enriches her virtue
	To sustain all beings.
爻辞：	**Yao Text**
初六：	Initial Six
履霜，	Treading on hoarfrost,
坚冰至。	Solid ice will come.
六二：	Second Six
直方大，	Straight, square, and great.
不习无不利。	Not from learning.
	Nothing is unfavorable.
六三：	Third Six
含章可贞，	Hiding excellence,
	Appropriate to be steadfast and upright.
或从王事，	Probably serving a king;
无成有终。	Claim no credit,
	Carrying things through to the end.

Chapter One
The *Book of Changes*: A Treasure of Chinese Intellectual History and Its Impact on 20th-Century Western World

  Fourth Six   六四：
   Tie up a bag.   括囊，
   No fault, no praise.   无咎，无誉。
  Fifth Six   六五：
   A yellow lower garment.   黄裳，
   Supreme good fortune.   元吉。
  Top Six   上六：
   Dragons fighting in the wilderness;   龙战于野，
   Their blood is blue-yellow.   其血玄黄。
  All Sixes   用六：
   Favorable to be perseveringly steadfast and upright.   利永贞。

Wen Yen   《文言》：
(Confucius's Commentary on the Words of the Text)

  Kun is most soft;   坤至柔而动也刚，
  Yet in action it is firm.
  It is most still,   至静而德方。
  Yet in nature, square.
  Through following she obtains her lord,   后得主而有常，
  Yet still maintains her nature and thus endures.
  She contains all beings   含万物而化光。
  And is brilliant in transforming.
  This is the way of Kun—How docile it is,   坤道其顺乎！
  Bearing Heaven and moving with time!   承天而时行。
  The family that heaps goodness upon goodness   积善之家必有余庆，
  Is sure to have an abundance of blessings.
  The family that piles evil upon evil   积不善之家必有余殃。
  Is sure to have an abundance of misery.
  Murder of a ruler by his minister,   臣弑其君，
  Or a father by his son,   子弑其父，
  Does not result from a single day and night.   非一朝一夕之故，
  Its causes have accumulated bit by bit   其所由来者渐矣，
  Through the absence of early discrimination.   由辨之不早辨也。
  The *I* says, "Treading on hoarfrost, solid ice will come."   《易》曰："履霜，坚冰至"，
  It shows the natural sequence of cause and effect.   盖言顺也。
  "Straight" indicates correctness.   "直"其正也，

"方"其义也。	"Square" indicates righteousness.
君子敬以直内，	The superior person respects herself
	In keeping her inner life straight.
义以方外，	And rectifies herself
	In making her outer action square.
敬义立而德不孤。	When respecting and rectifying are established,
	Then fulfillment of virtue will be free from isolation.
"直方大，	"Straight, square, and great.
不习，	Not from learning.
无不利"，	Nothing is unfavorable."
则不疑其所行也。	It shows she has no doubt in what she does.
阴虽有美，	Although yin possesses beauty,
"含"之以从王事，	It is concealed.
	Engaging in a king's service,
弗敢成也。	Claims no credit for oneself.
地道也，	This is the Tao of Earth,
妻道也，	The Tao of a wife,
臣道也。	And the Tao of one who serves the king.
地道"无成"而代"有终"也。	The Tao of Earth is to make no claim on its own,
	But to bring everything to completion.
天地变化，	Changing and transforming of Heaven and Earth
草木蕃。	Bring forth all plants flourishing.
天地闭，	If Heaven and Earth restrain their function,
贤人隐。	Then an able person would withdraw from the light.
《易》曰："括囊，无咎，无誉"，	The *I* says, "Tie up a bag. No fault, no praise."
盖言谨也。	It counsels caution.
君子"黄"中通理，	A superior person should hold the quality of Earth—Yellow is central and moderate,
正位居体，	Understanding and considerate.
美在其中，	Correcting her position and perfecting her action,
而畅于四支，	Her beauty lies within.
发于事业，	It permeates her whole being
美之至也。	And manifests in all her doing.
	This reveals the perfection of beauty.
阴疑于阳必战，	When yin competes against yang,

A contest is certain.	
Since no yang is considered,	为其嫌于无阳也,
Then a dragon is mentioned.	故称"龙"焉。
Since no category is changed,	犹未离其类也,
Then blood—a yin symbol—is noted.	故称"血"焉。
Blue and yellow is Heaven and Earth in fusion.	夫"玄黄"者,天地之杂(色)也,
Heaven is blue, Earth yellow.	天玄而地黄。

The Significance of Kun

This gua is one of the eight among the sixty-four accomplished gua that is made up by doubling one of the eight primary gua. Here, the accomplished gua is Kun, Responding, the primary gua is Earth. The *I Ching* describes the relationship of yin and yang, the two primary and fundamental forces in the universe. They are opposite but mutually complementary. The ancient Chinese believed that too much yang and too little yin is too hard, without elasticity and likely to be broken. Too much yin and too little yang is too soft, without spirit and likely to become inert. Yin and yang must coordinate and support each other. Qian represents the most yang; Kun represents the most yin. In the *I Ching* all sixty-four gua are derived from the principle of the mutual coordination and complementarity of yin and yang. One of the commentaries says,

Yin is the most gentle and submissive; when put in motion, it is strong and firm.

Yin is the most quiet and still; when taking action, it is able to reach a definite goal.

How can this be? Yin is gentle but not weak. It is submissive, without necessarily giving up its initiative. Yin receives yang qualities from nurturing the yang.

The host of the gua is the yielding line at the second place. Kun represents the Tao of Earth, the second place is the symbolic place for Earth. Kun illustrates the Tao of the subordinate, the second place is the symbolic place for subordinates. This place possesses the four virtues of the yin aspect—yielding, submissive, central, and correct. It is thus the most suitable as the host of this gua. The Decision advises that choosing one's own predetermined path will not work out well, but following another's wise lead will meet with success. It indicates the Tao of the subordinate or the responsive.

Generally, in the *I Ching*, the fifth place is the host of the gua. It is central to the upper gua and represents the position of a king or leader. The fourth place is directly underneath the king, it represents the position of a minister. The second place is also special, because it is central to the lower gua. Because it is far from the king, it is regarded as an official's position. If one takes this place, then one's role is as a servant to one's lord. In the lower gua, the second line is a yin element at a yin place, indicating a perfect situation for Responding. It represents all the yin aspects of a sage's quality by following the Tao of Heaven and establishing the Tao of Humanity.

(1) Initial Six. Kun alternates to Turning Back (The 24th Hexagram, Fu)

This line is a yin element at the bottom of the gua. Yin symbolizes cold; bottom symbolizes the ground. This gua represents tenth month of the Chinese lunar calendar. In northern China, hoarfrost appears during this month. When people see hoarfrost on the ground, they know that winter is at hand. Thus the Duke of Zhou said, "Treading on hoarfrost, solid ice will come." The message is that from a small clue one should be aware of what is coming; then one can take preventive measures against possible trouble. This line indicates that King Wu followed the instructions of his father, King Wen, preparing to rescue the people from the brutality of the tyrant of the Shang Dynasty. All the signs showed that the right time was at hand.

(2) Second Six. Kun alternates to Multitude (The 7th Hexagram, Shi)

The second line is a yin element at a yin place, central and correct. The ancient Chinese believed that Heaven is round while Earth is square. The text suggests that Earth symbolizes a sage's virtue. Straightforward, square, and great are the features of Earth. In Chinese, square, when it is applied to morality, carries the connotation of upright. When one follows the way of Heaven as Earth does, one is great. Thus, a superior person should possess the virtues of straightness, uprightness, and submissiveness, like Earth responding to Heaven; then one is able to carry out the will of Heaven spontaneously, without effort. This line indicates that the Duke of Zhou assisted his brother, King Wu, in planning an expedition against the tyrant of the Shang Dynasty. The Duke of Zhou advised King Wu to cultivate the virtue of Earth. Being straight and square, one would be great. Then the expedition could be conducted with no effort, and nothing would remain unfavorable.

(3) Third Six. Kun alternates to Humbleness (The 15th Hexagram, Qian)

The third line, "Hiding excellence," suggests humility. When the yielding line at the third place changes into a solid line, this gua alternates to Humbleness. However, one's excellence cannot be hidden very long, sooner or later it will be discovered. According to this line, one who has talent should come forth to serve the people. When the right time presents itself, one should carry things through to the end and not hold any selfish motivation. This line indicates that the Duke of Zhou and King Wu were preparing an expedition against the tyrant of the Shang Dynasty. Through the experience of having their grandfather killed by the Emperor of Shang, they realized the importance of hiding one's excellence and firmly maintaining it. Their strategy was to serve the tyrant with humility while bringing their plan to completion. Confucius praises their wisdom.

(4) Fourth Six. Kun alternates to Delight (The 16th Hexagram, Yu)

The fourth line is a yin element at a yin place. It is at the bottom of the upper gua. Although the place is correct, it is not central. In the *I Ching*, Kun also represents cloth. Thus the text employs the image of a tied-up bag to explain an unfavorable situation. "Tie up a bag" vividly suggests that in an unfavorable situation one should restrain oneself. Be cautious in words and actions. Being cautious in an unfavorable situation, how can one be at fault? To be cautious is a preventive stance to avoid harm, but it is not productive. Therefore, there is no praise. This line indicates that in preparing an expedition against the Tyrant of Shang, the Duke of Zhou and King Wu not only humbled themselves but also were cautious in their words and actions, as if tying up a bag.

(5) Fifth Six. Kun alternates to Union (The 8th Hexagram, Bi)

The fifth line is the central place of the upper gua; a yellow garment is used. In the *I Ching*, Qian represents the upper clothes, and Kun represents the lower garments. A lower garment symbolizes humility. In the Chinese system of the five elements, Earth is in the central place, and its color is yellow. For this reason the lower garment is yellow. A yellow garment symbolizes that one in this place is able to walk in the central path and be humble. It is extremely auspicious. In the class-based society of ancient times, the formal attire of a scholar was a black robe with a yellow lower garment. (Scholars were of the social stratum between senior officials and the common people.) The robe was long, and covered the yellow garment. Humility is of an inner beauty, like the beauty of the yellow garment covered by the black robe. Thus Confucius's commentary says, ("There is beauty within.") This line indicates that the time to send an expedition against the Tyrant of Shang was near. The Duke of Zhou and King Wu realized that humility should not be dealt with as a strategy. It should become one's nature.

There is a story relating to this line. There was a lord named Nan Gua who plotted to rebel against the king. He performed a divination and obtained this gua. He was very happy that the text said, "A yellow lower garment. Supreme good fortune." He was certain that he would meet with success. Nevertheless, a duke admonished him, "Dear Lord, it must be a faithful and truthful action to be auspicious. Otherwise it will fail." His explanation was based on the theory of the five elements. According to this theory, yellow, the color of Earth, represents the center which guides one to act in accordance with the principle of Confucius's Golden Mean, that is, to act exactly right without excess or insufficiency. To rebel is to leave the central path; such an undertaking would be bound to fail.

(6) Top Six. Kun alternates to Falling Away (The 23rd Hexagram, Bo)

The top line reaches the extremity of the gua. In this gua all six lines are yin. The yin element approaches closer and closer; the yang element retreats again and again. The yang reaches its end point; it has no place to retreat, and so a struggle with the yin is unavoidable. It is a struggle between negative and positive, darkness and light. In Chinese tradition, the color of heaven is blue. Two dragons—one yang and the other yin—are fighting. Consequently, the colors of their blood—blue (Heaven) and yellow (Earth), merge. The message of this yao is that when one approaches an extreme, the path comes to an end. If one is ready to change, this is a turning point. Otherwise, one will fall apart.

This line indicates that four years after King Wen had passed away, in the year 1066 B.C., King Wu followed his father's instruction, sending a punitive expedition against the tyrant of the Shang Dynasty. At first, King Wu sent spies to Shang. It was reported that the rulers and administrators were dissipated and unashamed. King Wu thought that the time was not appropriate. Later, messages were sent back that all the righteous persons had been reproached and dismissed from their posts. King Wu believed that the time was still not mature. At last, the messenger came back and told how the people of Shang dared not speak. King Wu considered that the time was ready. At the same time there was a famine; people working in the fields preferred to go on an expedition. King Wu took three hundred chariots, forty-five thousand soldiers, and three thousand troops as a vanguard. Soldiers sang and danced, and morale was high. Eight different ethnic kingdoms came to join the campaign. King Wu charged the tyrant with four indictments: that he was licentious and dissolute, indulging himself with concubines; that he did not offer sacrifices to Heaven and his ancestors; that he did not trust righteous persons, even his own relatives; and that he housed criminals of all kinds and harbored the escaped slaves of neighboring kingdoms. In a decisive battle, 170,000 troops of the Shang Dynasty responded to King Wu's righteous movement and rose up against the tyrant. The cruel Shang Dynasty was brought down.

(7) All Sixes. Kun alternates to Initiating (The 1st Hexagram, Qian)

All sixes indicates that all yin lines alternate to yang lines. As already mentioned, there are two extra Yao Texts with the first and second guas, Qian and Kun. Qian represents Heaven, pure yang, and Kun represents Earth, pure yin. When one's divination obtains this yao, one should use the full potential of the Earth quality; then "great will be the end," meaning that all six yin lines alternate to yang lines. In the *I Ching*, yang represents great, and yin represents little. When six yin lines alternate to six yang lines, that is great. The function of Earth is to respond. Earth responds to the action of Heaven. When one accepts the pure yang energy from Heaven and acts in accordance with perfect timing, then one is able to produce myriad beings between Heaven and Earth. This is a perfect complement of yin energy with yang energy. This line is a continuation of the preceding gua. King Wu fulfilled the will of his father, King Wen, who responded to the will of Heaven. The Tyrant of Shang was overthrown. All the yin energy turned to yang. The Tao of Heaven was fulfilled, but there remained something not yet fulfilled. According to the Tao of Heaven, it was favorable to be steadfast and upright.

Chapter One
The *Book of Changes*: A Treasure of Chinese Intellectual History and Its Impact on 20th-Century Western World

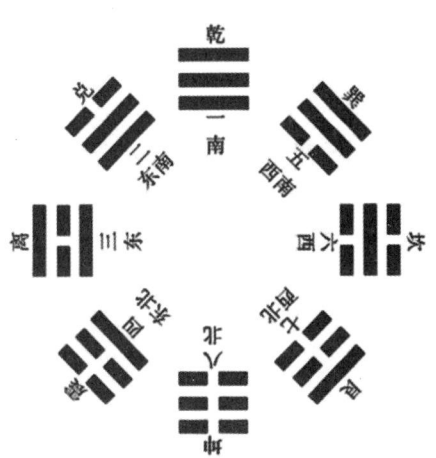

(Figure 2: Fuxi's "Earlier Heaven" bagua arrangement①)

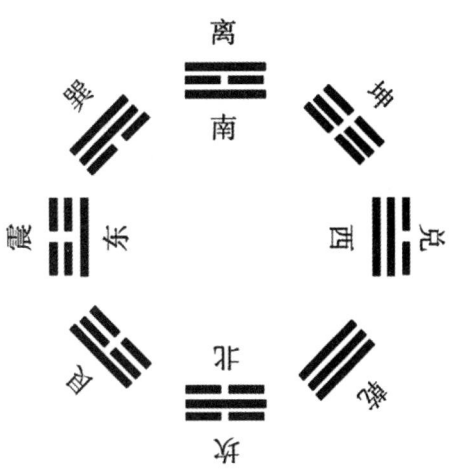

(Figure 3: King Wen's "Later Heaven" bagua arrangement②)

3. Zhun • Beginning 三、屯卦第三

 Kan·Cloud
Zhen·Thunder

Decision

 The beginning of a tiny sprout. 屯：

 Sublimely prosperous and smooth. 元亨，

 Favorable to be steadfast and upright. 利贞。

 Do not act lightly. 勿用，

 There is somewhere to go. 有攸往，

 Favorable to establish feudal lords. 利建侯。

Commentary on the Decision 《彖》：

 Beginning. 屯，

 The firm and yielding united at the very beginning; 刚柔始交而难生，

 Difficulties come into being.

 Movement in the midst of danger, 动乎险中，

 Great prosperity and smoothness come through steadfastness and uprightness. 大"亨贞"。

---

① From Chen, Deshu, *The Comprehensive Interpretation of the Authentic I Ching by Renowned Scholars over a century*, Bashu Publishing House, 2013, p. 46.

② Ibid., p. 48.

雷雨之动满盈。	The action of thunder and rain
	Filled things up everywhere.
天造草昧，	At the beginning of creation,
	There was irregularity and disorder.
宜"建侯"而不宁。	It was favorable to establish feudal lords,
	But unstable conditions still might arise.

《象》：   **Commentary on the Symbol**

云雷，	Clouds and thunder fill up.
屯。	In correspondence with this,
君子以经纶。	The superior person plans and sets things in order.

爻辞：   **Yao Text**

初九：	Initial Nine
磐桓，	Lingering and considering,
利居贞，	Favorable to abide in being steadfast and upright.
利建侯。	Favorable to establish feudal lords.
六二：	Second Six
屯如邅如，	Difficulty in advancing, hard to proceed.
乘马班如，	Mounting on horses, still not going forward.
匪寇，婚媾。	Not invading, seeking a marriage.
女子贞不字，	The maiden is chaste, marries not.
十年乃字。	After ten years, she marries.
六三：	Third Six
即鹿无虞，	Chasing deer, no guide
惟入于林中，	In the midst of woods.
君子几不如舍，	The superior person is alert:
	Give up!
往吝。	Going forward: humiliation.
六四：	Fourth Six
乘马班如，	Mounting on horses, still not going forward.
求婚媾。	Seeking a union.
往吉，	Going forward: good fortune.
无不利。	Nothing is unfavorable.
九五：	Fifth Nine

The beginning of one's abundance.	屯其膏，
Little things—	小贞吉，
Being steadfast and upright: good fortune.	
Great things—	大贞凶。
Being Steadfast: misfortune.	
Top Six	上六：
Mounting on horses,	乘马班如，
Still not going forward.	
Weeping grievously,	泣血涟如。
Shedding tears as if bleeding.	

The Significance of Zhun

This is an auspicious gua. It expounds the truth that a newly established situation is full of the potential to develop. On the other hand, it also contains latent difficulties. "Clouds over Thunder symbolizes Beginning"—this is the Chinese way to remember the structure of the gua. The structure presents a vivid picture of a tremendous power of energy, represented by thunder, lying at the base of clouds. In the Commentary on the Decision, Confucius says, "The action of thunder and rain filled things up everywhere." In his *Commentary on the Symbol* he says, "Cloud and thunder fill up." In both cases Confucius employs the image of clouds or rain instead of water. Clouds and rain have the same essence as water. Contemplating the symbol, Confucius says, "Clouds and thunder fill up," but he doesn't mention rain. The attribute of Thunder is action, but there is no action. However, the clouds do presage a storm. When dark clouds fill the sky, sooner or later rain will come. This gua holds the potential to create. Confucius advises that "the superior person plans and sets things in order." It is time to prepare to do something.

On the other hand, meditating on King Wen's Decision, Confucius says "The action of thunder and rain filled things up everywhere." Eventually the action comes—it is rain. Confucius then says, "At the beginning of creation there was irregularity and disorder." When I study this gua, I visualize the Chinese concept of genesis. Before Heaven and Earth were created, they were without form, void. During Creation, there were clouds, rain, and thunder. At first, there was irregularity and disorder. After the world was brought into being (the beginning), regularity and order were gradually established. Based on the idea of the union of yin and yang, Chinese scholars came to employ clouds and rain to suggest the actions of lovemaking. I can see this union appearing in the upper gua, which suggests clouds and rain. The fruit of this union is Thunder, the lower gua; in the *I Ching*, Thunder represents the eldest son. It is significant that this Chinese ideograph was selected to express the beginning of the world. In this ideograph the root is inscribed much longer than the sprout. Before sprouting, the root must penetrate deeply. The sages learned from nature that before effecting a plan, it is important to set things in order.

The host of the gua is the solid line on the bottom. King Wen's Decision on the gua says, "The beginning of a tiny sprout. … Favorable to establish feudal lords." One in this position is able to establish feudal lords to provide security. On the other hand, the solid line on the bottom symbolizes a beginning. Although it is firm and strong, it is on the bottom and carries two yielding lines. This situation indicates that a latent power will sprout, but in a difficult situation. The yang element at the fifth place lies in a supreme position—firm, central, and correct— and responds to the yin element at the second place. Everything is in order for it to be the host; however, since the name of the gua comes from the solid line at the bottom, that line makes a more suitable host.

Examining the structure, the lower gua is Thunder, indicating action and power. The upper gua is Water, indicating trouble. Thunder confronting Water delivers the message that when one faces difficulty at an initial stage, no matter how powerful one is, nothing should be taken lightly. This is the main theme of the gua. In this gua, the Duke of Zhou reaffirmed King Wen's guiding principle that care should be taken at the beginning of an undertaking. The time is favorable only for persevering in naming feudal lords in order to accumulate strength and laying the foundation of a new dynasty. His strength needed to grow as strong as a rock and as firm as a tree.

In the *I Ching*, in most cases, the act of marriage refers to a political alliance. The Duke of Zhou described the process of establishing feudal lords as difficult to advance, likening it to four horses drawing a cart at different paces. Three ferocious minority tribes came to him asking for an alliance. King Wen considered that the time was not auspicious and refused. The Duke of Zhou restated King Wen's instruction that, without first knowing the situation of the Shang Dynasty, launching an expedition would be like chasing deer without a guide in the midst of woods.

With time, the process of establishing feudal lords became like mounting on a horse but still not moving forward. King Wen took the initiative to form an alliance with Shang. As a result King Yi of the Shang Dynasty gave his younger sister to King Wen in marriage. The situation improved. Being in an alliance with the Shang Dynasty, the energy of the Zhou was obstructed. It was favorable only for small undertakings. In this gua, the Duke of Zhou repeated "Mounting on horses, still not going forward" three times. He grieved deeply, shedding tears as if bleeding.

(1) Initial Nine. Beginning alternates to Union (The 8th Hexagram, Bi)

Nine at the beginning is a solid line at the bottom of the lower gua, Thunder. The structure reveals two things. First, this line is at the initial stage of a process. Second, from this place one has great potential to move forward as thunder does. However, this element responds to the yin element at the fourth place, which is at the bottom of the upper gua, Water. Water has dark depths,

Chapter One
The *Book of Changes*: A Treasure of Chinese Intellectual History and Its Impact on 20th-Century Western World

suggesting difficulty. This place requires one to linger and consider. The timing is significant. Although there is difficulty ahead, it is a crucial time to start a new enterprise. In this situation, perseverance is critical.

The English translation of the Yao Text says, "Lingering and considering." In Chinese, the words for lingering and considering are pan huan. Pan is a huge rock, and huan is a big tree. When the Duke of Zhou saw a big tree growing on a huge rock, he realized that if there was sufficient life force then nothing could prevent the tree from growing. In the structure of the gua, there are several yin lines above the yang line, like a huge rock sitting above a tree. However, the tree eventually grows and stands firm on the rock. In ancient Chinese literature, a single word usually represented several thoughts. Huan meant pillar, and was also the name of the "Ode of Zhou," one of the pieces in *The Book of Songs*, a classic collection of folk songs compiled by Confucius. This ode praises the efforts of King Wu when he launched his expedition and eventually conquered the Tyrant of Shang. Later on, pan huan came to have the sense of lingering and considering. "Favorable to establish feudal lords" is an ancient Chinese expression equivalent to seeking support. If one plans to do something great, seeking support is a necessity.

(2) Second Six. Beginning alternates to Restricting (The 60th Hexagram, Jie)

Here the Duke of Zhou uses the image of the gua to tell a story. There are two yang elements and four yin elements. Six at the second place is a yin element symbolizing a maiden. She is enchanting two men. The one at the fifth place is her true lover; they have a common interest and mutual affection. Unfortunately, they are not close together. Another man, Nine at the beginning, is her close neighbor. He woos her. Two men woo one woman; the woman has to make a decision. Her decision is to stay faithful to her true love, to remain steadfast. Finally she marries the man she has truly loved.

The story derived from the structure of the gua. Six at the second place is a yin element at a yin place, central and correct. It responds to the yang element at the fifth place. These two elements, yin and yang, are a perfect match. But another yang element, at the bottom place, carries the second line. This yang element is a close neighbor. This situation makes it difficult for the yin element at the second place to advance. The yang element at the bottom is at a yang place, dominant and tyrannical. He would force the maiden to marry him. The maiden is in a central place; she prefers to walk the middle path. She acts exactly in accordance with the main theme of the gua, that nothing should be taken lightly. She remains firm in her will, patiently waiting. Eventually she obtains what she wants.

(3) Third Six. Beginning alternates to Already Fulfilled (The 63rd Hexagram, Jiji)

Here again, the Duke of Zhou tells a story. A group of people going hunting found a deer and chased it. The deer ran into the forest. Without the guidance of a forester, the wise man decided to give up; he let the deer flee like a bird. He knew that by going on, regret would follow. The Yao Text gives advice to one at the third place—at the top of the lower gua.

The upper gua is Water, symbolizing a difficult situation. We have here a yin element at a yang place, neither central nor correct. If one at this place does not remain content and intends to proceed, there will be difficulty ahead. Furthermore, the yin element at this place does not respond to the yin element at the uppermost place—they are both yin. If one at this place proceeds lightly, she will fall into dark depths. The text uses "chasing deer, no guide" as an analogy. Proceeding blindly with no guidance, one becomes lost. The message of this yao is that one should be wise enough, by knowing the situation, to make a proper choice of what to accept and what to avoid. Never act blindly.

(4) Fourth Six. Beginning alternates to Following (The 17th Hexagram, Sui).

Here the story of the marrying maiden continues. In this gua the position of the maiden shifts from the second to the fourth place—she is much closer to her true love. The situation is favorable and the time is right. The Duke of Zhou says, "Seeking a union. Going forward: good fortune. Nothing is unfavorable." But the maiden still hesitates. The problem is that she responds to the yang element at the bottom. On the other hand, she is much closer to the yang element at the fifth place. It is understandable that when two yang approach one yin, the yin becomes confused. In this situation Confucius encourages the maiden, "Go ahead. There is light." This decision is based on the structure of the gua. If one at this place proceeds, there is a yang element waiting. If she retreats, there are two yin elements behind. When one makes a decision, one should consider the most favorable position. The Chinese say, "A waterfront pavilion gets the moonlight first." The message of this yao is that when one is in a situation where it is difficult to decide between advancing or retreating, one should adopt a positive attitude in approaching the light.

(5) Fifth Nine. Beginning alternates to Turning Back (The 24th Hexagram, Fu).

To understand the significance of this yao, we must examine the structure first. The structure usually sheds light on a situation. In general terms, a yang element at the fifth place is usually auspicious because its place is central and correct and in a supreme position. But in this gua, the yang element at this place is lying in the middle of the upper gua, Water, the dark depths. Thus, Confucius says, "One's brilliance is not yet recognized." Accordingly, it is only favorable for small endeavors. Furthermore, the structure shows that the yang element at this place is surrounded by several yin elements. For this reason, the Yao Text recommended "being steadfast and upright," even in little ways. In the *I Ching*, where there is an auspicious omen, being steadfast and upright is often a prerequisite. The structure also shows that the yang element at this place responds to the yin element at the second place. However, the yin element at the second place is being cut off and is too weak to give support, because two yin elements lie between. These two yin elements leave the yang element stuck in an isolated position. In this situation, one should retreat and preserve one's energy, waiting for the right time.

(6) Top Six. Beginning alternates to Increasing (The 42nd Hexagram, Yi)

In this gua, "mounting on horses" appears three times. Here, however, the rider is weeping. Her grief is so deep that shedding tears is like bleeding. What is this story based upon? The yielding line on the top has ascended to the uppermost position. It is as if the sun has set beyond the western hills. The day is waning, and the road is ending. There is no way to go forward. In addition, this line does not respond to the yin element at the third place, indicating that there is no way to turn back. In the *I Ching*, the primary gua Water also signifies blood. The message of this gua is that, since one has already reached the uppermost position, one should not feel sorry about being unable to go forward or turn back. One must realize that when things reach an extreme they will alternate to the opposite. For this reason, the *I Ching* always calls for restraint before going too far.

4. Tai • Advance

四、泰卦第十一

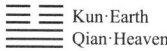
Kun·Earth
Qian·Heaven

Decision

    Advance.

    The little is departing,

    The great is arriving.

    Good fortune.

    Prosperous and smooth.

泰：

小往大来，吉，亨。

Commentary on the Decision

    Advance.

    The little is departing;

    The great is arriving.

    Good fortune.

    Prosperous and smooth.

    Heaven and Earth unite;

    All beings come into union.

    The upper and the lower link;

《彖》：

"泰，

小往大来，

吉，

亨"。

则是天地交而万物通也，

上下交而其志同也。

	Their wills are the same.
内阳而外阴，	The inner is the yang; the outer is the yin.
内健而外顺，	The inner is the strong; the outer is the gentle.
内君子而外小人，	The inner is the superior; the outer is the inferior.
	Thus,
君子道长，	The way of the superior is expanding;
小人道消也。	The way of the inferior is shrinking.

《象》: **Commentary on the Symbol**

天地交，	Heaven and Earth are moving together.
泰。	An image of Advance.
后以财成天地之道，	In correspondence with this,
辅相天地之宜，	The ruler gives full play to his ability and wisdom
	To complete the Tao of heaven and Earth,
以左右民。	And assists their suitable arrangement,
	to influence people.

爻辞： **Yao Text**

初九：	Initial Nine
拔茅茹，	Pulling out a reed,
以其汇，	Other roots come with it.
征吉。	Moving forward: good fortune.
九二：	Second Nine
包荒，	Embracing great rivers.
用冯河，	Fighting a tiger with bare hands.
	Crossing a river with bare feet.
不遐遗。	Abandon not the remote;
朋亡，	Cliques dissolve.
得尚乎中行。	Obtain esteem by walking the central path.
九三：	Third Nine
无平不陂，	No plain without undulation,
无往不复，	No past without return.
艰贞无咎。	In hardship,
勿恤其孚，	Being steadfast and upright: no fault.
于食有福。	Grieve not over your sincerity and truthfulness.

In inheritance there is happiness.

Fourth Six 六四：

Fluttering, fluttering. 翩翩，

Not affluent. 不富以其邻，

With your neighbors,

No admonishing, 不戒以孚。

Be sincere and truthful.

Fifth Six 六五：

King Yi married off his younger sister. 帝乙归妹，

This brought blessing. 以祉元吉。

Supreme good fortune.

Top Six 上六：

Castle wall returns into the moat. 城复于隍，

Use no multitude. 勿用师，

To your own county, make your self-blame known. 自邑告命，贞吝。

Being steadfast: humiliation.

The Significance of Tai

In this gua, the significance of the union of Heaven and Earth is employed to display the importance of union among people. When people communicate sincerely and truthfully, harmony is created, and things will be achieved easily and smoothly. In Chinese, this situation is called Tai, Advance. The Yao Text of this gua is extremely difficult to understand. Different scholars have varying ideas. To the Chinese, the opposite of Tai is Pi. To go from Tai (Advance) to Pi (Hindrance) or vice versa is a natural law, as is the waxing and waning of the moon. The wise prefer to live in harmony with the laws of Nature. Be content with one's fate, and never blame Heaven or others.

This gua also displays the wisdom of keeping a state of prosperity and preserving a period of bliss. In human society, starting any undertaking is difficult, but maintaining the achievement is even harder. One should not sleep on the accomplishment and feel complacent, but instead be aware that when the achievement reaches a climax, it begins to decline. The interconnection between Heaven and Earth sets the example for mutual communication between human beings. People with the same faith and goals should maintain their mutual love and care and support each other; then the blissful situation can last longer.

Two lines in this gua are qualified to be the host, either the yang at the second place or the yin at the fifth place. Because of its yang quality, the yang element at the second place is more suitable to be the host. This gua gives the image of that which is above, Heaven, coming down and that which is below, Earth, rising up. They unite in great compassion. This yang element and the yin element at the fifth place respond and support each other, suggesting a blissful condition in the natural environment. It is also applicable to social life.

This gua tells us that King Wen was ready to overthrow the Tyrant of Shang. Before taking action, King Wen recalled the rising and declining of the Shang Dynasty. In his Decision, he felt that the Shang Dynasty had already grown small and was about to end and the Kingdom of Zhou had gradually become great and was about to arrive. The situation was auspicious; progress and success awaited. The Duke of Zhou summarized the process of the rise and fall of the Shang Dynasty. Before King Tang, the originator of the Shang Dynasty, overthrew the Xia Dynasty in 1766 B.C., he launched eleven expeditions to exterminate the alliances of the Xia Dynasty. It was like pulling out a reed—other roots came with it; their roots were connected. The ancestors of the Shang embraced the wasteland as if fighting a tiger with bare hands and crossing a river with bare feet. They feared not the remote time and places and they eliminated selfishness in relationships and acted in accordance with the central path. But the descendants of the Shang disregarded the course of history, suggested by no plain without undulation and no past without return. They acted lightly, as a bird flutters, and lost their solidarity. After the Kingdom of Zhou became strong, King Yi of the Shang married off his younger sister to King Wen. This brought blessing and supreme good fortune to Zhou. However, it did not help the Shang Dynasty stop the castle wall from returning to the moat. Even while his self-blame was known to his people, the divination shows that the humiliation of the tyrant was close at hand. Advance is one of the twelve tidal gua[①], representing the first month of the Chinese lunar calendar. In the solar calendar, it is February.

(1) Initial Nine. Advance alternates to Growing Upward (The 46th Hexagram, Sheng)

The bottom line is the first line of the lower gua: ascending begins. When one starts an undertaking, it is better to have supportive coworkers. The three yang elements of the lower gua cherish the same ideals and follow the same path. Thus the Yao Text says, "Pulling out a reed, other roots come with it. Moving forward: good fortune."

(2) Second Nine. Advance alternates to Brilliance Injured (The 36th Hexagram, Mingyi)

This line is the host of the gua. The Yao Text employs a classic allusion to demonstrate the quality of Advance that ends with good fortune. It says, "Fighting a tiger with bare hands. Crossing a river with bare feet." This allusion was so well known that it was adopted in the

---

① Tidal Gua: The twelve tidal gua, also known as the twelve message gua, are the twelve accomplished gua that represent the waxing and waning of yin and yang energy over the course of a year. Each is associated with a month.

Chapter One
The *Book of Changes*: A Treasure of Chinese Intellectual History and Its Impact on 20th-Century Western World

<u>*Analects of Confucius*</u>:

> <u>*Once Confucius's disciple Zi-lu asked, "If Master had the conduct of the three armed services of a great state, whom would you have to act with you?"*</u>
>
> <u>*Confucius said, "I would not have him act with me who will fight a tiger with his bare hands or cross a river with bare feet, dying without any regret. My associate must be the one who proceeds to action full of watchful attention, who is good in stratagems and then carries them into execution."*</u>

<u>Advancing with watchful attention and stratagems is the true message of this line.</u>

Concerning the structure, this line is central, but it is a yang element at a yin place. The yang quality gives one at this place the disposition to be resolute and steadfast. The yin place bestows temperament of kindness and generosity. In this way, one is capable of bearing with the uncultured and relying on great courage—to fight a tiger with bare hands, cross a river with bare feet, and advance without fear of remote places. One is able to eliminate selfishness in relationships and to act in accordance with the central way. He is the one who gives full play of his ability and wisdom to complete the Tao of Heaven and Earth.

(3) Third Nine. Advance alternates to Approaching (The 19th Hexagram, Lin)

The solid line at the third place has reached the uppermost position of the lower gua. According to the law of Nature, after things proceed to the upper limit they begin to decline. Thus the Yao Text gives warning that there is no plain without undulation, there is no past without returning. Be upright in hardship; prosperity comes through sustaining.

(4) Fourth Six. Advance alternates to Great Strength (The 34th Hexagram, Dazhuang)

This line has already passed through the lower gua. It is a yin element at a correct yin place, and it responds to the yang element at the bottom place. Thus the Yao Text tells us that one at this place is able to be trustful and sincere with neighbors without being reminded. Furthermore, the yin element obtains the help and support of the yang element at the third place. The third line and the fourth line are the junction of the lower gua and the upper gua—Earth and Heaven. Their mutual relationship comes from the core of their hearts, because they are complementary yin and yang, reflecting the Tao of Heaven and Earth. In the *I Ching*, "not affluent" indicates a yielding line. Because a yielding line is a broken line, Confucius's commentary says, "solidarity has been lost." The fourth line together with the fifth and sixth lines from the upper mutual gua, which is Zhen, or Thunder. In certain cases Zhen symbolizes fluttering or means neighbor. The Yao Text thus says, "Fluttering, fluttering.... With your neighbors, no admonishing, be sincere and truthful." The message of this line warns that one who lives in a peaceful and safe situation still needs to be aware of an unfavorable potential. Always be kind and cooperative with neighbors and do not act lightly, as a fluttering bird.

(5) Fifth Six. Advance alternates to Needing (The 5th Hexagram, Xu)

The theme of this line is that King Yi of the Shang Dynasty married off his younger sister to King Wen. This theme also appears in the Yao Text of the fifth line of Marrying Maiden (The 54th Hexagram, Guimei). Before King Wen's son King Wu overthrew the Tyrant of Shang, King Wen had been a duke of the Shang Dynasty. The basis for "King Yi married off his younger sister" comes from the structure of this gua. This line is at the fifth place—a place for the king. It responds to the yang element at the second place—a place for a supportive subordinate. The yin quality of this line suggests a generous king who is gentle, kind, and humble. The corresponding yang element at the second place suggests a powerful and virtuous subordinate of the king. The upper mutual gua, Zhen (Thunder), represents an eldest son. The lower mutual gua, Dui (Lake), represents a youngest daughter. Because of the king's generosity and humbleness, he gave his youngest sister as a wife to his virtuous subordinate; from this act the blessing of supreme good fortune will come. "King Yi married off his younger sister" serves as a metaphor. The true message is that one should choose only able and virtuous persons with whom to work.

(6) Top Six. Advance alternates to Great Accumulation (The 26th Hexagram, Daxu)

The yielding line at the top reaches the final stage of Advance. A turning point from advance to Hindrance is waiting ahead. The Decision gives warning: the castle wall returned into the moat. It is the law of Nature: when things have proceeded to an extreme, they return to their opposite. It is wise for one to know one's predestined fate. One should not try to alter natural law by using force. Recognize the situation. In ancient times when there were serious calamities an emperor often issued a "self-blame decree," a mea culpa, to calm people's indignation. Through self-examination and by being central and steadfast, wait for another cycle from Hindrance to Advance. Out of the depths of misfortune comes bliss. Be patient; there is always hope.

五、同人卦第十三　　　　　5. Tong Ren · Seeking Harmony

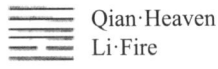
Qian·Heaven
Li·Fire

Decision

同人：	Seeking harmony among people,
同人于野，	Prosperous and smooth.
亨。	Favorable to cross great rivers.
利涉大川。	Favorable for the superior person
利君子贞。	To be steadfast and upright.

Commentary on the Decision

 Seeking Harmony.

 The yielding obtains the proper place.

 It is central

 And corresponds with Qian, the Initiating.

 This is Seeking Harmony.

 Seeking Harmony says:

 Seeking harmony among people.

 Prosperous and smooth.

 Favorable to cross great rivers.

 It is because Qian, the Initiating,

 Is progressing and advancing.

 Brilliance with strength,

 Central and corresponding.

 This is the correct way for the superior person.

 Only the superior person is able

 To convey the wills of all under Heaven.

Commentary on the Symbol

 Heaven with Fire.

 An image of Seeking Harmony.

 In correspondence with this,

 The superior person makes classifications of people

 According to their natures

 And makes distinctions of things

 In terms of their categories.

Yao Text

 Initial Nine

  Seeking harmony out of the gate.

  No fault.

 Second Six

  Seeking harmony within a clan.

  Humiliation.

 Third Nine

  Hiding fighters in the bushes

  Ascend to the high hills.

《彖》：

 "同人"，

 柔得位得中而应乎乾，

 曰"同人"。

 "同人"曰：

 "同人于野，

 亨，

 利涉大川"，

 乾行也。

 文明以健，

 中正而应，

 君子正也。

 唯君子为能通天下之志。

《象》：

 天与火，

 同人。

 君子以类族辨物。

爻辞：

 初九：

  同人于门，

  无咎。

 六二：

  同人于宗，

  吝。

 九三：

  伏戎于莽，

  升其高陵，

三岁不兴。	Three years,
	Unable to go into action.
九四:	Fourth Nine
乘其墉,	Mounting on high city walls,
弗克攻,	Unable to attack.
吉。	Good fortune.
九五:	Fifth Nine
同人,	Seeking harmony,
先号咷而后笑,	Begins with crying and weeping,
	Ends with laughing.
大师克,相遇。	The great multitude succeeds in meeting.
上九:	Top Nine
同人于郊,	Seeking harmony in the countryside.
无悔。	No regret.

The Significance of Tong Ren

The Decision says, "Seeking harmony among people." This is the main theme of the gua. Seeking harmony should be done with absolute unselfishness and among the majority. This was the ancient lofty ideal of a world of harmony. Seeking harmony among people, in Chinese, is tong ren yv ye. Tong ren means seeking harmony. Yv means at, in, or among. And ye is the place beyond the suburbs. Thus, most English translations give ye as "the open." However, ye also means the folk or the people, as contrasted with the government. Considering the theme of this gua, it is more suitable to employ people for ye. In this way, it brings more sense to the Decision: "Seeking harmony among people. Prosperous and smooth."

The outer gua is Qian (Heaven), symbolizing firmness and strength. With this quality, it is favorable for a person to cross great rivers, to overcome difficulties. The inner gua is Li (Fire), symbolizing a quality of inner brightness. In this situation, the host is the yielding line at the second place. It plays a leading role. It is a yin element at a yin place, central and correct. Thus, Confucius's Commentary on the Decision explains that the yielding obtains the proper place and corresponds with Qian. This yin line in the center of the lower gua indicates that one at this place possesses a high morality and is gentle and sincere, humble and modest, and willing to seek harmony with other people. It responds to the solid line at the fifth place, which is also central and correct. These two lines symbolize an ideal condition where the time is auspicious, the situation is favorable, and the people are in harmony. This ideal situation results from the circumstance of overcoming hindrance.

Tong Ren reveals the truth that if people deal with each other in a spirit of equality, then peace and advancement are possible. Otherwise, there will be conflict and obstruction. The first three lines of this gua represent the fact that from sameness differences originate. The next three lines tell us that sameness derives from differences. Thus, at the fifth line, people are at first weeping and full of regret and then laughing to celebrate the victory. In ancient times, people called the piping times of peace the Great Harmony.

This gua symbolizes the historical incident in which King Wen formed alliances with neighboring clans to battle the rebellious Rong clan. King Wen proclaimed that seeking harmony with people of other clans would be prosperous and smooth. The Duke of Zhou recounts how there was no hindrance in seeking alliances with different clans, yet seeking alliances exclusively within his own clan caused isolation and brought about unfavorable results. At the very beginning, the alliance took defensive action by placing troops on a high hill and hiding fighters in the bushes. For three years there was no trouble. Later, the alliance besieged Rong's city walls. After great struggles it was victorious. What began with weeping ended with laughing. At last, the alliance gathered in Zhou's countryside. There was no regret about the struggles that resulted in success.

(1) Initial Nine. Seeking harmony alternates to Retreat (The 33rd Hexagram, Dun)

The Yao Text of this line is "Seeking harmony out of the gate." When this line moves from yang to yin, then the lower gua alternates from Fire to Mountain. In the *I Ching*, Mountain also represents a gate. This line indicates the beginning of seeking harmony. The yang element has a firm and strong character, but it does not respond to the fourth line since they are both yang. Here it symbolizes a lack of personal consideration between them. Seeking Harmony out of the gate suggests action in public, not in secret. The acts are open and aboveboard. The ancient Chinese believed that seeking harmony in a closed place would be to act with selfish motives. Thus Confucius says, "Going out of the gate to seek harmony. Who would find fault with this?"

(2) Second Six. Seeking Harmony alternates to Initiating (The 1st Hexagram, Qian)

This is the host of the gua, as indicated by Confucius when he says, "The yielding obtains the proper place. It is central and corresponds with Qian, the Initiating." The content of the Yao Text is very clear: seeking harmony within the clan is selfish and stingy; it brings about humiliation. The yielding line at the second place is central and correct; it responds to the yang element at the fifth place. Generally, this condition represents a perfect situation and is very auspicious. However, in this gua it is not that positive. Seeking harmony exclusively in a family shows one's selfishness. It focuses on a personal relationship. Acting out of selfishness and personal considerations, how can one seek harmony with the community?

(3) Third Nine. Seeking Harmony alternates to Without Falsehood (The 25th Hexagram, Wuwang)

The third line is at the top of the lower gua, Li (Fire); it gives an image of ascending. This line is located within the inner gua, symbolizing hiding. Li also means weapon and fighter. When the third line moves from yang to yin, the lower gua alternates to Zhen (Thunder), which represents bushes. Thus the Yao Text says, "Hiding fighters in the bushes ascend to the high hills. Three years, unable to go into action." The three years derives from the fact that this is the third line. It does not mean exactly three years, but rather a long period of time.

This line is a yang element at a yang place—not central. One at this place has an irritable, bad temper. This yang element does not correspond with the yang element at the fifth place. It is close to the yin element at the second place, which has a good relationship with the yang element at the fifth place: they are complementary. The yang element at the fifth place is much more powerful than the yang element at the third place, owing to its central, correct, and superior location. One at the third place knows that there is no way to win a face-to-face fight with the one at the fifth place. So he ascends to the high hills to assess the geographical situation and hides fighters in the bushes. The one at the fifth place is much stronger; thus, Confucius says, "The opponent is too firm.... Be content with things as they are."

(4) Fourth Nine. Seeking Harmony alternates to Household (The 37th Hexagram, Jiaren)

The Yao Text says, "Mounting on high city walls." This line comes from the lower mutual gua, Xun (Wind), which also suggests the meaning of a high wall. The fourth line is on top of the lower mutual gua; it gives an image of mounting. The fourth line is a yang element at a yin place, neither central nor correct. It corresponds to the yang element of the bottom line but does not respond—they are both yang. Thus, this yang is closer to the yin element at the second place, and the yang element at the third place stands between them like a high wall. One at the fourth place knows that during a time of seeking harmony it is not good to take controversial actions. Thus, Confucius says, "Bind with morality and justice.... Good fortune due to return to the truth."

(5) Fifth Nine. Seeking Harmony alternates to Brightness (The 30th Hexagram, Li)

The Yao Text of this line bears a significance to the second line of the third gua, Beginning. In Beginning, the yin element at the second place wants to respond to the yang element at the fifth place, but they are blocked by two yin elements at the third and fourth places. Here, the yin element at the second place wants to respond to the yang element at the fifth place, but they are blocked by two yang elements at the third and fourth places. This time the blockage is two yang elements; great struggles are necessary to overcome it. To explore the significance of this line, the text continues the story of the previous two lines.

The yang element at the fifth place is central and correct, responding to the yin element at the second place. They are complementary yin and yang. However, the third line is hiding fighters in the bushes, and the fourth line is mounting on the high walls. These two lines, both strong yang elements, create a blockage. The second line is a yin element, gentle and weak. Therefore, one at the fifth place needs to use extraordinary strength to overcome the obstruction caused by the third and the fourth lines.

The message of this line is that when two people resonate with each other, while they might be separated physically, their hearts are still united. People might be kept apart by different kinds of obstructions that cause them to weep. But when they remain truthful in spirit, nothing can really separate them. After they experience the difficulty of separation, they are able to appreciate the true joy of union.

Confucius once said,

> Whether in charge of a government or being a hermit,
> Or keeping quiet or making comment,
> When two people become one in their hearts
> They are as sharp as a knife that is able to cut iron.
> They cherish the same idea and follow the same path;
> Their words are like the perfume and fragrance of orchids.

(6) Top Nine. Seeking Harmony alternates to Abolishing the Old (The 49th Hexagram, Ge)

The uppermost line is at the edge of the outer gua. In the *I Ching*, Initiating also represents the countryside. Thus, the Yao Text says, "Seeking harmony in the countryside." In ancient times, there were few people in the countryside. The yang element at the uppermost place wants to seek harmony with others, but there is no one to respond. Being content with the reality, although one's will is not yet fulfilled, one has the patience to wait for the right time. There is no regret.

Extensive Readings

A. The Fascination of *Zhouyi*[①]
《周易》的魅力

Richard Rutt
理查德·拉特

Why has this stark Bronze Age manual exerted such a powerful fascination for so many people throughout the centuries?

---

① Excerpted from Richard Rutt, *The Book of Changes*, Rutledge, 2002.

Philosophy and Cosmology

Once *Zhouyi* had been converted into *Yijing* by the addition of the *Ten Wings*, the ideas expressed in the Wings drove the hexagram and line statements into the background. Interest in the divinatory processes petered out as interest in mathematics and philosophy expanded.

The outline history of these changes is not hard to discern. The *Zuo Commentary* describes interpretations created by an early understanding of divination, but moral and metaphysical elements were already beginning to be considered. This change of emphasis coincided roughly with the lifetime of Confucius, not because of any personal connection with him, but because the spirit of the age favoured such development. A few centuries later, with the blossoming of abstract and ethical thought, it became natural for each hexagram to seem to represent the characteristics of a particular point in the everchanging continuum of time and space, a point which the authors of the *Ten Wings* called *shi* "the time" or "the occasion." This philosophy eventually became Confucian orthodoxy, but it was wholly a superimposition on the teachings of Confucius. Though some have discerned a theory of change in a remark he made while standing by a riverside, "What passes away is like this stream: day and night there is no break" (*Analects* ix.16.), he was reflecting on the passage of time, not on cosmology.

Han scholars were intrigued by the mysteriousness of the oracles and the mathematical patterns created by the hexagrams. These two aspects of *Zhouyi* led to scholars being grouped into what are now called two "schools": *yili* "meaning-principle" and *xiangshu* "form-number." Men like Zheng Xuan (127-200) and Wang Bi (226-249), primarily concerned with the meanings of the hexagram and line statements, represented *yili*, while Yu Fan (164-233) was an early exponent of the blend of mathematics and symbology that informed the *xiangshu* concern with the structure of the hexagrams.

The status of *Yijing* as an imperially canonized classic encouraged such men to study it. They fell under its spell, but the spell was cast more by the *Ten Wings* than by *Zhouyi*. It would be centuries before the Chinese would again think of the book in any other light than that with which it was suffused by the wings, especially the *Great Treatise*. Wang Bi, while arguing strongly for the direct meaning of the text to be considered, was convinced that the true meaning was abstract. Not only did he transmit the text; his influence set the general course of *Yijing* study for nearly two thousand years.

The *Great Treatise* itself is primarily about cosmology. Its doctrine can be summarized under nine points, which contain some surprising hints of ideas now associated with Plato, Jung and modern physics:

1. All things are between the poles of heaven and earth.
2. The principle of all being (dao) is the constant alternation and interaction of the positive

heavenly pole (yang) and the negative earthly pole (yin).

3. This polarity creates plus/minus, male/female, light/dark, proactive/reactive, firm/yielding and other polarities, the yin/yang of whose constant alternation and flux all things are constituted.

4. The polarities produce archetypal figures, seen in heaven as changing asterism patterns, on earth as geometric, geographical and biological patterns.

5. The archetypal figures can be traced analogically in all entities, and their flux gives rise to events, including birth, growth and death.

6. Ancient sages were inspired to create the hexagrams as analogues of the archetypal figures, in which polarity is expressed by firm (whole) and yielding (broken) lines, while flux is expressed by the changing places of the lines within the hexagrams.

7. The sages added oracular statements or prognoses indicating the changes to be expected in the lines and in analogous turns of events.

8. To achieve all this the sages needed communication with spirits. Spirits stand outside the yin/yang polarity and are involved in the use of *Zhouyi* because they control the random counting of the yarrow wands, by which the figure (hexagram) analogous to any given situation (time) can be ascertained,

9. The wise man therefore accepts dao and uses the hexagrams to help himself make right decisions.

Westerners may find this schema strangest at the point where patterns are discerned in the skies, the earth and man. Britons especially, because they live in a land of few cloudless nights, their sight further dimmed by ubiquitous artificial lighting that pollutes the darkness, find it hard to imagine the clear night skies of north-east Asia, where the brilliant patterns of the asterisms gave primitive man some of the first linear designs he discerned. The stratification of rocks and soil showed him parallel lines, his own body taught him symmetry. Such details in the *Great Treatise* are perceptive and accurate.

......

These abstractions, with the help of a broadening connotation for yi "change,"[1] bolstered the theory that the hexagrams portrayed the ever-changing nature of the world and everything in it. The hexagrams became, in Joseph Needham's memorable expressions, a "stupendous universal filing-system" for "pigeon-holing novelty," into which anything and everything could be fitted. Daoists had their version, Buddhists eventually had theirs, while alchemists found the whole arrangement very useful. Since government departments were organized to accord with the universe and its changes — rites and agriculture belonged to spring, punishments to autumn,

---

[1] See Richard Rutt, *The Book of Changes*, Rutledge, 2002, p.85.

and so on — *Yijing* was applied to the bureaucratic system. Though the oracles never mention the four seasons, hexagrams were discovered to relate to them too. Since numbers to the power of 2, together with multiple symmetries, turn up everywhere in mathematical and physical structures, Chinese scholars found no difficulty in applying the 64 hexagrams to everything from the structure of crystals to the solar system.

......

Yijing was thus held to contain the answers to all the questions the human mind could formulate, in science, metaphysics and morals. In the nineteenth century Westerners repeatedly reported that if any new invention appeared in China, Chinese scholars regarded it as only a matter of time before the relationship of the new invention to the hexagrams would be discovered. In 1901 Herbert Allen Giles (1845–1935), who in 1897 became professor of Chinese at Cambridge after twenty-five years in the British Consular Service in China, wrote: "No one really knows what is meant by the apparent gibberish of the *Book of Changes*. This is freely admitted by all learned Chinese, who nevertheless hold tenaciously to the belief that important lessons could be derived from its pages if only we had the wit to understand them."

Joseph Needham holds that nothing did so much to delay scientific thought in China as this filing-system approach. He suggests that the longevity and persistence of *Yijing* as a universal symbolic system was largely due to the congruence of the hexagrams with the concerns of a bureaucratic social order. This social order was designed for an agrarian society dominated by needs of irrigation and flood control — needs that were by nature cosmic and ever-changing. The same filing-system suited both government and natural science. The great thinkers of the Song period bequeathed a rich store of *Yijing* studies, including philology, philosophy and the history of the text. Their thought too was largely based in the *Ten Wings* rather than the *Zhouyi* oracles. Each expounded *Yijing* according to his own predilections. Shao Yong (1011–1077), heir to the *xiangshu* approach, explored the mathematics of the hexagrams. Ouyang Xiu (1007–1072), critical and rational, distinguished the core text from the *Ten Wings* and recognized that Confucius could not have written all the latter. Zhou Dunyi (1017–1073), a philosopher, compiled the typical cosmology of the period. Su Shi (1037–1101), better known as the genial poet Su Dongpo, wrote a notable commentary using *Yijing* as a philosopher's guide. Their contemporary Cheng Yi (1033–1107) wrote his commentary *Yizhuan* in the intellectual tradition of Wang Bi — the *yili* approach. In the next century Zhu Xi (1130–1200) insisted that the book's purpose was fundamentally divinatory; but the sense that *Yijing* was a book of wisdom became deeply entrenched as a result of his teaching.

These Song writers — most of all Zhu Xi — became the arbiters of Confucian orthodoxy for the Ming Dynasty. The Qing Dynasty approach was dominated by the Kangxi emperor's fascination with *Yijing* as a moral and political guide. In other fields scholars of the period made great strides in textual studies, but not in relation to *Zhouyi*. No new work could be done there until the discovery of oracle bones in 1899 opened up new vistas in the study of pre-Han Chinese. These made possible the new direction Chinese *Yijing* studies began to take with the work of Gu Jiegang and his fellows in the 1920s, and "contextual criticism" became the prevailing mode of academic studies.

Contextual criticism still goes back behind the *Ten Wings*, but some western sinologists are studying the history of *Yijing* philosophy from Han times onward; the beguiling patterns of the hexagrams and their combinatorial ramifications have lost none of their appeal; yarrow-wand divination has had a revival worldwide; and the "pigeon-holing" of scientific discoveries is seen in a new light as molecular biologists toy with the correspondence between the hexagrams and the sixty-four codons of DNA.

B. Foreword to *I Ching*[①]
《易经》序言

Carl Gustav Jung
卡尔·古斯塔夫·荣格

The Chinese mind, as I see it at work in the *I Ching*, seems to be exclusively preoccupied with the chance aspect of events. What we call coincidence seems to be the chief concern of this peculiar mind, and what we worship as causality passes almost unnoticed. We must admit that there is something to be said for the immense importance of chance. An incalculable amount of human effort is directed to combating and restricting the nuisance or danger represented by chance. Theoretical considerations of cause and effect often look pale and dusty in comparison to the practical results of chance. It is all very well to say that the crystal of quartz is a hexagonal prism. The statement is quite true in so far as an ideal crystal is envisaged. But in nature one finds no two crystals exactly alike, although all are unmistakably hexagonal. The actual form, however, seems to appeal more to the Chinese sage than the ideal one. The jumble of natural laws constituting empirical reality holds more significance for him than a causal explanation of events that, moreover, must usually be separated from one another in order to be properly dealt with.

The manner in which the *I Ching* tends to look upon reality seems to disfavor our causalistic procedures. The moment under actual observation appears to the ancient Chinese view more

---

① Excerpted from Richard Wilhelm and Cary F. Baynes, trans., *I Ching: Or, Book of Changes*, 3rd. ed., Princeton University Press, 1967.

of a chance hit than a clearly defined result of concurring causal chain processes. The matter of interest seems to be the configuration formed by chance events in the moment of observation, and not at all the hypothetical reasons that seemingly account for the coincidence. While the Western mind carefully sifts, weighs, selects, classifies, isolates, the Chinese picture of the moment encompasses everything down to the minutest nonsensical detail, because all of the ingredients make up the observed moment.

Thus it happens that when one throws the three coins, or counts through the forty-nine yarrow stalks, these chance details enter into the picture of the moment of observation and form a part of it—a part that is insignificant to us, yet most meaningful to the Chinese mind. With us it would be a banal and almost meaningless statement (at least on the face of it) to say that whatever happens in a given moment possesses inevitably the quality peculiar to that moment. This is not an abstract argument but a very practical one. There are certain connoisseurs who can tell you merely from the appearance, taste, and behavior of a wine the site of its vineyard and the year of its origin. There are antiquarians who with almost uncanny accuracy will name the time and place of origin and the maker of an object d'art or piece of furniture on merely looking at it. And there are even astrologers who can tell you, without any previous knowledge of your nativity, what the position of sun and moon was and what zodiacal sign rose above the horizon in the moment of your birth. In the face of such facts, it must be admitted that moments can leave long-lasting traces.

In other words, whoever invented the *I Ching* was convinced that the hexagram worked out in a certain moment coincided with the latter in quality no less than in time. To him the hexagram was the exponent of the moment in which it was cast—even more so than the hours of the clock or the divisions of the calendar could be—inasmuch as the hexagram was understood to be an indicator of the essential situation prevailing in the moment of its origin.

This assumption involves a certain curious principle that I have termed synchronicity, a concept that formulates a point of view diametrically opposed to that of causality. Since the latter is a merely statistical truth and not absolute, it is a sort of working hypothesis of how events evolve one out of another, whereas synchronicity takes the coincidence of events in space and time as meaning something more than mere chance, namely, a peculiar interdependence of objective events among themselves as well as with the subjective (psychic) states of the observer or observers.

The ancient Chinese mind contemplates the cosmos in a way comparable to that of the modern physicist, who cannot deny that his model of the world is a decidedly psychophysical structure. The microphysical event includes the observer just as much as the reality underlying the *I Ching* comprises subjective, i.e., psychic conditions in the totality of the momentary situation. Just as causality describes the sequence of events, so synchronicity to the Chinese mind deals with the coincidence of events. The causal point of view tells us a dramatic story about how D came into existence: it took its origin from C, which existed before D, and C in its turn had a father, B, etc. The synchronistic view on the other hand tries to produce an equally meaningful picture of coincidence. How does it happen that A', B', C', D', etc., appear all in the same moment and in the same place? It happens in the first place because the physical events A' and B' are of the same quality as the psychic events C' and D', and further because all are the exponents of one and the same momentary situation. The situation is assumed to represent a legible or understandable picture.

 Now the sixty-four hexagrams of the *I Ching* are the instrument by which the meaning of sixty-four different yet typical situations can be determined. These interpretations are equivalent to causal explanations. Causal connection is statistically necessary and can therefore be subjected to experiment. Inasmuch as situations are unique and cannot be repeated, experimenting with synchronicity seems to be impossible under ordinary conditions. In the *I Ching*, the only criterion of the validity of synchronicity is the observer's opinion that the text of the hexagram amounts to a true rendering of his psychic condition. It is assumed that the fall of the coins or the result of the division of the bundle of yarrow stalks is what it necessarily must be in a given "situation," inasmuch as anything happening in that moment belongs to it as an indispensable part of the picture. If a handful of matches is thrown to the floor, they form the pattern characteristic of that moment. But such an obvious truth as this reveals its meaningful nature only if it is possible to read the pattern and to verify its interpretation, partly by the observer's knowledge of the subjective and objective situation, partly by the character of subsequent events. It is obviously not a procedure that appeals to a critical mind used to experimental verification of facts or to factual evidence. But for someone who likes to look at the world at the angle from which ancient China saw it, the *I Ching* may have some attraction.

C. The *Yijing* in Early Postwar Counterculture in the West[①]
《易经》与西方战后早期反文化运动

Geoffrey Redmond
杰弗里·雷德蒙

1. Introduction: The Rise of the *Yijing* in the Early Postwar Anglophone World
In the 1960s, as the result of an improbable sequence of events, a 3,000-year-old Chinese compilation of mostly obscure fragments, the *Yijing*, or the *Book of Changes*, suddenly became

---

① Excerpted from "Chapter 12: The *Yijing* in Early Postwar Counterculture in the West", in Wai-ming Ng ed., *The Making of the Global Yijing in the Modern World: Cross-Cultural Interpretations and Interactions,* Springer, 2022.

a bestseller in the West. This chapter examines the impact of the *Yijing* in the 1960s and 1970s in the Western world. While the *Yijing* was the most fashionable Chinese classic during these decades, its rise was part of a deeper trend toward appreciation of Chinese culture through its ancient writings.

......

In the Sixties and Seventies, ancient wisdom was cool. Most read the *Yijing* in the hope of finding sagely advice that could help them with their own problems; some found it useful enough that they became lifelong devotees. With the interest in heterodox spirituality, mysticism attracted considerable attention in this period. Not only the *Yijing*, the *Dao De Jing* also appealed to this. From its beginnings in early China, the ambiguity of the *Yijing* texts and the open-ended meaning of the diagrams permitted interpretations to blossom, a process that only accelerated during its new foreign residences. ...

Despite its apparent popularity, the *Yijing* was never an easy read in any of its versions. Until recently, Western scholars had tended to avoid it, not only because of its obscure language, but also because its divinatory use associated it in some minds with other areas of rejected knowledge such as astrology and Tarot. This same association was attractive to practitioners, who were unconcerned with the anti-occult prejudices of academics and thus freer to investigate the arcane works that were resurfacing in the Sixties and Seventies. In this atmosphere, scholarly interest developed more slowly than popular interest. It is almost certain that some who later became scholars were initially attracted by this aura of mystery, though not publicly admitting it once they were established.

2. The *Yijing* and the Counterculture in the Sixties and Seventies

The characteristic Sixties-Seventies rhetoric was more hyperbolic in contrast to the measured language of Jung and his followers. Here is an example from Jay Stevens's valuable history of LSD (or "acid," a hallucinogenic drug), in which he described the ambitions of the Sixties-Seventies youth culture as:

> *two philosophies...on how the world might be remade. One path...seizing political power and using the vantage to raise consciousness and save the world. The other path proposed an attack on consciousness itself using a controversial and soon outlawed family of psychochemicals – the psychedelics.*①

The two modes of salvation—political reform and transformation of consciousness— have been with us since ancient times. Confucius and Plato advocated for proper governance, while

---

① Jay Stevens, *Storming Heaven: LSD and the American Dream*, Perennial Library, 1988, p. xii.

Chapter One
The *Book of Changes*: A Treasure of Chinese Intellectual History and Its Impact on 20th-Century Western World

Laozi, Shakyamuni Buddha and Jesus sought to improve the world by correcting disordered ways of thought.

The syncretism of the Sixties and Seventies came with a conscious sense of being members of a novel culture that was composed of diverse elements, including non-Western spirituality, opposition to the Vietnam war, socialism, laissez-faire sexual mores, long hair, bare feet, casual or eccentric dress, listening to rock music, and drug use. Probably no one embraced all these but made their own selections from the menu.

Put more broadly, imagination was unfettered, opening minds to many things including the *Yijing*. It seems likely that a reason for this strange text seeming relevant across long spans of time and distance is in part because it straddles the political and the personal. Its prognostications are suggestive, advocating morality but not prescribing rigid rules. In practice, the *Yijing* is interactive, almost dialectical, as a means of finding a wise response to a specific situation. Lines were selected by a slow process and then pondered in solitude or explored mutually between inquirers and diviners. Ethical wisdom in China was conceived as an ability possessed to perfection only by the ancient sages. It was this ability that the *Yijing* and the classics generally were thought to teach, equipping the refined person (junzi 君子) to respond properly as situations arose. Indeed, the *Yijing* was itself the creation of sages and culture heroes, intended to help those with less wisdom cultivate their own morality.

......

The first translation of Chinese poems that were actually readable was probably Ezra Pound's (1885–1972) *Cathay* (1915), a slender booklet of gem-like translations. He also translated the more difficult *Shijing* (*Classic of Poetry*), but this lengthy and more difficult work never caught on with the Western literati. His best-known work is probably the *Cantos*, written between 1915 and 1963. The current edition is 824 pages interspersed with quotations from Chinese classics, and notably, some Chinese characters supposedly written by his wife (Pound 1970). Given its density and Pound's unfortunate politics, this work achieved sustained attention mainly among literary critics, though probably many, like myself, read selections from it.

Interestingly, Pound's interest in China, particularly Confucianism, was serious enough to lead him to study the language and even translate the *Analects*. While some doubted that Pound actually knew Chinese, his recently published correspondence demonstrates the effort he put into learning it, with the help of Chinese friends.[①] In contrast to the flowery translations of the Victorian era, Pound's translations were terse, setting a precedent for trying to match the tone of the Chinese original. Given his eccentric life and poetry, Pound's example helped start the

---

[①] Qian, Zhaoming ed. *Ezra Pound's Chinese Friends: Stories in Letters*, Oxford University Press, 2008.

association of Chinese literature and philosophy with non-conformity. This culminated with the *Yijing*—having the compact gray volume in one's hand or bookshelf instantly proclaimed one's individualism, as did wearing a black turtleneck or long hair. While there is irony in thinking that a common behavior could signal individualism, there is some truth in it. For many, the *Yijing* and other newly available spiritual texts were not simply symbols; they were seeking new ways to think.

......

The counterculture was a reaction to the supposedly stifling conformity of the 1950s, and is often considered to have begun with the cultural rebellion that called itself the "Beat Generation," a variation of the "Lost Generation" applied by Gertrude Stein to an earlier avant-garde. The Beat movement had its own fashions—affecting a black turtleneck (roll-top) sweater and a beard marking one as a Beatnik. Jazz, later supplanted by folk rock, was its preferred music. Women had to make do with the turtleneck; the prominent Beats were male, with a few notable exceptions such as Diane Di Prima. The Beat Generation was actually a literary movement with its authors becoming celebrities for their antinomian poems or novels. Most of their writings were ephemeral, but the works of Alan Ginsberg, Jack Kerouac, and Gary Snyder are still read, if less often. The Beats produced an odd combination of Buddhism, drug use and promiscuous, and often homoerotic, sex. This combination of transgressive art with an equally transgressive lifestyle caught the public interest and foreshadowed the Sixties and Seventies. ...

In the Sixties and Seventies, spiritual practices previously disdained in the West, including shamanism, polytheism, divination, channeling, meditation, mantras, vegetarianism, and living in communes, to give an incomplete list, were now permitted. Asian religions had been subjects of academic study, but actual belief and practice of them were assumed to be incompatible with scholarly objectivity. Divination was then often simply entertainment, such as fortune cookies or newspaper astrology columns. The *Yijing* was easily adapted as yet another way of divining, enhanced by the allure of being ancient, but new in the West.

Simply for convenience, I will refer to divination, including the *Yijing*, as part of the category referred to as "occult," that is the seeking of knowledge not accessible by ordinary means. A useful term introduced by James Webb and further examined by Wouter Hanegraaff is "rejected knowledge," emphasizing its history of suppression in the West that began with the competition of early Christianity and paganism, and was later perpetuated by both the religious establishment and the scientific community.

Blended with these intellectual restrictions was a set of social restrictions that were expressed by a rigid dress code, including ties for men and high-heeled shoes for working women. Sexuality could only be hinted at in speech, writing and visual culture, but in the Sixties

Chapter One
The *Book of Changes*: A Treasure of Chinese Intellectual History and Its Impact on 20th-Century Western World

and Seventies, there was a widespread release of inhibitions, beginning with rock music and the legalization of sexually explicit texts and images. Divination was another forbidden subject that came into the open, along with channeling and other supernatural practices.

3. Carl G. Jung and the *Yijing*

One of the most influential advocates of Asian spirituality in the West was the Swiss psychiatrist Carl G. Jung (1875–1961). Known mainly for his archetypal psychology and a variety of now familiar notions such as introversion/extroversion and archetypes, he also assimilated many aspects of ancient and Asian cultures into his theories. His approach of treating the Chinese classic as a way of accessing the unconscious mind has been predominant in Western reading of the *Yijing* ever since.

Jung's Foreword to the Wilhelm-Baynes *Yijing* (1950) established the framework for its Western interpreters up to the present day. While written before the rise of the counterculture, it was essential to the success of the Wilhelm-Baynes translation. Read carefully, Jung's (1950, p. xxi) first sentence establishes that the *Yijing* can be understood outside its Chinese context: "Since I am not a sinologue, a foreword to the *Book of Changes* from my hand must be a testimonial of my individual experience with this great and singular book." Thus, Jung takes the *Yijing* beyond the realm of detached scholars to something to be experienced directly, as he did. This appealed to the counterculture with its distrust of authority. What is implied is that one can ignore scientific skepticism and try out the *Yijing* to discover its truth for oneself.

……

The main interest of this book is Jung's further development of his ideas about Chinese thought, somewhat stereotyped, but with a genuine appreciation as well. Here, for example, Jung anticipates the countercultural view, in contrast to Western science: "The East has taught us another wider, more profound and higher understanding, that is, understanding through life."[①] This was exactly the hope of the Sixties and Seventies, that wisdom thought to be lacking in Western culture was to be found in other cultures, particularly early or indigenous ones.

…Indeed, one of the most salient features of the then spirituality was its discovery that spirituality could involve actions as well as abstract ideas. For the *Yijing*, it was tossing coins and selecting a hexagram or lines. For Buddhism, it was sitting or walking meditation. The Daoism of the *Dao De Jing* did not have explicit instructions but proposed a different way of thinking. Even the Woodstock Music Festival could be considered a practice as it involved being outdoors, nudity and a relaxation of interpersonal boundaries. …

---

① Richard Wilhelm trans., *The Secret of the Golden Flower*, revised from 1931 Edition, Princeton University Press, 1962, p. 82.

These contrasted with the church services that bored many of the Sixties-Seventies youth as they sat through, consisting mostly of sitting, listening, and reciting with some kneeling and standing, depending on the denomination. Communion is a practice, but still mainly cerebral and impersonal. Confession is a practice, but felt as intrusive by many. The passivity of church services as well as their inability to induce an altered state led to a quest for a more experiential spirituality. This was not universal, but a basic difference between the spiritual seeking of the counterculture and that of their parents' generation. At least as presented in Western language accounts, Eastern spirituality seemed more active.

The *Yijing* is a physical book, but it was intended to be used in an active process to gain insight into a particular life situation. Consultation of the book ideally involved action: sitting facing north, lighting incense, tossing coins or sorting yarrow sticks, finding the selected passage, and most important of all, pondering the answer. The book itself was often personified as a sage with whom the inquirer interacts. Of course, when a diviner was involved, the consultation was more direct.

……

While Jung's psychology has sometimes been attacked as unscientific, he did complete medical training in psychiatry and was concerned to present evidence for his theories. The tension Jung revealed between science and the reconsideration of rejected knowledge was also inherent in the Sixties-Seventies culture as well. Despite the fascination with rejected knowledge, most were not willing to completely abandon scientific thinking.

One way to evade this issue was to claim that the metaphysics of the *Yijing*, particularly yin and yang, anticipated quantum physics. This line of argument was common in China as well, as expressed by Jung:

> *The ancient Chinese mind contemplates the cosmos in a way comparable to the modern physicist, who cannot deny that his model is a decidedly psychophysical structure.*

This statement is highly dubious—physics as practiced by physicists consists of equations and is quite unlike consulting the *Yijing*. Many still believe this, though not any physicists so far as I know. Despite the efforts of scientists, philosophers and mystics, the gap between matter and consciousness remains. …

To explain the *Yijing*, Jung proposes his famous concept of synchronicity, which, … refers to external events that seem correlated with mental ones, despite there being no causal connection, in other words, meaningful coincidence. …

So far as I know, pre-modern Chinese texts do not advance anything analogous to this explanation of the *Yijing*; since it was created by sages, it was just assumed to work. Everyone has had synchronicity as a subjective experience. …The matter of psychological differences between cultures remains a fraught one and Jung's casual remarks about the Chinese mind are best set aside.

His contribution to the understanding of the *Yijing*, a text for which he expresses the greatest respect, is considerable, but it was to the Western understanding he contributed, not that of traditional China.

As with any grand theory, Jung's had weaknesses. Yet, even if he did not get everything right, his influence remains indispensable to understanding the *Yijing* in psychological terms, now the dominant mode in the West. When one reads writings by contemporary divinatory practitioners of Tarot, astrology and other systems, almost all are written in the language of popular psychology and Jungian ideas quite often appear. While the psychologization of divination is inevitable, one result is to diminish the sense of mystery. The world has become disenchanted—but not entirely. Or so it seems. During the Sixties and Seventies, a great effort was made to re-enchant it, and the *Yijing* was a part of this re-enchantment. It still is.

4. The Meaning of the *Yijing* for the Postwar Generation

Not only the hippies, the entire counterculture also had ample reasons to want a way of life that did not involve war and early death, with anxieties intensified by the recent war in Korea and the ongoing war in Vietnam. These terrible events did much to shake faith in Western civilization. The burst of hedonism in the Sixties and Seventies, however, was transient and did not resolve the underlying angst.

The hippie movement was at root based on fashion, not on any lasting values. In photographs, hippies have very long hair, may be dancing, and wear wild clothes, such as tie-dyed T-shirts. These affectations replaced the more somber Beatnik vogue for black turtlenecks and berets. For most, the hippie look was simply a safe gesture of rebellion. The more extreme hippies, such as those in San Francisco's notorious Haight-Ashbury district, were heavily drug-addicted, with a dysfunctional lifestyle not at all appealing at close range. Rather than being spiritual, many were petty criminals indulging in shoplifting, euphemistically referred to as "liberating the purloined items." This slang exemplifies the shallow references to revolution that were common in the era.

…It is important, however, to keep in mind that those seduced by the excesses of the Sixties and Seventies were a minority. In contrast, the *Yijing* and other newly available spiritual works were mind-expanding in safe ways. Many, including myself, benefited greatly from our engagement with these texts. If there is a way to sum up the Sixties and Seventies, it was a time of opportunities and dangers, with the *Yijing* being one of the opportunities.

……

A more serious question is whether the use of the *Yijing* in the Sixties and Seventies had any real relation to how it was understood in traditional China. After all, there is nothing in the Chinese classic about the countercultural themes of free sex, drug use, or social transformation. The best answer, I think, is that there was more to the Beat Generation than, to use a common slogan, "sex, drugs, and rock and roll." Many were seriously interested in learning about other cultures and self-exploration. The latter was Zhu Xi's approach to the *Yijing*, although the West did not have this rich commentarial tradition to augment their studies.

While practitioners' interest in the *Yijing* may be waning, scholarly interest seems to be reviving. The unearthing of previously unknown manuscripts beginning in the 1970s has since revitalized the study of early China, and also provided background for work on the later history of these texts. Shaughnessy's meticulous publication of the important excavated *Zhouyi* texts, *Unearthing the Changes: Recently Discovered Manuscripts of the Yi Jing (I Ching) and Related Texts* (2014), greatly facilitates study of its early meanings.

In traditional China, the *Yijing* was usually approached through the commentaries of Wang Bi, Cheng Yi, and Zhu Xi. Richard John Lynn's translation, based on Wang's commentary, has been available for several years. Very recently, the commentaries of Cheng and Zhu have been translated by L. Michael Harrington—*The Yi River Commentary on the Book of Changes* (2019)—and Joseph Adler—*The Original Meaning of the Yijing: Commentary* (2019)—respectively. These are indispensable for further scholarship on the later tradition of *Yijing* interpretation. Also essential is Richard J. Smith's comprehensive account of the commentarial tradition from its beginnings to modern times—*Fathoming the Cosmos and Ordering the World: The Yijing (I-Ching or Classic of Changes) and its Evolution in China* (2008) and *The I Ching: A Biography* (2012). Thus, for the first time, Anglophone readers have the essential materials needed for serious study of the *Yijing* in Chinese intellectual history.

Exercises

I. **Vocabulary Practice**

Explain the meaning of the underlined terms:

1. 元、亨、利、贞
2. 西南得朋，东北丧朋
3. 磐桓 (pan huan)
4. 同人于野

Chapter One
The Book of Changes: A Treasure of Chinese Intellectual History and Its Impact on 20th-Century Western World

II. Comprehension

A. Read Confucius's commentary on the words of the text of Qian hexagram and answer the following questions:

5. What does the underlined "dragon lying low, do not use" mean?
6. What enable the sage not to be proud in a superior position and not distressed in a lowly one?

B. Read Alfred Huang's explanation of the significance of "Qian" and discuss the meaning of "timing" in King Wen's exposition of the six yaos of the Qian hexagram.

C. Read Alfred Huang's explanation of the significance of "Kun" and answer the following questions:

7. Why did the ancient Chinese emphasize yin and yang as the two primary and fundamental forces in the universe?
8. What metaphors of clothes are used to explain the meaning of Kun hexagram?

D. Read Alfred Huang's explanation of the significance of "Zhun" and answer the following questions:

9. How do the structures or images of the "second six" and "fourth six" tell a story about the main theme of the "Zhun" hexagram?
10. What does the story about (not) chasing the deer signify about the "third six" of "Zhun"?

E. Read Alfred Huang's explanation of the significance of "Tai" and answer the following questions:

11. How does the overall image of "Tai" show its thematic significance?
12. How is the allusion in the "second nine" used in the *Analects*?

F. Read Alfred Huang's explanation of "Tong Ren" and answer the following questions:

13. Which yao is the host line? How does its image in the hexagram suggest the theme of "seeking harmony among people"?

III. Application and Interpretation

A. Translate the underlined parts of Extensive Readings, compare the *Yijing* and the Western philosophical ideas and then write a short essay on the "stupendous universal filing-system" of the *Yijing*.

B. How did Carl Jung compare the perspective of reality in the *Yijing* with Western "causalistic procedures"? Explore more from Extensive Reading C and other resources, then find the psychological framework Jung attempted to articulate through such a comparison. How does this case explain ancient classics' role in shaping modern intellectuality or spirituality?

C. Focus on the underlined parts of Extensive Reading C, and then write a short essay to argue about the *Yijing*'s possible impact on the modern world and people. You could use the following questions as thinking lines that lead you through the writing process:

14. How did the *Yijing* get involved in the Western counterculture during the sixties and seventies?

15. Why did the author say the *Yijing* was "one of the opportunities" of the postwar era?

16. How can you integrate what you have learned in this piece of reading and your study of the *Book of Changes* to form your argument?

Chapter Two

Confucianism: Historical Context, Core Tenets, and Global Influences

> **导读**
>
> 本章课文节选了"四书"中《论语》和《孟子》片段。六篇拓展性阅读材料从以下篇目而来：A篇为司马迁所著《史记·孔子世家》的英译；B篇为当今中西比较哲学家安乐哲撰写的《儒家自然宇宙论》；C篇出自当代美国儒学研究者艾文荷为伊莱娜·布鲁姆译《孟子》所作的序言；D篇《人类与社会》出自约翰·诺布洛克编译的《荀子》；E篇《孔子——良善治者》的作者是美国当代学者威廉·阿普尔顿；F篇《儒家思想与英国浪漫主义时期的政治思想》的作者是英国当代学者克里斯·默里。

Introduction

1. An Overview of Confucian Thought

Confucianism, often regarded as the backbone of Chinese culture, has profoundly shaped Chinese society, politics, and ethics for thousands of years. At the heart of Confucianism lie the foundational texts such as the *Analects*, the *Mencius*, the *Great Learning*, and the *Doctrine of the Mean*. These classics form the bedrock upon which the edifice of Confucian philosophy is constructed. Eminent figures like Confucius, Mencius, and Xunzi have left an indelible mark on subsequent generations with their profound insights and teachings. Central to Confucian thought are the values of benevolence (ren), righteousness (yi), propriety (li), wisdom (zhi), and faithfulness (xin). It advocates for personal cultivation, harmonious family relations, enlightened state governance, and the ideal of a world in harmony, known as the Great Unity (datong).

Confucianism's emphasis on moral integrity, social responsibility, and the betterment of the individual for the greater good resonates not only within China but has also reached across the globe. Since the 16th century, as the East met the West and cultural exchanges intensified, Confucian ideas began to make their way into Europe. The Enlightenment thinkers of the time found inspiration in these Eastern philosophies, which have continued to influence global cultural discourse to this day.

The widespread dissemination of Confucianism is a testament to its universal appeal and adaptability. As a philosophical system, it offers a comprehensive framework for understanding human relationships, social order, and the pursuit of a just and peaceful society. Its teachings have transcended geographical and cultural boundaries, engaging with diverse intellectual traditions and providing a rich source of wisdom for the modern world.

In the following sections, we will delve into the specifics of Confucian thought as presented in the Basic Readings and Extensive Readings, exploring the depth and breadth of its philosophical insights and its relevance to contemporary issues. Through an examination of key texts and interpretations, we aim to provide a nuanced understanding of Confucianism's enduring legacy and its contributions to the human experience.

2. Foundations of Confucian Wisdom: Insights from the *Analects* and the *Mencius*

The Basic Readings of this chapter is a curated selection of excerpts from the Confucian canon, capturing the principal ideas of Confucius and Mencius. It serves as a window into the heart of Confucian philosophy, reflecting the teachings that have shaped Chinese thought for centuries.

The *Analects*, a compilation of sayings and ideas attributed to Confucius and his disciples, are explored to understand the essence of learning and its timely application. The text emphasizes the joy of learning and the importance of practice, encapsulated in the famous words, "To learn something and then to put it into practice at the right time: is this not a joy?" (1.1). It underscores the value of continuous self-improvement and the cultivation of virtue, as highlighted in the passage, "A gentleman is not a pot" (2.12), which suggests the depth and breadth of a gentleman's character.

The *Analects* also delve into the concept of the "gentleman" (junzi), detailing the qualities that define this paragon of virtue. The text outlines the importance of gravity, loyalty, and faithfulness, and the courage to correct one's mistakes, as stated, "A gentleman who lacks gravity has no authority and his learning will remain shallow" (1.8). These attributes are central to the Confucian ideal of personal development and social harmony.

The significance of propriety (li) is another key theme, with Master You's insight that "When practicing the ritual, what matters most is harmony" (1.12). This passage reflects the belief that rituals should be performed with an inner sense of harmony, not merely as outward displays of conformity.

Mencius, in his work, expands on the inherent goodness of human nature, a departure from the more implicit suggestions by Confucius. Mencius argues that everyone is born with the potential for goodness, which can be cultivated through moral education and self-cultivation. His discourse on the importance of benevolent governance (renzhi) is a cornerstone of his political philosophy, advocating for rulers who prioritize the well-being of their people.

Moreover, the Basic Readings include explorations of the moral sentiment of "shame" (xiu), as Mencius suggests, "A man without humanity cannot long bear adversity and cannot long know joy" (4.2), indicating that moral integrity is essential for enduring life's challenges and experiencing genuine happiness.

The selected passages also touch upon the Confucian view of the state and the role of the ruler, as seen in Duke Ding's inquiry about the relationship between ruler and minister, to which Confucius replies that both should interact with courtesy and loyalty, respectively (3.19).

In summary, the Basic Readings provide a comprehensive introduction to the core tenets of Confucianism, illustrating how these ancient teachings offer a blueprint for personal cultivation and the establishment of a harmonious society. Through these readings, we gain insight into the profound impact of Confucian thought on Chinese culture and its potential relevance to contemporary ethical and social issues.

3. Interpreting Confucianism: Historical Contexts and Cross-Cultural Dialogues

The Extensive Readings of this chapter broadens our understanding of Confucian thought by presenting a rich tapestry of interpretations and applications across various periods and cultural contexts. This section delves into the multifaceted nature of Confucianism, offering diverse perspectives that highlight the philosophy's adaptability and enduring relevance.

For instance, Szuma Chien's "Records of the Historian" provides an intricate account of Confucius's life, detailing his social and political challenges, as well as his unwavering commitment to moral rectitude and the dissemination of his teachings. This historical narrative not only humanizes Confucius but also illustrates the societal backdrop against which his ideas took root and flourished.

Roger T. Ames' "Confucian Natural Cosmology: An Interpretive Context" offers a comparative philosophical exploration, drawing parallels and contrasts between Confucian thought and Western philosophical traditions. It examines the concept of a natural order in the universe and how Confucianism perceives the relationship between humanity and the cosmos, distinct from the transcendental perspectives often found in Western philosophy.

In the preface by Philip J. Ivanhoe and the compilation by John Knoblock, we encounter fresh insights into Mencius and Xunzi, two seminal Confucian scholars whose works expand upon Confucius's teachings. Mencius's emphasis on the innate goodness of human nature and the role of moral sentiment in ethical development is juxtaposed with Xunzi's more pragmatic view of human nature as inherently inclined towards self-interest, thus necessitating the guidance of ritual and education.

Moreover, the section explores the confluence of Confucian thought with Western political science and romanticism. Chris Murray's work examines how Confucianism resonated with British political discourse during the Romantic era, offering a lens through which to view debates on governance and social order. The writings of William Appleton and Chris Murray reveal how Confucian principles were seen as a potential framework for social stability and moral leadership, particularly in contrast to the upheavals of the French Revolution and the subsequent quest for order in Britain.

Lastly, the Extensive Readings also include examinations of Confucius as a paradigm of virtuous governance, as explored by William Appleton. This study of Confucius as an exemplary ruler provides a historical comparison to contemporary political figures, inviting a reflection on the qualities that define effective and ethical leadership.

In sum, the Extensive Readings enriches our comprehension of Confucianism by situating it within a global dialogue, demonstrating its interaction with other intellectual traditions, and showcasing its continued significance in modern political and philosophical discourse. Through these varied readings, we gain a more nuanced appreciation of the breadth and depth of Confucian thought and its impact on diverse cultural and intellectual landscapes.

《论语》选篇[①] Selections from the *Analects*[②]

学而第一

1.1 子曰："学而时习之，不亦说乎？有朋自远方来，不亦乐乎？人不知，而不愠，不亦君子乎？"

1.8 子曰："君子不重，则不威；学则不固。主忠信。无友不如己者。过，则勿惮改。"

Chapter 1

1.1 The Master said: "To learn something and then to put it into practice at the right time: is this not a joy? To have friends coming from afar: is this not a delight? Not to be upset when one's merits are ignored: is this not the mark of a gentleman?"

1.8 The Master said: "A gentleman who lacks gravity has no authority and his learning will remain shallow. A gentleman puts loyalty and faithfulness foremost; he does not befriend his moral inferiors. When he commits a fault, he is not afraid to amend his

---

① 选自李泽厚：《论语今读》，合肥：安徽文艺出版社，1998年。

② Excerpted from *The Analects of Confucius*, trans. Simon Leys, W. W. Norton & Company, 1997.

ways."

1.12 Master You said: "When practicing the ritual, what matters most is harmony. This is what made the beauty of the way of the ancient kings; it inspired their every move, great or small. Yet they knew where to stop: harmony cannot be sought for its own sake, it must always be subordinated to the ritual; otherwise it would not do."

1.16 The Master said: "Don't worry if people don't recognize your merits; worry that you may not recognize theirs."

Chapter 2

2.4 The Master said: "At fifteen, I set my mind upon learning. At thirty, I took my stand. At forty, I had no doubts. At fifty, I knew the will of Heaven. At sixty, my ear was attuned. At seventy, I follow all the desires of my heart without breaking any rule."

2.12 The Master said: "A gentleman is not a pot."

2.18 Zizhang was studying in the hope of securing an official position. The Master said: "Collect much information, put aside what is doubtful, repeat cautiously the rest; then you will seldom say something wrong. Make many observations, leave aside what is suspect, apply cautiously the rest; then you will seldom have cause for regret. With few mistakes in what you say and few regrets for what you do, your career is made."

Chapter 3

3.4 Lin Fang asked: "What is the root of ritual?" The Master said: "Big question! In ceremonies, prefer simplicity to lavishness; in funerals, prefer grief to formality."

3.19 Duke Ding asked: "How should a ruler treat his minister? How should a minister serve his ruler?" Confucius replied: "A ruler should treat his minister with courtesy, a minister should serve his ruler with loyalty."

Chapter 4

4.2 The Master said: "A man without humanity cannot long bear adversity and cannot long know joy. A good man rests in his humanity, a wise man profits from his humanity."

4.15 The Master said: "Shen, my doctrine has one single

1.12 有子曰："礼之用，和为贵。先王之道，斯为美；小大由之。有所不行，知和而和，不以礼节之，亦不可行也。"

1.16 子曰："不患人之不己知，患不知人也。"

为政第二

2.4 子曰："吾十有五而志于学，三十而立，四十而不惑，五十而知天命，六十而耳顺，七十而从心所欲，不逾矩。"

2.12 子曰："君子不器。"

2.18 子张学干禄。子曰："多闻阙疑，慎言其余，则寡尤；多见阙殆，慎行其余，则寡悔。言寡尤，行寡悔，禄在其中矣。"

八佾第三

3.4 林放问礼之本。子曰："大哉问！礼，与其奢也，宁俭；丧，与其易也，宁戚。"

3.19 定公问："君使臣，臣事君，如之何？"孔子对曰："君使臣以礼，臣事君以忠。"

里仁第四

4.2 子曰："不仁者不可以久处约，不可以长处乐。仁者安仁，知者利仁。"

4.15 子曰："参乎！吾

道一以贯之。"曾子曰："唯。"子出，门人问曰："何谓也？"曾子曰："夫子之道，忠恕而已矣。"

公冶长第五

5.13 子贡曰："夫子之文章，可得而闻也；夫子之言性与天道，不可得而闻也。"

5.21 子曰："宁武子，邦有道，则知；邦无道，则愚。其知可及也，其愚不可及也。"

5.23 子曰："伯夷、叔齐不念旧恶，怨是用希。"

雍也第六

6.11 子曰："贤哉，回也！一箪食，一瓢饮，在陋巷，人不堪其忧，回也不改其乐。贤哉，回也！"

6.18 子曰："质胜文则野，文胜质则史。文质彬彬，然后君子。"

6.23 子曰："知者乐水，仁者乐山。知者动，仁者静。知者乐，仁者寿。"

6.26 宰我问曰："仁者，虽告之曰：'井有仁焉。'其从之也？"子曰："何为其然也？君子可逝也，不可陷也；可欺也，不可罔也。"

6.30 子贡曰："如有博施于民而能济众，何如？可谓仁乎？"子曰："何事于仁，必也圣乎！尧舜其犹病诸！夫仁者，己欲立而立人，己

thread running through it." Master Zeng Shen replied: "Indeed." The Master left. The other disciples asked: "What did he mean?" Master Zeng said: "The doctrine of the Master is: Loyalty and reciprocity, and that's all."

Chapter 5

5.13 Zigong said: "Our Master's views on culture can be gathered, but it is not possible to hear his views on the nature of things and on the Way of Heaven."

5.21 The Master said: "When the Way prevailed in the country, Lord Ning Wu was intelligent. When the country lost the Way, Lord Ning Wu became stupid. His intelligence can be equaled; his stupidity is peerless."

5.23 The Master said: "Boyi and Shuqi never remembered old grievances and seldom provoked resentment."

Chapter 6

6.11 The Master said: "How admirable was Yan Hui! A handful of rice to eat, a gourd of water for drink, a hovel for your shelter—no one would endure such misery, yet Yan Hui's joy remained unaltered. How admirable was Yan Hui!"

6.18 The Master said: "When nature prevails over culture, you get a savage; when culture prevails over nature, you get a pedant. When nature and culture are in balance, you get a gentleman."

6.23 The Master said: "The wise find joy on the water, the good find joy in the mountains. The wise are active, the good are quiet. The wise are joyful, the good live long."

6.26 Zai Yu asked: "If one were to tell a good man that goodness lies at the bottom of the well, should he jump to join it?" The Master said: "Why should he? A gentleman may be misinformed, he cannot be seduced: he may be deceived, he cannot be led astray."

6.30 Zigong said: "What would you say of a man who shows the people with blessings and who could save the multitude? Could he be called good?" The Master said: "What has this to do with goodness? He would be a saint! Even Yao and Shun would be found deficient in this respect. As for the good man: what he wishes to achieve for himself, he helps others to achieve; what he wishes to obtain for himself, he enables others to obtain—the ability simply to take one's own aspirations as a guide is the recipe for goodness."

欲达而达人。能近取譬，可谓仁之方也已。"

Chapter 7

述而第七

7.8 The Master said: "I enlighten only the enthusiastic; I guide only the fervent. After I have lifted up one corner of a question, if the student cannot discover the other three, I do not repeat."

7.8 子曰："不愤不启，不悱不发。举一隅不以三隅反，则不复也。"

7.14 When the Master was in Qi, he heard the Coronation Hymn of Shun. For three months, he forgot the taste of meat. He said: "I never imagined that music could reach such a point."

7.14 子在齐闻韶，三月不知肉味，曰："不图为乐之至于斯也。"

7.16 The Master said: "Even though you have only coarse grain for food, water for drink, and your bent arm for a pillow, you may still be happy. Riches and honors without Justice are to me as fleeting clouds."

7.16 子曰："饭疏食饮水，曲肱而枕之，乐亦在其中矣。不义而富且贵，于我如浮云。"

7.17 The Master said: "Give me a few more years; if I can study the Changes till fifty, I shall be free from big mistakes."

7.17 子曰："加我数年，五十以学易，可以无大过矣。"

7.27 The Master fished with a line, not with a net. When hunting, he never shot a roosting bird.

7.27 子钓而不纲，弋不射宿。

Chapter 8

泰伯第八

8.2 The Master said: "Without ritual, courtesy is tiresome; without ritual, prudence is timid; without ritual, bravery is quarrelsome; without ritual, frankness is hurtful. When gentlemen treat their kin generously, common people are attracted to goodness; when old ties are not forgotten, common people are not fickle."

8.2 子曰："恭而无礼则劳，慎而无礼则葸，勇而无礼则乱，直而无礼则绞。君子笃于亲，则民兴于仁；故旧不遗，则民不偷。"

Chapter 9

子罕第九

9.4 The Master absolutely eschewed four things: capriciousness, dogmatism, willfulness, self-importance.

9.4 子绝四——毋意，毋必，毋固，毋我。

9.17 The Master stood by a river and said: "Everything flows like this, without ceasing, day and night."

9.17 子在川上，曰："逝者如斯夫！不舍昼夜。"

9.28 The Master said: "It is in the cold of winter that you see how green the pines and cypresses are."

9.28 子曰："岁寒，然后知松柏之后凋也。"

Chapter 11

先进第十一

11.17 The Head of the Ji Family was richer than a king, and

11.17 季氏富于周公，而

求也为之聚敛而附益之。子曰："非吾徒也。小子鸣鼓而攻之，可也。"

11.21 子路问："闻斯行诸？"子曰："有父兄在，如之何其闻斯行之？"

冉有问："闻斯行诸？"子曰："闻斯行之。"

公西华曰："由也问闻斯行诸，子曰，'有父兄在'；求也问闻斯行诸，子曰，'闻斯行之'。赤也惑，敢问。"

子曰："求也退，故进之；由也兼人，故退之。"

11.25 子路、曾晳、冉有、公西华侍坐。

子曰："以吾一日长乎尔，毋吾以也。居则曰：'不吾知也！'如或知尔，则何以哉？"

子路率尔而对曰："千乘之国，摄乎大国之间，加之以师旅，因之以饥馑；由也为之，比及三年，可使有勇，且知方也。"

夫子哂之。"求！尔何如？"

对曰："方六七十，如五六十，求也为之，比及三年，可使足民。如其礼乐，以俟君子。"

"赤！尔何如？"

对曰："非曰能之，愿学焉。宗庙之事，如会同，端章甫，愿为小相焉。"

yet Ran Qiu kept pressuring the peasants to make him richer still. The Master said: "He is my disciple no more. Beat the drum, my little ones, and attack him: you have my permission."

11.21 Zilu asked: "Should I practice at once what I have just learned?" The Master said: "Your father and your elder brother are still alive; how could you practice at once what you have just learned?"

Ran Qiu asked: "Should I practice at once what I have just learned? The Master said: "Practice it at once."

Gongxi Chi said: "When Zilu asked if he should practice at once what he had just learned, you told him to consult first with his father and elder brother. When Ran Qiu asked if he should practice at once what he had just learned, you told him to practice it at once. I am confused; may I ask you to explain?"

The Master said: "Ran Qiu is slow, therefore I push him; Zilu has energy for two, therefore I hold him back."

11.25 Zilu, Zeng Dian, Ran Qiu, and Gongxi Chi were sitting with the Master.

The Master said: "Forget for one moment that I am your elder. You often say: 'The world does not recognize our merits.' But, given the opportunity, what would you wish to do?"

Zilu rushed to reply first: "Give me a country not too small, but squeezed between powerful neighbors; it is under attack and in the grip of a famine. Put me in charge: within three years, I would revive the spirits of the people and set them back on their feet."

The Master smiled. "Ran Qiu, what about you?"

The other replied: "Give me a domain of sixty to seventy—or, say, fifty to sixty leagues; within three years I would secure the prosperity of its people. As regards their spiritual wellbeing, however, this would naturally have to wait for the intervention of a true gentleman."

"Gongxi Chi, what about you?"

"I don't say that I would be able to do this, but I would like to learn: in the ceremonies of the Ancestral Temple, such as a diplomatic conference for instance, wearing chasuble and cap, I would like to play the part of a junior assistant."

"And what about you, Zeng Dian?"

Zeng Dian, who had been softly playing his zithern, plucked one last chord and pushed his instrument aside. He replied: "I am afraid my wish is not up to those of my three companions."

The Master said: "There is no harm in that! After all, each is simply confiding his personal aspirations."

"In late spring, after the making of the spring clothes has been completed, together with five or six companions and six or seven boys, I would like to bathe in the River Yi, and then enjoy the breeze on the Rain Dance Terrace, and go home singing."

The Master heaved a deep sigh and said: "I am with Dian!"

The three others left; Zeng Dian remained behind and said: "What did you think of their wishes?"

The Master said: "Each simply confided his personal aspirations."

"Why did you smile at Zilu?"

"One should govern a state through ritual restraint; yet his words were full of swagger."

"As for Ran Qiu, wasn't he in fact talking about a full-fledged state?"

"Indeed; have you ever heard of 'a domain of sixty to seventy, or fifty to sixty leagues'?"

"And Gongxi Chi? Wasn't he also talking about a state?"

"A diplomatic conference in the Ancestral Temple! What could it be, if not an international gathering? And if Gongxi Chi were there merely to play the part of a junior assistant, who would qualify for the main role?"

Chapter 12

12.3 Sima Niu asked about humanity. The Master said: "He who practices humanity is reluctant to speak."

The other said: "Reluctant to speak? And you call that humanity?"

The Master said: "When the practice of something is difficult, how could one speak about it lightly?"

"点！尔何如？"

鼓瑟希，铿尔，舍瑟而作，对曰："异乎三子者之撰。"

子曰："何伤乎？亦各言其志也。"

曰："莫春者，春服既成，冠者五六人，童子六七人，浴乎沂，风乎舞雩，咏而归。"

夫子喟然叹曰："吾与点也！"

三子者出，曾晳后。曾晳曰："夫三子者之言何如？"

子曰："亦各言其志也已矣。"

曰："夫子何哂由也？"

曰："为国以礼，其言不让，是故哂之。"

"唯求则非邦也与？"

"安见方六七十如五六十非邦也者？"

"唯赤则非邦也与？"

"宗庙会同，非诸侯而何？赤也为之小，孰能为之大？"

颜渊第十二

12.3 司马牛问仁。子曰："仁者，其言也讱。"

曰："其言也讱，斯谓之仁已乎？

子曰："为之难，言之得无讱乎？"

12.5 司马牛忧曰："人皆有兄弟，我独亡。"子夏曰："商闻之矣：死生有命，富贵在天。君子敬而无失，与人恭而有礼。四海之内，皆兄弟也——君子何患乎无兄弟也？"

12.17 季康子问政于孔子。孔子对曰："政者，正也。子帅以正，孰敢不正？"

子路第十三

13.3 子路曰："卫君待子而为政，子将奚先？"

子曰："必也正名乎！"

子路曰："有是哉，子之迂也！奚其正？"

子曰："野哉，由也！君子于其所不知，盖阙如也。名不正，则言不顺；言不顺，则事不成；事不成，则礼乐不兴；礼乐不兴，则刑罚不中；刑罚不中，则民无所措手足。故君子名之必可言也，言之必可行也。君子于其言，无所苟而已矣。"

13.18 叶公语孔子曰："吾党有直躬者，其父攘羊，而子证之。"孔子曰："吾党之直者异于是：父为子隐，子为父隐。——直在其中矣。"

宪问第十四

14.30 子曰："不患人之

12.5 Sima Niu was grieving: "All men have brothers; I alone have none." Zixia said: "I have heard this: life and death are decreed by fate, riches and honors are allotted by Heaven. Since a gentleman behaves with reverence and diligence, treating people with deference and courtesy, all within the Four Seas are his brothers. How could a gentleman ever complain that he has no brothers?"

12.17 Lord Ji Kang asked Confucius about government. Confucius replied: "To govern is to be straight. If you steer straight, who would dare not to go straight?"

Chapter 13

13.3 Zilu asked: "If the ruler of Wei were to entrust you with the government of the country, what would be your first initiative?"

The Master said: "It would certainly be to rectify the names."

Zilu said: "Really? Isn't this a little farfetched? What is this rectification for?"

The Master said: "How boorish can you get! Whereupon a gentleman is incompetent, thereupon he should remain silent. If the names are not correct, language is without an object. When language is without an object, no affair can be effected. When no affair can be effected, rites and music wither. When rites and music wither, punishments and penalties miss their target. When punishments and penalties miss their target, the people do not know where they stand. Therefore, whatever a gentleman conceives of, he must be able to say; and whatever he says, he must be able to do. In the matter of language, a gentleman leaves nothing to chance."

13.18 The Governor of She declared to Confucius: "Among my people, there is a man of unbending integrity: when his father stole a sheep, he denounced him." Confucius said: "Among my people, men of integrity do things differently: a father covers up for his son, a son covers up for his father—and there is integrity in what they do."

Chapter 14

14.30 The Master said: "It is not your obscurity that should distress you, but your incompetence."

14.34 Someone said: "To repay hatred with kindness—what do you think of that?" The Master said: "And what will you repay kindness with? Rather repay hatred with justice, and kindness with kindness."

Chapter 15

15.24 Zigong asked: "Is there any single word that could guide one's entire life?" The Master said: "Should it not be reciprocity? What you do not wish for yourself, do not do to others."

15.29 The Master said: "Man can enlarge the Way. It is not the Way that enlarges man."

Selections from the *Mencius*[①]

3A3

Duke Wen of Teng asked about governing the state. Mencius replied, "The people's business may not be delayed. The ode says,

In the morning gather the grasses,

In the evening twist the ropes;

Be quick to climb to the housetop,

Begin to sow the hundred grains.

The way of the people is this: that when they have a constant livelihood, they will have constant minds, but when they lack a constant livelihood, they will lack constant minds. When they lack constant minds, there is no dissoluteness, depravity, deviance, or excess to which they will not succumb. If, once they have sunk into crime, one responds by subjecting them to punishment—this is to entrap the people.

When a humane man is in a position of authority, how could the entrapment of the people be allowed to occur? Therefore, an exemplary ruler will be respectful, frugal, and reverent toward his subjects, and must take from the people only in accordance with

不己知，患其不能也。"

14.34 或曰："以德报怨，何如？"子曰："何以报德？以直报怨，以德报德。"

卫灵公第十五

15.24 子贡问曰："有一言而可以终身行之者乎？"子曰："其恕乎！己所不欲，勿施于人。"

15.29 子曰："人能弘道，非道弘人。"

《孟子》选篇[②]

滕文公上·三

滕文公问为国。

孟子曰："民事不可缓也。《诗》云：'昼尔于茅，宵尔索绹；亟其乘屋，其始播百谷。'民之为道也，有恒产者有恒心，无恒产者无恒心。苟无恒心，放辟邪侈，无不为已。及陷乎罪，然后从而刑之，是罔民也。焉有仁人在位罔民而可为也？是故贤君必恭俭礼下，取于民有制。阳虎曰：'为富不仁矣，为仁不富矣。'……"

---

① Excerpted from the *Mencius*, trans. Irene Bloom, Columbia University Press, 2009.

② 选自万丽华、蓝旭译注：《孟子》，北京：中华书局，2012 年。

the regulations. Yang Hu said, "One who would be wealthy will not be humane; one who would be humane will not be wealthy."

滕文公上·六

孟子曰："人皆有不忍人之心。先王有不忍人之心，斯有不忍人之政矣。以不忍人之心，行不忍人之政，治天下可运之掌上。所以谓人皆有不忍人之心者，今人乍见孺子将入于井，皆有怵惕恻隐之心，非所以内交于孺子之父母也，非所以要誉于乡党朋友也，非恶其声而然也。由是观之，<u>无恻隐之心，非人也</u>；无羞恶之心，非人也；无辞让之心，非人也；无是非之心，非人也。恻隐之心，仁之端也；羞恶之心，义之端也；辞让之心，礼之端也；是非之心，智之端也。人之有是四端也，犹其有四体也。有是四端而自谓不能者，自贼者也；谓其君不能者，贼其君者也。凡有四端于我者，知皆扩而充之矣，若火之始然，泉之始达。苟能充之，足以保四海；苟不充之，不足以事父母。"

3A6

Mencius said, "All human beings have a mind that cannot bear to see the sufferings of others. The ancient kings had such a commiserating mind and, accordingly, a commiserating government. Having a commiserating mind, and effecting a commiserating government, governing the world was like turning something around on the palm of the hand.

"Here is why I say that all human beings have a mind that commiserates with others. Now, if anyone were suddenly to see a child about to fall into a well, his mind would be filled with alarm, distress, pity, and compassion. That he would react accordingly is not because he would hope to use the opportunity to ingratiate himself with the child's parents, nor because he would seek commendation from neighbors and friends, nor because he would hate the adverse reputation [that could come from not reacting accordingly]. From this it may be seen that one who lacks a mind that feels pity and compassion would not be human; one who lacks a mind that feels shame and aversion would not be human; one who lacks a mind that feels modesty and compliance would not be human; and one who lacks a mind that knows right and wrong would not be human.

"The mind's feeling of pity and compassion is the sprout of humaneness; the mind's feeling of shame and aversion is the sprout of rightness; the mind's feeling of modesty and compliance is the sprout of propriety; and the mind's sense of right and wrong is the sprout of wisdom.

"Human beings have these four sprouts just as they have four limbs. For one to have these four sprouts and yet to say of oneself that one is unable to fulfill them is to injure oneself, while to say that one's ruler is unable to fulfill them is to injure one's ruler. When we know how to enlarge and bring to fulfillment these four sprouts that are within us, it will be like a fire beginning to burn or a spring finding an outlet. If one is able to bring them to fulfillment, they will be sufficient to enable him to protect 'all within the four seas'; if one is not, they will be insufficient even to enable him to serve his parents."

3B2

Jing Chun said, "Truly, Gongsun Yan and Zhang Yi were great men, were they not? When they were angry, the lords would tremble in fear; when they dwelled in peace, the fires of conflict throughout the world were extinguished."

Mencius said, "How can they be considered great men? Have you, sir, not studied the Book of Rituals? When a man is capped, his father gives him orders. When a woman is married, her mother gives her orders, accompanying her to the door and cautioning her, 'You are going to your home. You must be reverent, you must be cautious. Do not disobey your husband.' To consider compliance to be correct is the way of women.

"One who dwells in the wide house of the world, occupies his proper place in the world, and carries out the great Way of the world: when he is able to realize his intentions, carries them out for the sake of the people of the world, and when he cannot realize them, practices the Way alone. He cannot be led astray by riches and honor, moved by poverty and privation, or deflected by power or force. This is what I call a great man."

4A8

Mencius said, "Is it possible to speak with those who are not humane? Mistaking danger for peace and calamity for profit, they take pleasure in what occasions their ruin. If, despite their inhumanity, it were possible to talk with them, would we have this ruin of states and this destruction of families?

"There was a boy who was singing,

When the waters of the Cang-lang are clear,

I can wash my cap strings.

When the waters of the Cang-lang are muddy,

I can wash my feet.

"Confucius said, 'Listen to him, my little ones. When it is clear, it washes cap strings; when it is muddy, it washes the feet.

滕文公下·二

景春曰："公孙衍、张仪岂不诚大丈夫哉？一怒而诸侯惧，安居而天下熄。"

孟子曰："是焉得为大丈夫乎？子未学礼乎？丈夫之冠也，父命之；女子之嫁也，母命之，往送之门，戒之曰：'往之女家，必敬必戒，无违夫子！'以顺为正者，妾妇之道也。居天下之广居，立天下之正位，行天下之大道；得志，与民由之；不得志，独行其道。富贵不能淫，贫贱不能移，威武不能屈，此之谓大丈夫。"

离娄上·八

孟子曰："不仁者可与言哉？安其危而利其菑，乐其所以亡者。不仁而可与言，则何亡国败家之有？有孺子歌曰：'沧浪之水清兮，可以濯我缨；沧浪之水浊兮，可以濯我足。'孔子曰：'小子听之！清斯濯缨，浊斯濯足矣。自取之也。'夫人必自侮，然后人侮之；家必自毁，而后人毁之；国必自伐，而后人伐之。《太甲》曰：'<u>天作孽，犹可违。自作孽，不可活</u>。'此之谓也。"

This is all determined by the water itself.' A man must demean himself; only then will others demean him. A family must destroy itself; only then will others destroy it. A state must attack itself and only then will others attack it. This is what is meant when the 'Taijia' says, When Heaven makes misfortunes, it is still possible to escape them. When the misfortunes are of our own making, it is no longer possible to live."

离娄上·十七

淳于髡曰："男女授受不亲，礼与？"

孟子曰："礼也。"

曰："嫂溺，则援之以手乎？"

曰："嫂溺不援，是豺狼也。男女授受不亲，礼也。嫂溺，援之以手者，权也。"

曰："今天下溺矣，夫子之不援，何也？"

曰："天下溺，援之以道。嫂溺，援之以手。——子欲手援天下乎？"

4A17

Chunyu Kun said, "Is it a matter of ritual propriety that, in giving and receiving things, men and women should not touch one another?"

Mencius said, "This is according to ritual."

"If one's sister-in-law is drowning, may one save her with his hand?"

"If one's sister-in-law were drowning and one did not save her, one would be a wolf. For men and women, in giving and receiving, not to touch one another is according to ritual. To save a sister-in-law from drowning by using one's hand is a matter of expedience."

"Now the whole world is drowning, and yet you do not save it. Why is this?"

"When the world is drowning, one saves it through the Way. If one's sister-in-law is drowning, one saves her with one's hand. Would you like me to save the world with my hand?"

万章上·一

万章问曰："舜往于田，号泣于旻天，何为其号泣也？"

孟子曰："怨慕也。"

万章曰："'父母爱之，喜而不忘。父母恶之，劳而不怨。'然则舜怨乎？"

曰："长息问于公明高曰：'舜往于田，则吾既得

5A1

Wan Zhang asked, "When Shun went to the fields, weeping and crying out to merciful Heaven, why was it that he wept and cried?"

Mencius said, "It was from grief and longing."

Wan Zhang said, "When his father and mother love him, he should be glad and never forget them. If his father and mother hate him, though he may suffer, he should not be aggrieved. Was Shun then aggrieved?"

Mencius said, "Chang Xi asked Gongming Gao, 'As to Shun's going to the fields, I have heard your instructions, but I do

Chapter Two
Confucianism: Historical Context, Core Tenets, and Global Influences

not know about his weeping and crying out to merciful Heaven and to his parents.' Gongming Gao said, 'This is something you do not understand.' Gongming Gao thought that the mind of the filial son could not be so dispassionate as this. [Shun said] 'In devoting my strength to tilling the fields, I am fulfilling my duties as a son, nothing more. What is there in me that causes my father and mother not to love me?'

"The sovereign, Yao, caused his children, nine sons and two daughters, his officers, oxen and sheep, granaries and storehouses, to be prepared to serve Shun in the channeled fields, and he was sought out by many of the men of service in the realm. It was the intention of the sovereign to have Shun join him in overseeing the realm and then to transfer it to him. But because he was not in harmony with his parents, Shun was like a poor man with no home to return to.

"To have the approval of the men of service of the realm is something everyone desires, yet this was not enough to dispel his sorrow. To have the love of women is something every man desires, and Shun had as wives the two daughters of the sovereign, yet this was not enough to dispel his sorrow. Wealth is something everyone desires, and he had the wealth that comes with possessing the realm, yet this was not enough to dispel his sorrow. Honor is something that everyone desires and he had the honor of becoming the Son of Heaven, but this was not enough to dispel his sorrow. The reason why the approval of men, the love of women, wealth, and honor were not enough to dispel his sorrow was that it was a sorrow that could be dispelled only by being in harmony with his parents.

"A person when young longs for his father and mother; when he comes to know the love of women, he longs for young and beautiful women; when he has a wife and child, he longs for his wife and child. When he has an office, he longs for his ruler, and if he does not gain the regard of his ruler, he burns within. The person of great filial devotion longs throughout his life for his father and mother. In the great Shun there was manifested one who, at the age

闻命矣。号泣于旻天，于父母，则吾不知也。'公明高曰：'是非尔所知也。'夫公明高以孝子之心，为不若是恝。我竭力耕田，共为子职而已矣。父母之不我爱，于我何哉？帝使其子九男二女，百官牛羊仓廪备，以事舜于畎亩之中，天下之士多就之者，帝将胥天下而迁之焉。为不顺于父母，如穷人无所归。天下之士悦之，人之所欲也，而不足以解忧；好色，人之所欲，妻帝之二女，而不足以解忧；富，人之所欲，富有天下，而不足以解忧；贵，人之所欲，贵为天子，而不足以解忧。人悦之、好色、富贵，无足以解忧者，惟顺于父母可以解忧。人少，则慕父母；知好色，则慕少艾；有妻子，则慕妻子；仕则慕君，不得于君则热中。大孝终身慕父母。五十而慕者，予于大舜见之矣。"

尽心上·四十五

孟子曰："君子之于物也，爱之而弗仁；于民也，仁之而弗亲。亲亲而仁民，仁民而爱物。"

尽心上·四十六

孟子曰："知者无不知也，当务之为急；仁者无不爱也，急亲贤之为务。尧、舜之知而不遍物，急先务也；尧、舜之仁不遍爱人，急亲贤也。不能三年之丧，而缌、小功之察；放饭流歠，而问无齿决，是之谓不知务。"

尽心下·一

孟子曰："不仁哉梁惠王也！仁者以其所爱及其所不爱，不仁者以其所不爱及其所爱。"

公孙丑曰："何谓也？"

"梁惠王以土地之故，糜烂其民而战之，大败。将复之，恐不能胜，故驱其所爱子弟以殉之，是之谓以其所不爱及其所爱也。"

of fifty, still longed for them."

7A45

Mencius said, "The noble person loves living things without being humane toward them and is humane toward the people without being affectionate. That he is affectionate toward his family is what allows him to be humane toward the people and loving toward creatures."

7A46

Mencius said, "There is nothing that the wise do not know, but what is urgent for them is confronting what is fundamental. There is no one whom the humane do not love, but what is fundamental for them is earnestly caring for the worthy. Even in the cases of Yao and Shun, their wisdom did not extend to everything, but they earnestly attended first to what was fundamental. The humaneness of Yao and Shun did not involve loving every person, but they earnestly cared for the worthy.

"To be unable to observe the three years' mourning while devoting scrupulous attention to the three months' mourning and the five months' mourning; to be gluttonous in one's eating and immoderate in one's drinking while inquiring about not tearing the meat with one's teeth—this is what I call not knowing what is fundamental."

7B1

Mencius said, "How inhumane was King Hui of Liang! The humane begin with what they love and proceed to what they do not love. The inhumane begin with what they do not love and proceed to what they love."

Gongsun Chou said, "What do you mean?"

"For the sake of territory, King Hui of Liang pulverized his people and propelled them into war. In the wake of a great defeat, he engaged again, fearful he would not prevail. He importuned the son whom he loved until he buried him along with them. When I spoke of beginning with what one does not love and proceeding to what one loves, this is what I meant."

7B31

Mencius says, "All human beings have that which they cannot bear. Getting this attitude to reach to what they can bear is humaneness. All human beings have that which they will not do. Getting this attitude to reach to that which they will do is rightness. When human beings are able to bring to fulfillment the mind that desires not to harm others, their humaneness is inexhaustible, and when they are able to bring to fulfillment the mind that refuses to break through or to jump over a wall, their rightness is inexhaustible. If they can bring to fulfillment their reluctance to accept unsuitable modes of address, there will be no place in which they fail to manifest rightness. If a scholar speaks of something about which he was not to have spoken in order to gain some advantage by speaking, or if he fails to speak of something about which he might have spoken in order to gain some advantage from not speaking, this is in both cases like breaking through or jumping over the wall."

尽心下·三十一

孟子曰："人皆有所不忍，达之于其所忍，仁也；人皆有所不为，达之于其所为，义也。人能充无欲害人之心，而仁不可胜用也；人能充无穿窬之心，而义不可胜用也；人能充无受尔汝之实，无所往而不为义也。士未可以言而言，是以言餂之也；可以言而不言，是以不言餂之也。是皆穿窬之类也。"

Extensive Readings

A. Confucius[①]
《史记·孔子世家》选段

Szuma Chien
司马迁

Confucius was born in Zou, a village in the district of Changping in the state of Lu. His ancestors came from Song and one of them, Kong Fangshu, had a son named Boxia, whose son was Shuliaoghe. In his old age Shulianghe took a daughter of the Yan family, and after he had prayed at the shrine of Niqiu she gave birth to Confucius. That was in the twenty-second year of Duke Xiang of Lu. Because he was born with a hollow in the top of his head, he was given the

---

① Excerpted from Szuma Chien. *Selections from Records of the Historian I*, trans. Yang Hsien-yi and Gladys Yang, Foreign Languages Press, 2008.

personal name of Qiu, with the courtesy name Zhongni and the surname Kong.

Soon after his birth Shuliaoghe died and was buried at Mount Fang in the east of Lu. Later Confucius suspected that his father's grave was there, but his mother hid the truth from him. As a child, Confucius liked to play with sacrificial vessels, setting them out as if for a ceremony. After his mother's death, as a precaution, he had her coffin entombed in Wufu Lane. Then the mother of Wan Fu of Zou told him the whereabouts of his father's grave, and he had his mother buried with her husband at Mount Fang.

Confucius was still wearing the belt of mourning when he went to a feast for gentlemen given by the Ji clan. Yang Hu turned him away, saying, "The Ji clan is entertaining gentlemen: you are not included." At that Confucius withdrew.

……

Confucius was poor and humble. Growing up and working as keeper of the granaries for the Ji clan he measured the grain fairly; when he was keeper of the livestock the animals flourished; and so he was made minister of works. Subsequently he left Lu, was dismissed from Qi, driven out of Song and Wei (1024B.C.–209B.C.) and ran into trouble between Chen and Cai. Finally he returned to Lu.

Well over six feet, Confucius was called the Tall Man and everybody marvelled at his height. He returned to the state of Lu as it had treated him well. Nangong Jingshu asked the duke of Lu to let him accompany Confucius to Zhou, and the duke gave them a carriage, a pair of horses and a page boy. They went to Zhou to study rites and there met Lao Zi.

When Confucius was leaving, Lao Zi's parting words to him were, "I have heard that the rich and great offer farewell gifts of money while the good offer advice. I am neither rich nor great but, unworthy as I am, have been called good; so let me offer you a few words of advice." Then he said, "A shrewd observer, prone to criticize others, risks his own life. A learned man who exposes the faults of others endangers himself. A filial son must never thrust himself forward, and neither may a good subject."

……

When Confucius was thirty-five, Ji Pingzi, because of a cockfight between a bird of his and one owned by Hou Zhaobo, offended Duke Zhao of Lu. The duke led troops against him. Ji Pingzi fought back with the support of the houses of Mengsun and Shusun and defeated the duke, who fled to Qi where he settled at Ganhou. After this there was such confusion in Lu that Confucius went to Qi to serve as Gao Zhaozi's steward in the hope of getting an introduction to Duke Jing. He discussed music with the chief musician of Qi, heard the Shao Music and studied it, and for three months did not know the taste of meat. The men of Qi thought highly of him.

Duke Jing of Qi questioned him about government. His answer was, "Let the prince be a prince, the minister a minister, the father a father and the son a son."

The duke rejoined, "Well said! For indeed when the prince is not a prince, the minister not a minister, the father not a father, the son not a son, even if there were grain I might be unable to eat it."

……

In the fourteenth year of Duke Ding, Confucius, now fifty-six, appeared gratified when he was appointed both chief justice and prime minister.

His pupils said, "We have heard that a gentleman would show no fear in the face of calamity, no joy in the face of good fortune."

"True," replied Confucius. "But what of the saying, 'He delights in high position because he can show his humility'?" He executed Shaozheng Mao, a minister of Lu who had made trouble. After three months of his administration vendors of lamb and pork stopped raising their prices, men and women walked on different sides of the street, no one picked up anything lost on the road, and strangers coming to the city did not have to look for the officers in charge for everyone made them welcome.

When the men of Qi knew this they took fright and said, "With Confucius at the head of the state, Lu is bound to grow powerful; then we who are close to it will be the first to be swallowed up: We had better offer them some land."

But Zi Lu said, "Let us first see if we can't foil them. If that fails, it will not be too late to offer land."

So they chose eighty of the prettiest girls in Qi who could dance to the kang music, dressed them in gay costumes and sent them with sixty pairs of dappled horses as a gift to the duke of Lu. The dancers were displayed with the horses outside Gao Gate in the south city, and Ji Huanzi who went in disguise several times to see them was tempted to accept. He persuaded the duke to go there by a roundabout way, and they watched all day, neglecting state affairs.

Then Zilu said, "Master, it is time to leave!"

Confucius replied, "The duke will soon be sacrificing to heaven and earth. If he presents portions of the offerings to the ministers, I can stay."

But Ji Huanzi accepted the dancers from Qi, for three days no court was held, and no meat was offered to the ministers at the sacrifice.

So Confucius left, putting up for one night at Tun. Shi Yi, who had come to see him off, said, "This is not your fault, master."

Confucius retorted, "Shall I sing you a song?" And he chanted:

A woman's tongue

Can cost a man his post;

A woman's words

Can cost a man his head;

Then why not retire

To spend my last years as I please?

Upon Shi Yi's return Ji Huanzi asked, "What did Confucius say?"

When told, he said with a sigh, "I've offended the master because of a pack of girls."

……

Going on to Zheng, Confucius was separated from his followers. He was standing alone at the East Gate when a citizen of Zheng remarked to Zigong, "There is a man at the East Gate with a forehead like Yao, a neck like Gao Tao and shoulders like Zichan, and just three inches shorter below the waist than Yu. Lost as a stray dog he looks!"

When this was repeated to Confucius, he chuckled. "The appearance is unimportant," he said. "But it's true that I'm like a stray dog. That is certainly true!"

……

One day Confucius was playing the chimes when a man with a wicker crate passed the door and said, "Poor fellow, playing the chimes! He is self-willed but does not know himself. It is useless to talk with him."

Confucius practised playing the lute for ten days without attempting anything new. Shi Xiang, his tutor, said, "You can go ahead now."

"I have learned the tune but not the technique," said Confucius.

After some time Shi Xiang said: "You have mastered the measure now, you can go on."

But Confucius replied, "I have not yet caught the spirit."

Some time later the other said, "Now you have caught the spirit, you can go on."

"I cannot yet visualize the man behind it," answered Confucius.

Later he observed, "This is the work of a man who thought deeply and seriously, one who saw far ahead and had a calm, lofty outlook." He continued, "I see him now. He is dark and tall, with far-seeing eyes that seem to command all the kingdoms around. No one but King Wen could have composed this music."

Shi Xiang rose from his seat and bowed as he rejoined, "Yes, this is the lute-song of King Wen."

……

The next year Confucius went from Cai to Ye. Asked about government by the duke of Ye, he replied, "The art lies in attracting the people from far away and winning the hearts of those close by."

Chapter Two
Confucianism: Historical Context, Core Tenets, and Global Influences

Another time the duke of Ye asked Zilu his opinion of his master, but Zilu did not reply. When Confucius heard this he said, "Why didn't you tell him, 'He is a man who never wearies of studying the truth, never tires of teaching others, but who in his eagerness forgets his hunger and in his joy forgets his bitter lot, not worrying that old age is creeping on'?"

……

Knowing that his disciples were in low spirits, Confucius called Zilu and said to him, "The old song runs: 'I am neither rhinoceros nor tiger, yet I go to the wilderness.' Is our way wrong? Is that why we have come to this?"

"Maybe we lack humanity and therefore men do not trust us," replied Zilu. "Or perhaps we are not intelligent enough for them to follow our way."

"Do you really think so?" countered Confucius. "If the humane were always trusted, how do you account for what happened to Bo Yi and Shu Qi? If the intelligent always had their way, how do you explain the case of Prince Bigan?"

After Zilu left, Zigong came and Confucius put the same question to him. "The old song says, 'I am neither rhinoceros nor tiger, yet I go to the wilderness.' Is our way wrong? Is that why we have come to this?"

Zigong answered, "Master, your way is too great for the world to accept. You should modify it a little."

"A good farmer can sow but may not always reap a harvest," said Confucius. "A good craftsman can use his skill but may not be able to please. A gentleman can cultivate his way, draw up principles, recapitulate and reason, but may not be able to make his way accepted. Now your aim is not to cultivate your way but to please others. Your ambition is not high enough."

After Zigong had left, Yan Hui came and Confucius again put the same question to him.

"Master, your way is too great for the world to accept," said Yan Hui. "All the same, you should persist in it. What does it matter if they cannot accept it? That just shows that you are a superior man. We are at fault if we do not cultivate the true way. Yet if we cultivate it fully and it is not adopted, it is the rulers who are at fault. What does it matter if they cannot accept your way? That just shows that you are a superior man."

Confucius smiled with pleasure and exclaimed, "Well said, son of Yan! If you had great wealth, I should like to administer it for you."

B. Confucian Natural Cosmology: An Interpretive Context[①]
儒家自然宇宙论

Roger T. Ames
安乐哲

1. Distinguishing Confucian Cosmology from Greek Transcendentalism

The distinguished French sinologist Marcel Granet observes rather starkly that "Chinese wisdom has no need of the idea of God."[②] This characterization of classical Chinese philosophy is a premise that underlies the correlative mode of thinking, and that has had many iterations albeit in different formulations by many of our most prominent sinologists, both Chinese and Western alike. Contemporary New Confucian philosopher (xinruxuejia 新儒学家) Tang Junyi 唐君毅 for example states unequivocally that

> ...the Chinese as a people have not embraced a concept of "Heaven" (tian 天) that has transcendent meaning. The pervasive idea among Chinese with respect to tian is that it is inseparable from the world.[③]

Joseph Needham would also disassociate Chinese cosmology from assumptions about some underlying permanent structure when he claims that

> ...Chinese ideals involved neither God nor Law....Thus the mechanical and the quantitative, the forced and the externally imposed, were all absent. The notion of Order excluded the notion of Law.[④]

Indeed, our best interpreters of classical Chinese philosophy are explicit in rejecting the idea that Chinese cosmology begins from some independent, transcendent principle and thus entails the ontological reality/appearance distinction followed by the plethora of dualistic

---

[①] Excerpted from Roger T. Ames, *A Sourcebook in Classical Confucian Philosophy*, State University of New York Press, 2024.

[②] Marcel Granet, *La pensée chinoise*, Éditions Albin Michel, 1968, p. 478.

[③] Tang Junyi 唐君毅, *The Complete Works of Tang Junyi* 唐君毅全集, Vol. 11, Taipei: Xuesheng Shuju, p. 241: 中国民族无含超绝意义的天的观念。中国人对天有个普遍的观念，就是天与地是分不开的。

[④] Joseph Needham, *Science and Civilisation in China*, Vol. II, Cambridge: Cambridge University Press, 1956, p. 290.

Chapter Two
Confucianism: Historical Context, Core Tenets, and Global Influences

categories that arise within such a worldview.① The philosophical implications of this seemingly off-hand observation are fundamental and profound. One consequence of taking this insight into Chinese cosmology seriously is that it enables us to disambiguate some of the central philosophical vocabulary of classical Chinese philosophy by identifying equivocations that emerge when we elide the distinction between classical Greek cosmological assumptions and those indigenous to the classical Chinese worldview. Angus Graham cautions us about such equivocations, insisting that

> *...in the Chinese cosmos all things are interdependent, without transcendent principles by which to explain them or a transcendent origin from which they derive.... A novelty in this position which greatly impresses me is that it exposes a preconception of Western interpreters that such concepts as Tian "Heaven" and Dao "Way" must have the transcendence of our own ultimate principles; it is hard for us to grasp that even the Way is interdependent with man.*②

We will find that an important corollary to the absence of "God" in Chinese cosmology is the need for a different language in thinking about issues as basic as cosmic origins, the source of meaning in the world, and the nature of creativity itself.

Trying to be self-conscious about the cultural assumptions that we willy-nilly bring to our attempt to translate and understand the Chinese philosophical tradition raises an important issue: What is the distinction between a literal and an expository interpretation? If by "literal" we mean to accord with the exact or at least the primary meanings of terms without our own embellishment of them, then to translate *dao* 道 conventionally as "the Way" or *tian* 天 as "Heaven," far from being "literal" as many would claim, is a case of naïve exposition of the most egregious kind. After all, we must allow that in terms of both sense and reference, "the Way" and "Heaven" as understood within our own linguistic universe not only infer, but are indeed metonymic for the Abrahamic conception of "God" and all that it entails, a theological concept that has little relevance for traditional Chinese cosmology.③ Again, a failure of translators to be self-conscious and to take fair account of their own Gadamerian "prejudices" with the excuse that they are relying on an existing "objective" dictionary that gives us this equation between *tian* 天 and

---

① For the argument I have made against the relevance of strict philosophical transcendence for classical Confucian cosmology that includes a survey of similar characterizations of early Chinese cosmology in both Chinese and Western sources, see Roger T. Ames, *Confucian Role Ethics: A Vocabulary*, Albany: State University of New York Press, 2020, Chapter 5.

② A.C. Graham, "Replies" in Henry Rosemont Jr. (ed.), *Chinese Texts and Philosophical Contexts: Essays Dedicated to Angus C. Graham*, La Salle, IL: Open Court, 1991, p.287.

③ Metonymy is a figure of speech in which a word or phrase is substituted for another word or phrase with which it is closely associated, such as in the use of Beijing for the Chinese government.

"Heaven," is to fail to acknowledge that in the case of China at least, this lexical resource given its missionary origins, is itself so heavily colored with cultural biases that Chinese philosophy is for the most part taught in religion or Asian studies departments in our universities, and shelved in the religion or literature sections of our libraries.① To fail to be self-conscious as translators is to betray our readers not once, but twice. That is, not only do we fail to provide the "objective" reading of the text we have promised, but we also neglect to warn our unsuspecting readers of the cultural assumptions we willy-nilly insinuate into our translations.

If, as the dominant classical Greek metaphysical views would have it, unity and permanence are fundamental, then the phenomenal world experienced as unbounded change cannot be finally real. In this classical Greek worldview, of which A.N. Whitehead's interpretation of Plato as a metaphysical realist is a fair representative, "reality" must refer to that which grounds the world of appearances, while changing phenomena as mere appearances are at best misleading and illusory.② By contrast, there is little recourse to anything like this reality/appearance "two world" distinction in classical Chinese thought.③ The early Confucian thinkers showed little interest in the search for an ontological ground for phenomena. Tang Junyi insists that

> ... when Chinese philosophers speak of the world, they are thinking of the world that we are living in. There is no world beyond or outside of the one we are experiencing. ...They are not referencing "a world" or "the world," but are simply saying "worlding" or "world as such" without putting any indefinite or definite article in front of it.④

---

① Hans-Georg Gadamer uses "prejudices" not in the sense of blind prejudice, but on the contrary, in the sense that our prejudgments can facilitate rather than obstruct our understanding. Our assumptions can positively condition our experience. For Gadamer, we must always entertain these assumptions critically, being aware that the hermeneutical circle in which understanding is always situated requires of us that we continually strive to be conscious of what we are bringing to our experience. In thus being self-conscious in our interpretation of experience, we must pursue increasingly felicitous prejudgments that can inform our behaviors in better and more productive ways.

② Much good research is being done to rescue the artist Plato from the received idealist Plato, dominated as this latter interpretation has been by systematic metaphysics. But it is this received Plato filtered through the Church fathers and 20th century scientism that has exercised such important influence on the evolution of the Western cultural narrative.

③ For a discussion of this issue in some detail see David L. Hall and Roger T. Ames, *Thinking from the Han: Self, Truth, and Transcendence in Chinese and Western Culture*, Albany: State University of New York Press, 1998, pp. 123-146. Nathan Sivin, a most cautious interpreter of the classical Chinese world, has recently stated unequivocally that the "fundamental claim, which we usually refer to as appearance vs. reality, has no counterpart in China." See Nathan Sivin, *Medicine, Philosophy and Religion in Ancient China: Researches and Reflections*, Aldershot: Variorum, 1995, p. 3.

④ Tang Junyi, *The Complete Works of Tang Junyi*, Vol. 11, pp. 101-103: 中国哲人言世界，只想着我们所处的世界。我们所处的世界以外有无其他的世界……中国的哲人说世界，不说我们的世界是一世界 A World, 亦不说是这世界 The World, 而只是说世界，天地，World as Such 前面不加冠词，实是有非常重大的意义的。

Chapter Two
Confucianism: Historical Context, Core Tenets, and Global Influences

It is this assumption of metaphysical realists that they can make an object of the world and thereby decontextualize themselves that allows such deracinated philosophers to entertain an erstwhile "view from nowhere." And it is indeed this view from nowhere that stands as guarantor for the possibility of apodictic truth and certainty.

The intellectual milieu for early Chinese thinkers as it is captured in the vocabulary of the "Great Commentary" fascicle of the *Book of Changes* was a phenomenal world of process and change construed simply as *dao* 道: "the unfolding of the boundless field of experience," or *wanwu* 万物: "the ten thousand processes or events," or more simply put, "everything that is happening." Importantly, without any subject/object dualism, *dao* 道 as "experiencing" far from providing a view from nowhere, is always being construed from one particular perspective or another. These early thinkers were less inclined to ask what makes something real or why things exist, and more interested in how the complex relationships among the changing phenomena of their surroundings could be correlated to negotiate an optimum productivity. It is an achieved personal, social, and ultimately cosmic harmony more than teleological assumptions about origins or design that served these early thinkers as a fundamental guiding value.

2. Power and Creativity

David Hall introduces the distinction between the notions of "power" and "creativity" as one way of clarifying the meaning of such transactional and inclusive events, observing that

> ..."creativity" is a notion that can be characterized only in terms of self-actualization. Unlike power relationships that require that tensions among component elements be resolved in favor of one of the components, in relations defined by creativity there is no otherness, no separation or distancing, nothing to be overcome.[①]

Such a definition of creativity—or better, co-creativity between persons and their natural, social, and cultural environments—cannot be reconciled with notions of external causation that appeal to determination by some external agency. In fact, there is a persisting confusion regarding "creativity" that has attended all but the most recent thinking about religious experience within the *creatio ex nihilo* doctrines familiar in the Abrahamic religious culture.[②] Hall further avers that

> ...*creatio ex nihilo, as it is normally understood, is in fact the paradigm of all power*

---

① See David L. Hall, *Eros and Irony: A Prelude to Philosophical Anarchism*, Albany: State University of New York, 1982, p. 249.

② A. N. Whitehead has identified and attempted to address what he takes to be a serious incoherence in the relationship between world, God, and creativity in the Abrahamic tradition by making creativity itself more fundamental than God. This challenge is perhaps acknowledged by the fact that the Oxford English Dictionary introduces a new entry for "creativity" into its pages in a 1971 supplement with two of its three references to Whitehead's own *Religion in the Making*.

*relationships since the "creative" element of the relation is completely in control of its "other," which is in itself literally nothing.*①

The traditional theological all-powerful "Creator" God determines things, makes things. God, as Omnipotent Other who commands the world into being, is Maker of the world, but is not in any interesting sense its "Creator" because nothing novel emerges in the process. The aseity or self-sufficiency of God ascribes "Perfection" itself to Godhead, and hence nothing can be added to Him or taken away. Indeed, in such a world there is nothing new under the sun, and in Friedrich Schleiermacher's terms, gives us a religion of absolute dependence.② Any subsequent human acts of "creativity" that by definition ought to entail the spontaneous emergence of novelty can in fact only be secondary and derivative exercises of power.

Creativity understood in terms of the spontaneous emergence of novelty can only make sense in a world with ontological parity among things. Either everything shares in creativity, or the world is sharply divided into creators and their shadows, into Being and its mere appearances. In the latter world, the elements of novelty and spontaneity are fatally threatened. Such concerns are precisely what are at issue in the process understanding of creativity.

Power is to be construed as the production of intended effects determined by external causation. Creativity, on the other hand, is the spontaneous production of novelty, and is thus irreducible to an exhaustive causal analysis. Power is exercised with respect to and over others. Creativity is always reflexive and is exercised over and with respect to radically embedded "persons" who are inclusive of themselves and their environing others. And since persons in a processive world are always social, such creativity is a transactional and multi-dimensional undertaking.

Stated the other way around, it is the transactional, co-creative character of all creative processes that renders personal cultivation irreducibly social. In "creating" oneself as a committed and effective teacher, one is producing extraordinary students. And the standards in teaching demanded by exceptional students produce a committed and effective teacher. Both teacher and student are the cause and the effect in their transactional relationship. Since all persons are constituted by their relationships, self-creation means being trustworthy and true in one's associations. It is effectively integrating oneself within one's social, natural, and cultural contexts, the ground from which one's person as simultaneously self and other arise together to maximum

---

① David L. Hall, *Eros and Irony: A Prelude to Philosophical Anarchism*, Albany: State University of New York, 1982, p. 249.

② Friedrich Schleiermacher in *The Christian Faith* uses this language of "absolute dependence"— a self-abnegating deference to a self-sufficient, independent Deity—as a positive expression of religious humility. See *The Christian Faith*, ed. H.R. Mackintosh and J.S. Stewart, London: T & T Clark, 1999, p. 132.

benefit. Self-creation is not ultimately what things are, but how well and how productively they are able to fare in their synergistic alliances.

Focusing the Familiar (*Zhongyong* 中庸) provides us with a dramatic account of precisely this contextualized understanding of self-consummation:

> *Resolve (cheng* 诚*) is self-consummating and its way-making is self-directing. Resolve is the beginning and the end of things, and without this resolve, there would be nothing. It is thus that, for exemplary persons, it is resolve that is prized. But resolve is not simply the self-consummating of one's own person; it is what consummates everything. Completing oneself is achieving virtuosity in one's roles and relations (ren* 仁*); completing all things is advancing wisdom in the world (zhi* 知*). Such is the virtuosity achieved in one's natural propensities and the way-making that integrates what is more internal and what is more external. Thus when and wherever one applies this virtuosity, it is fitting.*①

What does *cheng* 诚—translated here as "resolve" but conventionally rendered "sincerity" or "integrity" mean as a technical cosmological term? The Song Dynasty scholar Xu Zhongche 徐中车 emphasizes the dynamic aspect of *cheng* 诚 by alluding to the phrase in *Zhongyong* "the utmost creativity is ceaseless" (*zhichengwuxi* 至诚无息), thus defining *cheng* as "ceaseless" (buxi 不息). Similarly, Tang Junyi understands the *Zhongyong*'s use of *cheng* 诚 as "continuity itself" (*jixubenshen* 继续本身).

Wing-tsit Chan in translating the *Zhongyong* for a Western audience insists that *cheng* 诚 in this text "is not just a state of mind, but an active force that is always transforming things and completing things, and drawing man and Heaven together in the same current."② Tu Wei-ming takes this reflection further in observing that the term *cheng* 诚 as it appears in *Zhongyong* "has been somewhat unjustifiably translated as 'sincerity'" since "the last thirteen chapters deal mainly with the metaphysical concept of *ch'eng* [*cheng*] (sincerity, reality, and truth)."③ In his monograph length study of this text, Tu collates earlier commentarial exegesis and insists that *cheng* 诚 must be understood as "creativity." In his own words, *cheng* 诚

> *...can be conceived as a form of creativity. ...it is that which brings about the transforming and nourishing processes of heaven and earth. As creativity, ch'eng [cheng] is*

---

① *Focusing the Familiar* 中庸 25: 诚者自成也，而道自道也。诚者物之终始，不诚无物。是故君子诚之为贵。诚者非自成己而已也，所以成物也。成己，仁也；成物，知也。性之德也，合外内之道也，故时措之宜也。

② Wing-tsit Chan, *A Source Book in Chinese Philosophy*, Princeton: Princeton University Press, 1963, p. 96.

③ Tu Wei-ming, *Centrality and Commonality: An Essay on Confucian Religiousness*, Albany: State University of New York Press, 1989, pp. 16-17.

"ceaseless" (pu-hsi [buxi 不息]). Because of its ceaselessness it does not create in a single act beyond the spatiotemporal sequence. Rather, it creates in a continuous and unending process in time and space…it is simultaneously a self-subsistent and self-fulfilling process of creation that produces life unceasingly.①

C. Introduction to the *Mencius*②
《孟子》序言

Philip J. Ivanhoe
艾文荷

1. The Man and the Work

Mencius records the teachings of the Chinese philosopher whose surname was Meng 孟 and personal name Ke 轲. Throughout East Asia, he is better known as Mengzi 孟子, or "Master Meng" (391–308 B.C.E); "Mencius" is the Latinized version of this more widely used appellation. Mencius lived during the later part of the Zhou Dynasty (traditional dates: 1122–249 B.C.E.), in a time known as the Warring States Period (403–221 B.C.E.). This was an age in which the older feudal order of the Zhou Dynasty had deteriorated. The Zhou king ruled in name only and his former empire was divided into different states, each with its own ruler, who continued to vie with the rulers of other states for supremacy. These state rulers often illegitimately claimed for themselves the title of king (wang 王) in an attempt to arrogate to themselves what rightfully belonged to the now enfeebled Zhou king. These features of Mencius's time often are reflected in the conversations he had with rulers of various states, for example his conversations with King Hui of Liang and King Xuan of Qi in the first part of Book I, about how they might realize their grand ambition to unite and rule over all of China. As readers will see from the translation, Mencius thought that only someone who possessed the moral qualities of a true king, someone worthy of the title, could successfully unify the empire, and in many of his conversations he tries to steer the attention of various state rulers from their desire for power to a concern with morality. Like Kongzi (Confucius) before him, Mencius defended the older Zhou form of life,

---

① Tu Wei-ming, *Centrality and Commonality: An Essay on Confucian Religiousness*, Albany: State University of New York Press, 1989, pp. 81-82.

② Excerpted from Philip J. Ivanhoe, "Introduction", in *Mencius*, trans. Irene Bloom, Columbia University Press, 2009, pp. ix-xx.

which of course entailed the preeminence of the Zhou king, but he did so in a new, intellectually more diverse and sophisticated context. He faced a wide range of formidable challengers to the Way (dao 道) Confucius had advocated–see for example 3A4, 3A5, 3B9, 6AI–6, and 7A26– and in response to their contending theories and ideas he developed innovative, powerful, and highly nuanced views about human nature, the mind, self-cultivation, politics and Heaven that had a profound and lasting influence on the later Confucian tradition and on East Asian culture in general.

......

Mencius had a place, though not a commanding position, among Confucian writings until its extraordinary ascent. This began toward the end of the Tang Dynasty (618–907), when thinkers such as Han Yu 韩愈 (768–824) and Li Ao 李翱 (fl.798) advocated *Mencius* as a particularly important resource for the revival of Confucianism, which had fallen into relative neglect in the face of a remarkable and rising tide of Daoist and Buddhist innovation and success. In the following, Song Dynasty (960–1279), the inimitable Zhu Xi 朱熹 (1130–1200) wrote a highly influential commentary on *Mencius* and included the latter, along with the *Analects*, *Great Learning*, and *Doctrine of the Mean*, as one of the *Four Books*—a collection that came to serve as the gateway to Confucian learning and the all-important civil service examination. <u>Largely as a result of these developments, in subsequent dynasties *Mencius* came to occupy a singularly important place in the Confucian scriptural pantheon.</u> In 1315, the Mongol court recognized it as a classic, which secured its preeminent position within the tradition; since that time the text has enjoyed unprecedented and unmatched influence and prestige. Among current scholars, it remains one of the most highly studied Confucian classics.

2. Ethical Views

Mencius's primary ethical concern, both theoretical and practical, was moral self-cultivation; he wanted people to improve themselves and believed they could do so with the right kind of attitude and effort. Like many Confucians, he was more a teacher or therapist than a theoretician, more interested in moving people toward a certain ideal than in crafting and presenting tight and careful valid arguments. This is not to say that he does not present interesting and at times compelling arguments, only that this was not his aim or ideal. Readers should keep in mind his more practical concerns as they seek to gain a sympathetic understanding of his philosophy and life.

<u>At the core of Mencius's theory of self-cultivation is a belief in the innate moral qualities and inclination of human nature. He is best known for his theory that human nature is good (xing shan 性善), and readers will find him discussing this topic in a variety of places in the text, most notably but by no means exclusively in the opening sections of the first part of book</u>

6. Mencius meant by this claim, first, that human beings possess certain observable and active resources for becoming good, what he calls moral "sprouts." In more modern terms, we might describe this part of his view as the claim that human beings innately possess some measure of other-regarding desires such as compassion and altruism. In addition, Mencius argues that if human beings exercise the most important and distinctive aspects of their nature—for example, their innate moral sensibilities and their abilities to reflect and think—according to what he regards as their natural functions, this will lead them to develop their moral sprouts into full and vibrant virtues. The key to this process of development is the mind (xin 心), and organ Mencius believed contained affective, cognitive, and volitional elements. Roughly, his view is that if we exercise our minds and reflect upon ourselves and our condition, we will discover not only that we do in fact care about other people, creatures and things, but also that focusing upon our moral sprouts leads us to act morally and offers us the most profound, stable, and enduring sources of satisfaction available to creatures like us. This satisfaction or joy in moral action, along with a parallel sense of disapproval and shame in bad action, can lead us to become good, but only if we exercise our minds to reflect upon and follow the "greater part" of our nature (6A15).

3. Political Views

Mencius was one of the first thinkers in the history of the world to insist that rulers and states exist to serve their people. The proper aim of a good state is the welfare of its people, and this is conceived in terms of the order, security, wealth, happiness, and education the people enjoy. Mencius believed the people are the only tangible indicator of a good governance, and elite members of society must look to the people as the most reliable gauge of the quality of their rule and heed what this guide reveals. Much to the chagrin of the rulers in his own time and a number of later Chinese emperors as well, Mencius further argued that rulers who fail to serve the people lose the mandate to rule and can even be forcibly removed by those more qualified to fulfill Heaven's plan for its people. These forceful and at times quite subtle views about the role the welfare of the people plays in justifying political rule did not include any clear correlates to Western ideas about a right to revolt or to elect those who govern. Nevertheless, Mencius's views about the wisdom and importance of the people have the potential to significantly enrich present-day political philosophy.

Like Confucius before him, Mencius offered nuanced and interesting ideas on what constitutes the welfare of the people. His views about the importance of family and intimate interpersonal relationships call for very different approaches to how one conceives of and seeks to ensure basic welfare. Like any Confucian, Mencius would adamantly reject the idea that simply providing for the material needs of people is in any way adequate. To treat someone in such a fashion is to treat that person as less than fully human. Confucians also place a tremendous

Chapter Two
Confucianism: Historical Context, Core Tenets, and Global Influences

emphasis on education as a chief concern of the government and a primary good for the people. One can see a number of ways in which a good education, and especially one with ethical content, can contribute both directly and indirectly to a person's welfare and to the welfare of the state as well and why it arguably should be one of the highest priorities of any decent society.

A number of current thinkers have focused on Mencius's views about human nature as a resource for developing Confucian conceptions of human rights. While one does not find an explicit discussion of rights or even clear cases of the concept of rights in the early Confucian tradition, Mencius's belief in a common, ethically charged nature unambiguously establishes what Donald J. Munro calls natural equality among human beings. Throughout the early tradition, one also finds the notion that human beings all are regarded by and can appeal to Heaven to bear testimony to their moral worth, no matter how badly they might be treated by others. These ideas offer a clear and solid foundation for developing a robust conception of basic rights.

Early Confucians describe a system of moral right and wrong, good and bad largely in terms of a set of virtues and a system of rituals and norms. These function to achieve many of the same goods as a system of rights and laws. Nevertheless, Confucians emphasize being humane (ren 仁) rather than the modern Western notion of justice. They clearly have a concept of justice, in terms of what is due to a person given her or his social role and circumstance and simply in virtue of being a fellow human being, but their sense of justice is distinctive and needs to be carefully distinguished from its modern Western counterparts. As Munro has shown, early Confucians most definitely have a sense of equal human worth and dignity, clear views about the ability to make and adhere to moral choices, and to take on and assign blame, praise, and responsibility. Together, these and other ethical ideas and practices constitute a distinctively Confucian way of life that is importantly different from the modern Western liberal view. Roughly, one might say that people have dignity and moral worth because of their innate moral nature, as members of families and a larger society, and because they possess the capacity to develop themselves to be good and so forth.

Those who argue that Confucianism cannot develop any robust conception of rights almost certainly are wrong. To make such a case, one would have to show that the tradition is unable to adapt, develop, and change. Anyone who has made even the slightest effort to study, understand, and appreciate the rich, creative, and still vibrant history of Confucianism will find such a claim both naïve and implausible; like all great traditions, Confucianism has demonstrated a remarkable ability to transform itself as well as those who participate in it. The view that Confucianism is somehow incapable of developing or accommodating any conceptions of rights must recognize that, for most of its history, the Western tradition lacked any robust sense of basic rights. The notions of rights, autonomy, and free will all are modern developments. Unless one can show that such developments could only take one unique route, there is no conceptual reason that prevents the Confucian tradition—or the Daoist, Buddhist, and Hindu traditions—from following its own path to a related or largely similar idea. I suggest, however, that rather than simply looking to find, develop, or apply the modern Western liberal notion of rights within the Confucian tradition, we might all the best be served by working to describe an alternative Confucian foundation and conception of rights. Surely this would be better than groping for some weak conception of rights within traditional culture, as some have done, or seeking to graft onto a vital and rich tradition an alien and unfamiliar ideal. Seen in this light, the Confucian tradition, and Mencius's philosophy in particular, have tremendous potential for contributing to and enhancing our understanding of the notion of human rights. …

4. Wider Influence on Culture

Mencius's influence on Chinese culture extends far beyond his contributions to ethical, political, and religious thought, impressive as they are. His example as a defender of Confucianism and Chinese culture in general was an important reason he and his ideas proved to have such a remarkable legacy. Mencius was the first thinker to defend Confucius's Way against a range of articulate challengers. In so doing, he established a precedent and inspiring example that later Confucians would follow and explicitly appeal to throughout the history of the tradition. Later thinkers often invoke the trope of being forced to respond to, challenge, and oppose some new threat to the Confucian tradition and Chinese society; they thus cast themselves as latter-day versions of Mencius, who, we are told, far from being "fond of argument," was "compelled" to engage in it in order to defend the Way (3B9).

Another reason *Mencius* has endured and exerted such a profound influence on Chinese culture is its remarkable literary qualities. It is one of the most elegant and accessible classical Chinese texts and abounds with memorable and clever stories, powerful and at times haunting images, and wonderful turns of phrase. It is an abundant source for the distinctive feature of the Chinese language called set phrases (cheng yu 成语): expressions, usually of four characters, still used in modern oral and written Chinese to invoke complex ideas in terse yet highly evocative and often amusing ways. For example, the phrase "climbing a tree in search of a fish" (yuan shu qiu yu 缘树求鱼①) is from 1A7 and is used to describe actions that are hopeless and wrongheaded; the phrase "pulling at the sprouts and help them grow" (ba miao zhu zhang 拔苗助长) is from 2A2 and describes actions that foolishly aim to rush a natural process and as a result harm the cause one seeks to advance. Simply by invoking these four-character expressions, speakers or authors conjure up and continue parts of the rich Mencius legacy.

---

① 应为"缘木求鱼",见《孟子·梁惠王上·七》。

......

A final and more amorphous influence is no less real or important, and that is the powerful current of humanity running throughout Chinese culture. Mencius's view of human nature and its potential for good has penetrated deeply and resides in the marrow and bones of the Chinese people; it finds expression in a wide range of cultural phenomena. There is an often unexpressed imperative echoing down through Chinese history calling on every person, from the most powerful to the most humble, to cultivate and manifest fundamental decency, kindness, and ethical nobility. Whereas people in Western culture tend to reserve the worst approbation for those who are unjust, the Chinese reserve such condemnation for those who are uncaring or unfeeling, and there is something to their preference. The latter ideal is more within any person's ability, and failing on this standard may well show a more fundamental lack of one of the most basic and cherished qualities of human beings. We in the West seem to share something like this view as well, at least in our more popular appraisals—think of the character Scrooge—and after all, we use the word humanity both to designate ourselves as a species and to describe one of our best qualities. In any event, Mencius was the first to sound this call and illustrate it with moving parables such as King Xuan sparing the ox (IA7), the story of the child and the well (2A6), and the desolation of Ox Mountain (6A8).

Mencius's irrepressibly optimistic appraisal of human nature and his endorsement of the human spirit are perhaps the greatest legacy of his philosophy; the fact that most Chinese people and many scholars of Chinese culture would simply call these ideas Confucian or Chinese only testifies to the degree to which his ideas have permeated this magnificent civilization and East Asian cultures more generally.

D. Man and Society[①]
人类与社会

John Knoblock
约翰·诺布洛克

1. Human Nature

For Ru philosophers the question of human nature was of great importance since they placed on the individual the whole success of society. Confucius himself was ambiguous in his teachings about man's nature. He objected when Ji Zicheng 棘子成 contended that a gentleman

---

[①] Excerpted from *Xunzi—A Translation and Study of the Complete Works*, vol. 1, translated and edited by John Knoblock, Standford University Press, 1988.

is nothing more than the stuff of which he is made. To Confucius the embellishments of culture were important: "shorn of its fur, the pelt of a tiger or leopard is no different from that of a dog or sheep" (*LY*, 12.8). He indicated that by nature all men were essentially alike. It is the process of education that causes them to become different (*LY*, 17.2, 15.39). He granted that some were so stupid that they could not be changed and others so wise that instruction was unnecessary (*LY*, 17.3). Since men differ but little in inborn nature, Confucius stressed that education should be open to all. He himself never failed to offer instruction to anyone who sought it eagerly (*LY*, 7.7).

……

It seems clear that Confucius must have regarded man's inborn nature as a mixture of good qualities that education must develop and bad qualities that it must suppress. This is in any case certainly the view of his disciples. Wang Chong 王充 reports that the disciples Fu Zijian 宓子贱, Qidiao Kai 漆雕开, and Gongsun Nizi 公孙尼子 shared with Shi Shi 世硕 the view that human nature contains both good and evil elements: "If one emphasizes what is good in inborn nature, if one cultivates and regulates it, then its goodness will increase" (*Lunheng* 论衡, 3.12a). The same is true of the evil in man's nature. The explanation is to be found in the fact that "in everyone's inborn nature there are both Yin and Yang elements, and good and evil qualities depend on what is cultivated" (*Lunheng*, 3.12a). Wang Chong explains that the inborn nature with which we are initially endowed by Nature as our ming 命, "lot" or "fate," is determined by the particular mixture of fine and coarse qi vapor of which we are composed.

Mencius held that man's nature was good, as proved by the fact that everyone has in him the "Four Beginnings": a sense of compassion for others, a sense of shame, a sense of modesty and courtesy, and a sense of right and wrong. Mencius cited the example of the spontaneous reaction of all people to a child about to fall into a well. Anyone that is human will try to rescue it. Mencius thus concluded that since the most important of the Ru virtues are prefigured in the Four Beginnings, man's inborn nature must be good (*Mengzi*, 2A.6). <u>Xunzi explicitly rejects Mencius' analysis as flawed and devoted his book "Man's Nature Is Evil" to refuting Mencius' view.</u> Realism forced Mencius to admit there was a "small part" in man's nature that the gentleman suppresses with his mind. Ordinary men remain ordinary because they do not use their minds to think and so find no answers (*Mengzi*, 6A15). Xunzi argues that the "conscious effort" implied by such use of the mind shows that goodness is not a part of inborn nature, but is acquired. This, in Xunzi's view, allows man to overcome his nature, just as Mencius admits the great man overcomes the "small part" of his nature.

Whatever their arguments about man's inborn nature, all Ru philosophers agreed that to develop the good and suppress the bad, it was necessary to know the teachings of the sages, to observe the restrictions of ritual, to incorporate the harmony of music, to cultivate one's inner

Chapter Two
Confucianism: Historical Context, Core Tenets, and Global Influences

power, and to develop a sense of what is right. Because all of these had to be learned—no one was born knowing them—Xunzi concluded that man's nature is that of the pretty man. Yet all men had the potential to become a sage, if they would accumulate good.

2. Evil

Against these terms of ethical value, there was a rich vocabulary to describe evil and wickedness. Xunzi uses four terms to express evil: liu 流 wayward; yin 淫 wanton; jian 奸 wicked; and e 恶 evil. The term liu has as its root meaning "stream, outflow of a spring." By extension it designates what "flows" or "drifts"; applied to persons, it means "a drifter, vagrant"; in terms of a person's ideals, one who holds no fixed values, no principles, in short, one who is "wayward."

……

The term Xunzi uses to describe man's inborn nature is e "evil." Translating e as "evil" often overstates its meaning since the Chinee dose not carry the sinister and baleful overtones of the English word. It is applied, for instance, to "bad relations" with another state, which should "not be prolonged," as opposed to "good relations, which should not be lost," because bad relations may get out of hand, like a fire burning on a plain (Zuo, Yin 6). An officer, fearing the duke's anger, murdered him, showing that "he had no regard for his lord in his heart and so proceeded in his evil movements" (Zuo, Huan 2). The character also means "ugly" as opposed to "beautiful." We have seen Confucius use it this way to refer to the qualities of men. It also means "dislike" as opposed to "like," "hate" as opposed to "love," "bad" as opposed to "good," and generally what men have a natural revulsion to in contrast to what they have a natural desire for. It is in the latter sense that Xunzi typically employs the term; he argues that the desires inherent in man's nature will, if unchecked, produce results that are ugly and bad that men will dislike and hate. He specifies that the "evil" is "what is wrong through partiality, what wickedly contravenes natural order, rebellion, and chaos" ("Xing'e," 23.3a①). This clearly indicates that the inborn nature of man must be judged evil not because its inborn qualities are sinister or baleful, but because they lead to evil results. It is precisely because man's nature is evil that good is possible ("Xing'e," 23.2b②).

For Xunzi, the problem of evil was linked to the problem of desire. The essential emotional nature of man is such that he feels love and hate, delight and anger, and joy and sorrow ("Zhengming," 22.Ib; "Tianlun," I7.3). When hungry, he desires something to eat; when cold, warm clothing; and when weary, rest ("Xing'e," 23.Id). Men like what is beneficial and dislike what is harmful. They want honor and hate disgrace. They desire strength and hate weakness.

---

① 所谓恶者，偏险悖乱也。
② 人之性恶明矣，其善者伪也。

They enjoy comfort and security, and they hate danger ("Rongru," 4.8; "Jundao," 12.8; "Ruxiao," 8.11). What men like and what they hate are common to all men, even those who seem quite exceptional ("Wangzhi," 9.3; "Rongru," 4.3). From the fact that desires are the same for all men, it follows that if society were not hierarchical, there could be no unity because men would be unwilling to serve each other since none would listen to the commands of another. The result would be contention and civil disorder, which would lead to universal poverty. Inequality is the norm of Nature. Kingship and the division of men into social classes are necessary conditions of order. "Just as there is Heaven and Earth, so too there exists the distinction between superior and inferior" ("Wangzhi," 9.3①). The sage kings knew this and instituted their government of regulations, ritual principles, and moral duty.

3. The Purposes of Society

Many Ru were reluctant to discuss the other "great affair" of state, warfare, but even here the proper instruments are "inner power, just punishment, punctilious observance, right conduct, ritual propriety, and good faith. By inner power, one bestows generous kindness. By the just application of punishment, one corrects what is wrong. By punctilious observance, one serves the spirits. By right conduct, one raises up what is beneficial. by ritual propriety, one acts in natural accord with the seasons. With good faith, one tends the things in one's change" (Zuo, Cheng 16). We have a definition of the seven "virtues possessed by true martial prowess" given by the king of Chu: "The true meaning of military prowess is to be seen in the suppression of cruelty, in the sheathing of weapons, in the safeguarding of the great Mandate, in the firm establishment of accomplishment, in giving repose to the people, in producing harmony among the multitude of states, and in producing abundance of resources" (Zuo, Xuan 12). Xunzi devoted a book to the principles of warfare. He continued the tradition represented in these words. A True King does not engage in aggression. Like King Wen in chastising the errant state of Chong, he displays his moral force, and his enemies are overawed. Without quitting the trenches, his troops triumph.

There was very little dispute between the Mohists and Ru as to the purposes of society. Mo Di argued that the state was to care for the people, to preside over the altars of soil and grain, and to bring order to the nation (9 "Shang xian," II 尚贤，中，2.5a). The tests of a good state derive from its purposes: it is rich, its population is numerous, and its application of punishments and the administration of its government are well ordered. Mo Di develops a well-argued strategy by which to achieve this result (8 "Shang xian," I 上，2.12). "In their exercise of government, the sage kings of antiquity distinguished men on the basis of their inner power and elevated those that were worthy. Those who had ability were raised up, given high office, with rank and honor,

---

① 有天有地而上下有差。

remunerated with a generous stipend, entrusted with important matters, and empowered to see orders carried out" (8 "Shang xian," I, 2.3a).

……

Xunzi develops his theories concerning the proper organization of society in several of his books. He observes that the nature of man being what it is, if society were not a hierarchy, no one would be willing to follow the orders of anyone else. The essential work of society could not be done. There could be no unity. "Two men of equal eminence cannot attend each other; two men of the same low status cannot command each other—such is the norm of Heaven" ("Wangzhi," 9.3①). Since desires are limitless and material goods limited, were power and positions equally distributed, then the result would be that no man's desires would be satisfied. This would certainly lead to contention, which could only result in poverty. Society emerged because the Ancient Kings abhorred such disorder.

The Ancient Kings thus created the basic institutions of society on the basis of the family. Unequal positions were the base. Xunzi quotes with approval a passage from the *Documents* ("lü xing" 吕刑, 19.30b): "There is equality only insofar as they are not equal." This was expressed by the division of society into social classes so that "there were gradation of wealth and eminence of station sufficient to bring everyone under supervision." The basic institutions of government were expressed in regulations and ordinances. Such institutions were themselves based on their idea of justice expressed in the precepts of ritual principles. The success of the enterprise rested on men of moral excellence. The imperatives of the sage kings consisted in this: "Select good and worthy men for office, promote those who are honest and reverent, reward filial piety and brotherly affection, gather under your protection orphans and widows, and offer assistance to those in poverty and need" ("Wangzhi," 9.4②).

Xunzi recognizes four levels of moral excellence. There is the sage 圣人, who represents the pinnacle of human qualities. The great sages had founded human society, had bestowed on humanity all its treasures, and had developed the institutions that enable man to reach his noblest expressions. But the last sages had died almost a thousand years earlier. The Duke of Zhou is the last man Xunzi clearly regards as a sage. Confucius is not accorded that status in unequivocal terms. No ruler of his time aspired to be a sage. Rather, Xunzi discusses what would happen if a humane man 仁人 were to be ruler. Such a man need not be a sage, but his moral excellence must be high.

Xunzi does not include the humane man as one of his four categories. The sage is humane,

---

① 夫两贵之不能相事，两贱之不能相使，是天数也。
② 选贤良，举笃敬，兴孝弟，收孤寡，补贫穷。

but so is the gentleman and the worthy. It is a term that allows him to move from the category of the perfect excellence of the sage to that of the outstanding excellence of the worthy. The Chinese word xian 贤, conventionally translated "worthy," probably originally meant on who was morally steadfast, but it is applied generally to those who are wise, skillful, and morally worthy even in the *Odes*. The opposite is not someone who is "not worthy," but one who "does not resemble" 不肖—referring particularly to a son who does not resemble his father. It implies a lack of filial piety. Persons who are "unworthy" by "not resembling" are blameworthy, violent, stupid, and low.

Lower than the sage and the worthy in Xunzi's scheme is the junzi gentleman. The gentleman is the goal of all teaching and self-cultivation. He combines wide comprehension with high moral character. Xunzi devotes a substantial portion of his works to developing his ideas of the true character of the gentleman, how one becomes a gentleman, and why the rulers of his time should employ gentlemen. The common contrast in Xunzi, as in other philosophers, is between the gentleman, who has cultivated himself, and the xiaoren 小人, the small or petty man, who does not develop his talents.

Usually equivalent to the gentleman, but in Xunzi clearly representing a morally less developed person, is the shi, "knight" or "scholar." The first task of learning is to create a "scholar," but its final end to create a sage ("Quanxue," 1.8①). For Xunzi, moral worth is tied to self-cultivation. Self-cultivation requires an understanding of ritual principles and cannot easily succeed without a teacher to lead one through the Classics. But, by repeating what his teacher has said, by grasping the meaning of the Classics, by incorporating the dictates of ritual in every facet of his conduct, any man can become morally excellent. "If he obtains a worthy teacher, then what he hears will be the way of Yao, Shun, Yu, and Tang. If he obtains good men as his friends, then what he sees will be conduct that is marked by loyalty, trust, respect, and politeness. Each day he will advance in true humanity and in morality without his being conscious of it because his environment has caused it" ("Xing'e," 23.9②). For Xunzi, the environment created the man. It alone was critical. He taught that the accumulation of small acts and deeds through the course of our lives determines where we take our stand and what we accomplish. Learning and self-cultivation are the basis of everything else. Brought to completion, the gentleman is a whole man who can form a Triad with Heaven and Earth, as did the great sages. The gentleman becomes a different man: "The exigencies of time and place and considerations of personal profit cannot influence him, cliques and coteries cannot sway him, and the whole world cannot deter him" ("Quanxue," 1.14③).

---

① 其义则始乎为士，终乎为圣人。
② 身日进于仁义而不自知也者，靡使然也。
③ 是故权利不能倾也，群众不能移也，天下不能荡也。

E. Confucius, The Good Governor[①]
孔子——良善治者

William Appleton
威廉·阿普尔顿

The BABEL CONTROVERSY[②] was long a-dying, but while the reverberations of the dispute were slowly attenuated some opinions on China became generally accepted. Missionaries and travelers alike, from the sixteenth century on, in addition to noting such curiosities as the Great Wall, the manufacture of porcelain, and cormorant fishing, concurred in their praise of China's peaceful and stable government.[③] By 1660 its reputation in this respect was established. In the decades that followed, China also became renowned for superior morality, and in the person of Confucius these two merits were fused. Under the stimulus of Jesuit narratives and translations, and the enthusiasm of various essayists and philosophers, the cult of the sage began.

"Sancte Confuci, ora pro nobis!" La Mothe le Vayer exclaimed in a moment of exaltation. He was not alone in his fervor, for the sage represented to many the good governor and enlightened moralist. Though the voyagers of the sixteenth and early seventeenth centuries had stressed the order and tranquility that prevailed in Canton and Amoy, a contrast perhaps to the tension of Elizabeth's England and the turmoil of Philip the Second's Iberian empire, they did

---

① Excerpted from William Appleton, *A Cycle of Cathay: The Chinese Vogue in England During the Seventeenth and Eighteenth Centuries*, Columbia University Press, 1951.

② The "Babel controversy" refers to the debates and discussions among scholars, theologians, and linguists regarding the Biblical account of the Tower of Babel, as described in the Book of Genesis. This narrative describes how humanity, speaking a single language, attempted to build a tower to reach heaven. In response, God confounded their language, causing them to no longer understand one another, and subsequently scattered them across the earth. Key aspects of the Babel controversy include: 1. The different interpretation of the Biblical text, particularly the nature of the "confounding" of languages. Some interpreted it literally, while others considered more metaphorical or allegorical readings; 2. Search for a primitive language: The controversy spurred interest in the idea of a "primitive" or original language that existed before the Babel incident, with some scholars speculating that it could be linked to ancient languages, including Hebrew or even Chinese; 3. Cultural and historical implications: Scholars explored how the story reflected on human unity and diversity, as well as the theological implications of God's actions in scattering humanity; 4. Linguistic studies: The controversy also influenced early linguistic studies to examine Eastern and Western languages and consider the possibility of a universal language; 5. Philosophical and Theological Debates: Scholars like Sir Thomas Browne engaged with pondering the implications of language change and continuity throughout history.

③ Ch'ien Chung-shu, "China in the English Literature of the Seventeenth Century," *Quarterly Bulletin of Chinese Bibliography*, I. No. 4 (1940), 351-84; Ten-Chung Fan, "Chinese Culture in England from Sir William Temple to Oliver Goldsmith," *Harvard University Summaries of Ph.D. Theses 1931*, pp. 223-226.

not clearly relate this to the morality of its governors. However, as the missionaries arrived in increasing numbers and sought to orient themselves for a more lasting stay, they were forced to appraise the nature of this government more carefully. The China they found, despite its recent conquest by the Manchus, was administered by a scholar-class steeped in Confucian traditions. Anxious to consolidate their rule, the usurpers had shrewdly enlisted the support of the most conservative element of the empire, and under K'ang Hsi Confucian studies were rigorously pursued. It was a policy that played into the hands of the Jesuits.

……

Such a figure[①] fitted admirably into the European philosophical background. In France as early as 1642 La Mothe le Vayer in his *Vertu des payens* had refused to consign Plato, Socrates, and Confucius to the perpetual fires. In England such later works as Dryden's *Religio Laici* showed how favorable the philosophical climate was for a tolerant reception of the sage. The Horatian via media of the well-tempered classicists was certainly not far removed from the Confucian Doctrine of the Mean. Noting this receptiveness, the missionaries, in their anxiety to justify themselves, flooded Europe with translations of the Chinese classics and the writings of the sage. In *Sapientia Sinica* (1662) they introduced the *Ta Hsueh* (*Great Learning*) and *Lun Yü* (*Analects*) of Confucius to the Western world. Adding his *Chung Yung* (*Doctrine of the Mean*) to these earlier translations, and including also his biography and a chronology of China since 2697 B.C., they dedicated the ensuing composite, *Confucius Sinarum Philosophus* (1687), to no less a figure than Louis XIV.

……

In England, as well, the Confucian legend appealed to both orthodox and heterodox thinkers. Its materialism appealed to the English deists; the humanism and benevolent patriarchy endorsed by Confucius, and the perfected, if mummified, Chinese way of life gratified solid Tories and cautious Whigs. Confucius was the supreme apostle of the orderly status quo. It was the temper of the Augustans to find their Elysium not, as their descendants did, in the primitive innocence of the South Seas, but in the glories of a civilized past. With their instinctive Hobbesian distrust of a disorganized society, the classicists, both French and English, preferred the sage to the savage, the static to the dynamic. *The Morals of Confucius* (1691), as interpreted by Father Couplet, in most respects left unruffled the most die-hard principles of the Roi Soleil and the Stuarts.

……

The more philosophical maxims were scarcely more disturbing to the orthodox. The Preface to the *Morals* made the conventional assertion that the Chinese were not idolaters and paid

---

① Confucius as the spiritual leader of China's scholar-governors.

Chapter Two
Confucianism: Historical Context, Core Tenets, and Global Influences

adoration only to the Creator of the Universe, and the translators' choice of sayings was largely guided by the desire to point as nice a parallel as possible between the maxims of Confucius and those of the Christian church. A number, however, such as "The Natural Light is only a perpetual Conformity of our Soul with the Laws of Heaven,"[①] appealed to more liberal thinkers.

It is not difficult to see why such material attracted the attention of Sir William Temple, the most fulsome English admirer of China. Though John Webb had attempted to spark English interest earlier, Temple's enthusiasm for China and Confucius was of a more persuasive and contagious kind. His opinions were the distillation of a naturally cool scholarly mind, and his judgment of the Chinese merits was tempered by a lifetime of participation in public affairs.

……

Though Temple in his writings touched upon many aspects of Chinese culture and history, his main concern was with the cult of this sage. Primarily, he admired Confucius because, like Socrates, he had turned men away from dizzy metaphysical speculation to the contemplation of a practical social morality of universal applicability. In his essay *Of Heroic Virtue* Temple's admiration achieved its fullest expression.

……

The sum of his writings seem to be a body or digestion of ethics, that is, of all moral virtues, either personal, economical, civil or political; and framed for the institution and conduct of men's lives, their families, and their governments, but chiefly of the last: the bent of his thoughts and reasonings running up and down this scale, that no people can be happy but under good governments, and no governments happy but over good men; and that for the felicity of mankind, all men in a nation, from the Prince to the meanest peasant, should endeavor to be good, and wise, and virtuous, as far as his own thoughts, the precepts of others, or the laws of his country can instruct him.[②]

In praising this gregarious and materialistic code of ethics which measured man's morality largely in terms of social progress, the skeptical Temple found himself in agreement with such staunch Catholics as Father Intorcetta who, in the Sinarum Scientia Politico-Moralis (Goa, 1669), with its appended life of Confucius, laid the same stress on the humanitarianism of the sage and its beneficial results. His morality, after all, had brought about something close to an earthly paradise—government by the intellectually elect, who were chosen through a rigid system of competitive examinations and were subject to constant critical scrutiny while in office.

---

① *The Morals of Confucius, a Chinese Philosopher.* London: Printed for Randal Taylor near Stationers Hall, 1691, p. 138.

② Sir William Temple, *The Works of Sir William Temple.* Vol. 3. Originally published London: F.C. and J. Rivington, 1814. Reprinted by Wentworth Press, 2019, pp. 332-333.

Upon these foundations and institutions, by such methods and orders, the kingdom of China seems to be framed and policed with the utmost force and reach of human wisdom, reason and contrivance; and in practice to excel the very speculations of other men, and all those imaginary schemes of the European wits, the institutions of Xenophon, the republic of Plato, the Utopias, or Oceanas, of our modem writers.

It was futile to trust to visionary Utopias, "witty fictions, but mere Chimeras," as Burton called them.① As Peter Heylyn observed in his *Cosmography*, China was a pleasing example of the realization of some of More's schemes. Temple also was more concerned with concrete achievements than with ideal visions, and in a moral-political development such as the followers of Confucius had achieved he found the hope of mankind. Fatally subject though earthly kingdoms were to alteration and decay, an empire founded on such principles might well rise above the ruins of time.

While Temple found other displays of heroic virtue among the great men of Peru, Scythia, and Arabia, his praise of them was far more temperate. He lauded the virtues of Mahomet, but branded the *Alcoran* "a wild fanatic rhapsody of his visions or dreams," a far cry from the order and clarity of Confucius' maxims. In the final analysis he acclaimed the Chinese sage and his followers as the wisest of people and turned an approving eye on the four maxims of their benevolent patriarchic rule: the avoidance of innovation; the necessity of putting national and not private interests first; the encouragement of industry and thrift; and last of all, the prevention of dangers from abroad. Further principles of Confucian statesmanship doubtless suggested to him such specific remedies to better the English government as that no peer be allowed a voice in the government before the age of thirty, and that no officeholder enjoy more than one civil or military appointment simultaneously.

Though Temple touched on other aspects of China (the asymmetrical "sharawadgi"② and the medical knowledge of the pulse), these are subsidiary references. His interest remained centered on Confucius, whose genius had been directed toward so practical an aim—government by the intellectually and morally elect. The Chinese sage played only a small part in the *Essay on Ancient and Modern Learning*; nevertheless, Temple clearly enrolled him among the heroes of antiquity.

Not polemic by design, the essay which precipitated the Battle of the Books was, however, far more than a retired statesman's graceful expression of a partiality for the culture of Rome and Greece. Unwittingly, perhaps, Temple was voicing a theory of history as well. His urbanity and

---

① Robert Burton, *The Anatomy of Melancholy*. Edited by A. F. Bullen. London: J. M. Dent & Sons, 1923, p.113.

② William Temple, "Of Gardening." In *The Works of Sir William Temple*. London: F.C. and J. Rivington, 1814, pp.237-238.

Chapter Two
Confucianism: Historical Context, Core Tenets, and Global Influences

experience as a man of affairs led him to distrust the easy optimism and confident vision of the scientists of Gresham College. The rise and fall of empires and the broad vistas of world history inspired him with the gravest doubts of the triumphal march of the arts and sciences. History was not progress onward and upward. Rather, it seemed to him, a tempestuous cyclic flux, in which heroic virtue periodically rose from its own ashes. No matter how often time obliterated the achievements of the great, new heroes sprang up to reduplicate their triumphs. ...

Temple's paeans to the Chinese and the sage did not, however, touch off a wave of enthusiasm. The English do not easily succumb to heroes and hero worship. Confucius might well be pleasing to the liberal philosophers of France and Germany, but John Bull did not take readily to rhapsody. He continued deferentially to peruse the glowing narratives of the missionaries, with their accounts of the superior Confucian morality and government, even if such panegyrics did not awaken in him the excited echoes they roused on the Continent. When Le Comte's *Memoirs and Observations* appeared in 1697, Confucius in the role of the good governor, the apostle of order and reason, was already a familiar figure.

......

All but the most atrophied Tories or the most extreme Whigs could have taken such political dicta within their stride. The doctrine of reason and natural morality was a far more slippery topic. Unquestionably it appealed to Temple, but he judged Confucianism primarily by its political manifestations. It was a philosophy for statesmen and for bringing about a near heaven on earth. Whether it could exalt men to a more lasting paradise was a question he left discreetly unexplored.

Continental authors, however, faced the problem more boldly. ...

Though the Jesuit's memoirs were condemned by the faculty of theology in Paris, such heresies could not be readily stamped out. Skepticism of revelation and formal religion was already rampant. Early studies in comparative religion had already begun, and such works as André Michel Ramsay's *Les Voyages de Cyrus* (1727) , widely reprinted in England, showed a widening admiration for the heathen sages. Rationalists revered a universe of inexorable mathematical order which allowed no place for the miracles, priestcraft, and superstition that clouded most religions. It was necessary to scrape them off like barnacles to discover the residuum of reason and real religion underneath. In this process of dissecting pagan sects Ramsay found their dogmas essentially those of Christianity, and in his "Discourse upon the Theology and Mythology of the Pagans" annexed to *Les Voyages* he paid particular tribute to the Chinese as he did in his later work, *The Philosophical Principles of Natural and Revealed Religion.*

The basic premise of Ramsay's *Les Voyages* is essentially that of Tindal's *Christianity as Old as Creation* (1731), the Bible of deism, as Leslie Stephen called it. This second great

English champion of Confucius and the Chinese was similarly concerned to prove that religions of nature, whether in China or Peru, are basically the same. Writing in the popular didactic form of a dialogue, Tindal asserted that God at all times had given men sufficient means of knowing whatever He required of them, the "observation of those duties to God and men which reason dictates."

> *To sum up all in a few words; as nature teaches men to unite for their mutual defense and happiness, and government was instituted solely for this end; so to make this more effectual, was religion, which reaches the thoughts, wholly ordained; it being impossible for God, in governing the world, to propose to himself any other end than the good of the governed; and consequently, whoever does his best for the good of his fellow creatures, does all that God or man requires.*[①]

The materialism of such a doctrine dovetailed neatly with Confucian morality, and Tindal's scathing disapproval of superstition and priestcraft in all its manifestations would have won him the sympathy of the literati. Doubtless he sensed this likeness among men of reason, for in describing the universal code of practical morality he found the sayings of Confucius and Christ almost interchangeable.

......

As depicted in one of the engravings of Du Halde's *Description... de la Chine* (1735), "a compilation of twenty-seven missionary accounts, Confucius is a grave, bearded Augustan, almost imperceptibly slant-eyed, meditating majestically in a neatly shelved European library of calf-bound books. Around this figure the Chinese legend had slowly accumulated. Dr. Johnson, in the course of his puffing for Cave's English edition of Du Halde, wrote with enthusiasm of Confucius. The sage had become generally admired as the representative of an efficiently run patriarchy and the spokesman for a sensible morality almost Euclidean in its logic and efficiency.

For a long time he remained almost unshaken on his pedestal. The eighteenth century reissue of the *Morals* included a greatly enlarged account of his life. Alexander Pope in *The Temple of Fame* nodded politely in his direction.[②] His extensive biography in *The Chinese Traveller* (1775) and Sir William Chambers' House of Confucius at Kew attested to his persistent fame.

---

① Matthew Tindal, *Christianity as Old as the Creation*. London: Facsimiles-Garl, 1730, pp. 24-25.

② Alexander Pope, *The Temple of Fame*, vol. II, pp. 107-108. In *The Guardian* 173 Pope discusses Temple's essay "Of Gardening" which is also referred to in his letter to Robert Digby of August 12, 1723.

F. Confucianism and the Politics of Romantic Britain[①]
儒家思想与英国浪漫主义时期的政治思想

Chris Murray
克里斯·默里

If missionaries contended that China was predisposed to accept Christianity, and expatriate politics in Asia motivated Marshman's and Morrison's translations, Confucian philosophy in turn found particular relevance in Romantic-period Britain. For very different reasons, Confucianism appealed to contemporary debates on domestic matters and foreign affairs, among both conservative thinkers and liberals. Some commentators viewed Confucianism within an imagined Orientalist arena where Britain should compete with France for scholarly supremacy. In domestic debates, Confucianism gained currency because the war-like age of Confucius bore cursory resemblance to the unrest of the Romantic period; therefore the philosopher offered answers to comparable problems. Marshman indicates this possibility in the introduction to *The Works of Confucius*. He opines that while Confucianism is "less splendid" than Greek philosophy, it is "superior in point of utility ... with respect to civilization and political order," as demonstrated by its sustained influence on Chinese government.[②]

The Romantic age was shaped by the French Revolution of 1789, which toppled the ancient régime of monarchy and aristocracy in pursuit of egalitarianism. In response to the Revolution, Britain declared war on France in 1792 as a matter of principle. The two nations were in conflict almost continuously until 1815. For fear that the Revolution would be replicated in Britain, William Pitt's Conservative government introduced repressive legislation. Restrictions were placed on public assembly in the 1795 Gagging Acts, the press was heavily censored, and the writ of Habeas Corpus was suspended from 1794 to 1795, and again from 1798 to 1801, to enable the internment of suspects without trial. The Act of Union was enforced in 1801, yet Pitt's government lost power in the prolonged debate over Catholic Emancipation. Liberals campaigned for governmental reform and universal suffrage, and protested the inhumanity of Britain's actions overseas, such as war and slavery. A gunman shot the King's carriage in 1795, and Prime Minister Spencer Perceval was assassinated in 1812. A volatile atmosphere prevailed throughout the

---

① Excerpted from "'Wonderful Nonsense': Confucianism in the British Romantic Period." *Interdisciplinary Literary Studies*, vol. 17, no. 4, 2015.

② Confucius, *The Works of Confucius; Containing the Original Text, with a Translation*, Joshua Marshman trans., Mission Press, 1809, p. cxxxix.

period. To some readers, Confucianism offered solutions.

Journalistic allusions to Confucian philosophy became more frequent following Marshman's and Morrison's translations, but did occur previously. References to Confucianism during the Romantic period often employ language that is politically charged and invoke a key term of radical debate, "reform." In his *History of Philosophy* (1791), based on Johann Jakob Brucker's *Historia Critica Philosophiae* (1742–1744), William Enfield claims that "by his sage counsels, his moral doctrine, and his exemplary conduct, [Confucius] obtained an immortal name as the reformer of his country" (2.575). In his *Universal History* (1802), published the year of a doomed peace treaty between Britain and France, William Fordyce Mavor intimates a wish for a Confucian figure to harmonize society:

> *Confucius seemed designed by heaven to reform, both by his doctrines and example, the corruptions which at this time prevailed as well in the civil as in the religious establishments of China. ... His chief design was to reform their hearts and lives...and, notwithstanding the great opposition which he met with from the influence of the mandarins and grandees, he had the satisfaction to see his excellent morality universally admired.*①

In *The Moral Instructor*, the American author Jesse Torrey accounts that Confucius

> [s]ent six hundred of his disciples into different parts of the empire, to reform the manners of the people. ... A few days before his last illness, he told his disciples with tears in his eyes, that he was overcome with grief at the sight of the disorders that prevailed in the empire.②

The opponent of "mandarins and grandees," moved by civic "disorders," Confucius is an egalitarian figure suited to radical discourse.

Confucianism illustrated reformist ideals, but could further serve as oblique criticism on Britain's existing regime. The Prince Regent—whose Orientalist pleasure-dome at Brighton Pavilion was under construction from 1802 to 1822—both revived the fad for chinoiserie and fell victim to the reception of Chinese culture. In his satirical verse pamphlet *The Queen's Matrimonial Ladder* (1820), William Hone portrays the Prince as "an old fat MANDARIN." George Cruikshank's illustrations depict the Regent as a teapot—uselessly, full of holes—in reference to the ritualistic, sinicized tea-drinking popularized by the Prince.③ Allusions to the virtuous leadership envisioned in Confucianism inevitably cast the Prince in unfavorable

---

① William Fordyce Mavor, *Universal History, Ancient and Modern: From the Earliest Records of Time to the General Peace of 1801*, vol. 11, R. Philips, 1804, pp. 306-307.

② Jesse Torrey, *The Moral Instructor and Guide to Virtue and Happiness.* New York: U. F. Doubleday, 1819, pp. 51-52.

③ William Hone, *The Queen's Matrimonial Ladder*, Kessinger Publishing, pp. 17-19.

Chapter Two
Confucianism: Historical Context, Core Tenets, and Global Influences

relief. Previously identified by liberals as a champion of reform, the Prince disappointed after his assumption of rule in 1811, and was a notorious drunkard and opium addict. The Prince's unpopularity for his failure to support Catholic Emancipation culminated with an incident at a dinner on St. Patrick's Day 1812. When the Marquis of Lansdowne toasted the Prince, other guests hissed. *The Morning Chronicle* published a sycophantic editorial to appease the Prince. The radical journalist Leigh Hunt (1784–1859) replied with an article for which he was libeled:

> *What person, unacquainted with the true state of the case, would imagine, in reading these astounding eulogies, that this Glory of the People was the subject of millions of shrugs and reproaches!…That this Maecenas of the Age patronized not a single deserving writer! That this Breather of Eloquence could not say a few decent extempore words—if we are to judge at least from what he said to his regiment on its embarkation to Portugal! That this Conquerer of Hearts was the disappointer of hopes! That this…Adonis in Loveliness, was a corpulent gentleman of fifty! In short, this delightful, blissful, wise, pleasurable, honourable, virtuous, true, and immortal PRINCE, was a violator of his word, a libertine over head and ears in debt and disgrace, a despiser of domestic ties, the companion of gamblers and demireps, a man who had just closed half a century without one single claim on the gratitude of his country or the respect of posterity!* (1.221)

Charles Lamb also satirizes the gluttonous libertine in his contemporaneous poem "The Triumph of the Whale," yet precedents for the dissolute Prince indicate political unease: Mary Wollstonecraft notes that "rapacious prowlers" such as Louis XVI (1754–1793) bring about "vile intrigues" (96).

In contrast with the despised Prince, journalists celebrated the exemplary life of Confucius and his power as a political symbol. This is the mythical Confucius deified in Chinese folk religion, the sum total of the Confucian principles and maxims, whose hagiography Marshman includes in his *Works of Confucius*. Often commentators overlook Confucian philosophy per se in favor of its paradigm in the demi-mythical Confucius himself. The first issue of *Analectic Magazine* (1813), edited by Washington Irving, reproduces Marshman's life of Confucius verbatim; Irving sourced the material in the *Monthly Magazine*. Marshman depicts the idealized Confucius, who devoted himself to philosophy from the age of fifteen, declined government employment, travelled China in search of worthy society, and "felt no inclination to engage in public affairs" because he would rather edit the Chinese classics.[1] "An undue quantity he did not

---

[1] Joshua Marshman, *Elements of Chinese Grammar; With a Preliminary Dissertation on the Characters, and the Colloquial Medium of the Chinese, and an Appendix Containing the Ta-Hyoh of Confucius with a Translation*, Mission Press, 1814, p. ix.

eat," Marshman translates from *Analects*①. Exiled for his outspoken politics, Confucius found closer Romantic counterparts in Thomas Paine—libeled in absentia②—and Hunt than the apostate Prince.

In 1813, the *Literary Panorama* dismisses Confucianism as a system that encourages a "dull passive morality," but eulogizes Confucius himself for his tireless efforts at self-edification, "that image of perfection, which he set before his imagination, and to which he endeavoured to conform his behavior":

> *An orderly, self-governed, social and benevolent person. Not an ascetic; Confucius did not fly mankind, nor resort to a desert, to shun the converse of his fellows. ... The perfection he sought was that of quietude, his eminence was that of letters, his superiority was that of teaching, his glory was his readiness in distinguishing right from wrong, and communicating the distinction to others, as they were competent to receive it.*③

Furthermore, the author praises Confucius' depiction of "the character of a legislator, or a leading man." This alludes to passages in the *Analects* that portray an inadequate ruler as, in Marshman's words, a "man light and contemptible in his outward deportment," who develops "no respectability of character;" he is "evil" and "silly"④. While the *Panorama* notes the Chinese sage's social conduct and austere diet, the "silly" ruler with "no respectability of character" evokes Hunt's "corpulent" Prince Regent. The Confucian tenet of filial piety reflects poorly on the Prince Regent's infamous treatment of his mentally ill father. Marshman explains the concept concisely: "To serve parents while living, to inter them with due solemnity, and afterward to worship or reverence them" (90). *Great Learning* discusses a princely paradigm of filial piety

---

① Joshua Marshman, *Elements of Chinese Grammar; With a Preliminary Dissertation on the Characters, and the Colloquial Medium of the Chinese, and an Appendix Containing the Ta-Hyoh of Confucius with a Translation*, Mission Press, 1814, p. 692.

② 托马斯·潘恩（Thomas Paine）是18世纪后期著名的政治思想家、革命家，以及资产阶级启蒙主义者。他在英国出生，但在美国独立战争期间扮演了重要角色，其著作《常识》（*Common Sense*）对美国独立思想的传播起到了关键作用。潘恩还参与了《独立宣言》的起草，并在法国大革命期间发挥了影响，协助起草了法国的《人权宣言》。"libeled in absentia"这句话指的是潘恩因为其著作《人权论》（*The Rights of Man*）在英国遭到叛国罪的起诉。在这本书中，潘恩批判了英国的君主制和贵族制度，支持法国大革命的理念。由于这些观点，英国政府对他进行了缺席审判，即在潘恩不在场的情况下进行了审理，并最终判处他煽动性诽谤罪，宣布他为逃犯，同时《人权论》也在英国被永久封禁。潘恩在英国被缺席审判并判有罪，这体现了当时英国对言论自由的压制和政治异见者的严厉对待。

③ "Anecdotes of the Conduct and Maxims of Confucius, the Chinese Sage," in *Literary Panorama* (1813), 12: 1233.

④ Joshua Marshman, *Elements of Chinese Grammar; With a Preliminary Dissertation on the Characters, and the Colloquial Medium of the Chinese, and an Appendix Containing the Ta-Hyoh of Confucius with a Translation*, Mission Press, 1814, p. 34.

Chapter Two
Confucianism: Historical Context, Core Tenets, and Global Influences

in Wen (1152–1056 BCE), successor① to King Wu in ancient Chinese history, as Morrison translates: "His venerable appearance commanded respect; his determined conduct [commanded] an attention to justice and propriety—such was the learned Prince"②. Thus at a time when the qualities of effective leadership were under scrutiny, Confucianism gained particular potency. Commentators also related the philosophy to a separate debate on the international prominence of British scholarship.

To introduce his *Works of Confucius*, Marshman situates his text within the extant corpus of European Sinology:

*It has been observed by the late Sir W. Jones of illustrious memory, that it is to our French neighbours, we have been hitherto indebted for almost every effort to elucidate the language and literature of China. The interests of the English nation however, no less than its literary honor, seem to demand that we also should use our utmost exertions in cultivating this department of literature.*③

Marshman's and Morrison's Confucian translations became associated with Britain's rivalries with France in empire and scholarship, and the intellectual achievements of Protestantism in competition with Catholicism. Depictions of Confucianism in Britain in the early Romantic period remained dominated by Jesuit accounts, which distort Confucian practice to suggest similarities with Catholicism. Hence in Bell's *New Pantheon* (1790)—an encyclopedic survey of world religions—a sacrifice to Confucius is portrayed as a Catholic mass. …The decisive blessing, in which Confucius' spirit is summoned to enter the sacrificial meat, resembles the believed transubstantiation of the Eucharist and wine into Christ's body and blood. Thus in Romantic Britain, Confucianism carried the taint of association with Catholics, who would remain subject to Penal Laws in Britain until 1829. By extension, Catholicism evoked xenophobia toward Continental Europe. In effect Confucianism was Catholic and therefore, loosely, French.

Journalists with little palpable interest in Chinese culture championed the efforts of Marshman and Morrison as national and religious victories. Hence the *Quarterly* writer who evaluates Marshman's Chinese texts as "nonsense" also celebrates the recent missionary translations for their Britishness: "in England we have reason to believe the Chinese language and literature have already

---

① 这里应该是作者的笔误，周文王是武王的 predecessor。
② Robert Morrison, *Horæ Sinicæ: Translations from the Popular Literature of the Chinese*, Black and Parry, 1912, p. 25.
③ Joshua Marshman, *Elements of Chinese Grammar; With a Preliminary Dissertation on the Characters, and the Colloquial Medium of the Chinese, and an Appendix Containing the Ta-Hyoh of Confucius with a Translation*, Mission Press, 1814, pp. ii–iii.

made much greater progress than on the continent."① The Protestant translations could retrieve Chinese culture from its associations with Catholicism. The *Quarterly* attacks French scholars—predominantly Jesuit priests—as incompetent, superficial, and even dishonest:

> *To few, if any of them, can be assigned the merit of having directed their philological studies to any one point of practical utility. ... Indeed the authenticity of many of their communications has often been called into question—less perhaps from the matter of them than from an apparently studied concealment of the means that might enable the learned and studious of Europe to examine the originals. ... In short, they have given us a profusion of the garnish of Chinese literature, but totally omitted the substantial and wholesome part of it.*②

......

In 1816 the *Quarterly* acknowledges that Marshman's translation has been attacked for its poor quality, but argues that this is made unimportant by the humanitarian significance of the missionaries' efforts in Asia. The Serampore Baptists display bravery and persistence:

> *We envy not the feelings of those who find amusement in holding up to ridicule the labours of the Baptist Missionaries; ours, we confess, have received a very different impression, which tells us that we shall not err greatly in placing the names of Marshman, Carey, Ward, and the rest of the Serampore missionaries, among the benefactors of the human race. ...Their progress in the various oriental languages is really wonderful; but so are their exertions, and their contempt of bodily suffering and personal danger.*③

The journalist praises Marshman as an innovator, who inspired the invention of the first movable, metal printing press for Chinese characters:

> *This discovery will prove of infinite importance to the Chinese, if their pride will only suffer them to adopt it; for we believe there is no nation on earth, not even our own, in which printing is carried out to so great an extent as in China.*④

In fact such a press had been invented in China some centuries earlier; national pride displaces journalistic accuracy. Similarly, the author forgets the publication's earlier misgivings about the work of Marshman and Morrison to celebrate them as having "completely torn away the veil that has so long enveloped the symbolic writing of China" (361). While in 1814 the *Quarterly*

---

① "Progress of Chinese Literature in Europe," *London Quarterly Review*, 1814, 11, p. 334.
② Ibid., p. 332.
③ "Missionary Chinese Works," *London Quarterly Review*, 1816, 15, pp. 350-351.
④ Ibid., p. 354.

Chapter Two
Confucianism: Historical Context, Core Tenets, and Global Influences

complains that Marshman's text "is not in the least calculated" to convey an idea of Chinese literature or assist a reader in learning the language (397), the writer of 1816 declares that, due to Marshman's work, "almost every European, who has made the least progress in the knowledge of the written character, has become enraptured with its beauties" (361). The journalist envisions not only a British readership, but a European one, in which the missionary texts occupy a space left by the inadequacy of French scholarship. As in the factual error concerning Marshman's printing press, this contradiction of the opinion expressed previously in the *Quarterly* is necessary to rhetoric that exaggerates British achievement in Asia while subtly deriding France's recent lack of progress in the region.

The *Quarterly* journalism of 1816 illustrates a political environment that paradoxically both encouraged and thwarted British scholarship in Chinese culture. The Baptists' translations arose as viable projects amid the diplomatic complexities of British Asia and were welcomed domestically as a sign of superiority over France. Yet the celebration of publication as an achievement in itself encouraged scholarship that was hurried or, as Wang and Ye term it, "immature." In the course of the nineteenth century, imperial presence in China would become a primary expression of Anglo-French rivalry. The grounds on which the Baptist translations were celebrated anticipate a pattern that emerged in the following decades: the rush to possess China in various ways resulted in failure to understand China. Wang and Ye observe the further irony that bungled scholarship made Confucian philosophy appear the infantile product of a low culture to Europeans. This suited imperialist rhetoric, by which British incursions into China often assumed the guise of educative assistance.[①] Gu moderates such a diametric view of European imperialism and Chinese victimhood with a perceptive argument that China became complicit in modern Sinologism because of its unconscious fetishization of the West, which arose in response to the insistence of Occidental cultures on their own preeminence.[②]

Exercises

I. Vocabulary Practice

Explain the meaning of the underlined terms:
1. 不患人之不己知，患不知人也。
2. 君子不器。

[①] Wang Hui, and Lamei Ye, "A Comparison of Robert Morrison's and Joshua Marshman's Translations of the Daxue," *Journal of Chinese Studies*, 2009, 49, pp. 422-424.

[②] Gu, Ming Dong, *Sinologism: An Alternative to Orientalism and Postcolonialism*, Routledge, 2013, p. 39.

3. 夫子之道，忠恕而已矣。

4. 文质彬彬。

5. 三月不知肉味。

6. 不义而富且贵，于我如浮云。

7. 钓而不纲，弋不射宿。

8. 毋意，毋必，毋固，毋我。

9. 逝者如斯夫，不舍昼夜。

10. 岁寒，然后知松柏之后凋也。

11. 吾与点也！

12. 四海之内，皆兄弟也。

13. 不患人之不己知，患其不能也。

14. 人能弘道，非道弘人。

15. 无恻隐之心，非人也。

16. 富贵不能淫，贫贱不能移，威武不能屈，此之谓大丈夫。

17. 沧浪之水清兮，可以濯我缨；沧浪之水浊兮，可以濯我足。

18. 天作孽，犹可违。自作孽，不可活。

19. 仁者以其所爱及其所不爱，不仁者以其所不爱及其所爱。

II. Comprehension

A. Read Extensive Reading A, Szuma Chien's depiction of Confucius and answer the following questions:

20. How did Confucius respond to Duke Jing of Qi's question about government? What political ideas are reflected in Confucius's answer?

21. What personality of Confucius have you figured out through Szuma Chien's depiction?

B. Read Extensive Reading B, Roger T. Ames's "Confucian Natural Cosmology: An Interpretive Context" and answer the following questions:

22. How is Chinese cosmology different from Greek Transcendentalism?

23. What is problematic about the ontological reality/appearance distinction? How has such a worldview influenced Western ideology?

24. What is the problem with a translation of Chinese philosophy that fails to recognize the Western cultural assumptions involved?

25. What is power? What is creativity? Why does the author insist that Confucianism has the spirit of creativity?

C. Read Extensive Reading C, Philip J. Ivanhoe's "Introduction to the *Mencius*" and answer the following questions:

26. What is Mencius's political idealization of the leadership?
27. What is the core of Mencius's theory of self-cultivation and human nature? How do you agree with it?
28. How does the author compare the Confucian idea of humane with the Western notion of justice? How do you understand his argument that "those who argue that Confucianism cannot develop any robust conception of rights almost certainly are wrong"?
D. Read Extensive Reading D, Knoblock's "Man and Society" and answer the following questions:
29. How did Xunzi refute Mencius's analysis of human nature?
30. How do you understand Xunzi's theory concerning the proper organization of society? How does the role of family come into the theorization?

III. Application and Interpretation

A. Focus on Extensive Reading E, William Appleton's "Confucius, The Good Governor" and complete the following tasks:
31. Translate the underlined passage "In praising this gregarious and materialistic code of ethics …" into Chinese.
32. Summarize the various aspects of Confucianism's influence on European thought during the 16th to the 18th centuries.
33. How does the case further your understanding of cross-cultural communication?
B. Focus on Extensive Reading F, Chris Murray's "Confucianism and the Politics of Romantic Britain" and complete the following tasks:
34. Translate the underlined passage "Confucianism illustrated reformist ideals…". Why does the author say that Confucianism served as an oblique criticism of the British regime, particularly the Prince Regent?
35. How does the author explain the unrest situations during the British Romantic period? And why was Confucianism relevant to British domestic and foreign affairs during this period?
36. Use the sources from Extensive Readings E and F and write an essay researching Confucianism's influence in the west since the Enlightenment period.

Chapter Three

Philosophical Daoism: Its Enduring Legacy and Contemporary Relevance

---

导读

本章课文节选了《道德经》部分章节和《庄子》第一章《逍遥游》及第二章《齐物论》。三篇拓展性阅读材料从以下篇目而来：A篇为美国汉学家安乐哲和郝大维所写《哲学导论：关联宇宙学——一个解释性背景》节选；B篇为当代学者伊丽莎白·哈珀撰写的《早期现代欧洲对〈庄子〉文本的（不）接受》；C篇《一位中国圣人》表达了19世纪爱尔兰著名作家奥斯卡·王尔德对庄子思想的赞誉。

Introduction

1. The Eminence of Daoist Philosophy in Chinese Intellectual History

Daoism, alongside Confucianism, stands as one of the twin pillars of traditional Chinese thought. Emerging during the Spring and Autumn and Warring States periods, Daoist philosophy provided a profound critique of the moral and social norms that were being established by Confucianism. Daoism's emphasis on the Dao, or the Way, as a natural and unforced process, offered a stark contrast to the more human-centric and ritual-focused Confucian ethos. Over time, Daoism has permeated various aspects of Chinese life, influencing not only philosophical discourse but also religious practices, artistic expression, and political theory. Its principles of harmony, balance, and the parity and interconnectivity of all things have left an indelible mark on the Chinese worldview.

2. The Quintessence of Daoist Thought and Its Significance in Modern Society

The Daoist school of thought, with its profound and enduring philosophy, offers a unique perspective on life and the universe, which remains relevant and significant in the modern world.

Chapter Three
Philosophical Daoism: Its Enduring Legacy and Contemporary Relevance

At the heart of Daoism lies the concept of the Dao, or "the Way," which represents the natural order and the underlying principles that govern all existence. The *Dao De Jing*, translated in the extensive reading A by Roger T. Ames and David L. Hall as "Making This Life Significant," provides a philosophical framework that emphasizes living in harmony with the Dao, embracing simplicity, and practicing non-action (Wu Wei) as a means to achieve balance and tranquility.

In today's fast-paced and complex society, where technological advancements and consumerism often overshadow the connection to nature and the self, Daoist thought provides a counterpoint to the dominant ethos. It encourages individuals to seek a more authentic and meaningful existence by aligning their lives with the natural rhythms of the world, fostering a sense of inner peace, and cultivating a deeper understanding of the interconnectedness of all things.

The essence of Daoism is its focus on the process of "becoming" rather than fixating on a static "being." It challenges the modern preoccupation with material success and the relentless pursuit of progress, proposing an alternative approach that values personal contentment, spiritual well-being, and ecological sustainability. Daoist principles, such as the mutual entailing of opposites and the cyclical nature of existence, offer insights into the impermanence of life and the inevitability of change, which can be profoundly comforting and liberating in an era characterized by uncertainty and constant transformation.

Moreover, the Daoist emphasis on self-cultivation and self-creation speaks to the modern quest for personal growth and self-improvement. It suggests that true fulfillment comes from within and is achieved through a process of self-discovery and alignment with one's own nature, rather than through external validation or the pursuit of societally defined goals.

In a nutshell, the quintessence of Daoist thought, according to Roger T. Ames and David L. Hall, is its timeless wisdom that resonates with the contemporary search for meaning, balance, and harmony in a world that often seems out of sync with the natural order. By offering a philosophy that values simplicity, spontaneity, and a life lived in tune with the Dao, Daoism provides a refreshing and transformative lens through which modern society can reevaluate its priorities and aspirations.

3. The Journey of Daoist Thought in 18th and 19th Century Britain

The Daoist philosophy's voyage to 18th and 19th century Britain was not a direct one. Initially, the Jesuit missionaries and early sinologists focused primarily on Confucian texts, viewing Daoism as either too complex or too foreign to reconcile with Christian doctrine. However, as Europe underwent the Enlightenment and then the Romantic movement, there emerged a new appetite for diverse philosophical ideas and a fascination with the exotic East.

The *Zhuangzi*, with its rich metaphors and parables, eventually found its way into the hands of European intellectuals, who were captivated by its profound insights into the nature of existence and the human condition. Figures like Oscar Wilde and scholars such as James Legge played pivotal roles in translating and interpreting Daoist texts, making them accessible to a Western audience. Wilde's review of Herbert Giles' translation of *Zhuangzi* in *The Speaker* highlighted the text's critique of conventional morality and societal norms, resonating with the European intellectual climate of the time.

This cross-cultural exchange was not merely about the importation of Eastern thought into the West; it represented a broader dialogue between different worldviews. The reception of Daoism in Britain was part of a larger trend of cultural exchange during a period of colonial expansion and global exploration. It challenged Europeans to think beyond their own philosophical traditions and consider alternative ways of understanding the universe and humanity's place within it.

The dissemination of Daoist thought in Britain also had a reciprocal effect, influencing Western philosophers and writers, who in turn reinterpreted and reimagined these ideas within their own cultural context. This exchange enriched the global philosophical discourse and demonstrated the universal appeal of Daoist principles, which transcend geographical and cultural boundaries.

In conclusion, this chapter provides an in-depth exploration of Daoist philosophy, its historical significance in China, its contemporary relevance in a world grappling with issues of sustainability and meaning, and its historical journey and impact in the 18th and 19th century Britain. It showcases the enduring legacy and evolving influence of Daoist thought across time and cultures.

《道德经》选篇[①]   Selections from *Dao De Jing*[②]

第一章

道可道也，非恒道也。
名可名也，非恒名也。

Chapter 1

Way-making (*dao*) that can be put into words is not really way-making,

And naming (*ming*) that can assign fixed reference to things is not really naming.

无名，万物之始也。有名，   The nameless (*wuming*) is the fetal beginnings of everything

---

① 选自老子：《道德经（帛书版：全本全译全析）》，秦复观注解，西安：三秦出版社，2024 年。

② Excerpted from *Dao De Jing "Making This Life Significant"—A Philosophical Translation*, trans. Roger T. Ames and David L. Hall, Ballantine Books, 2003.

that is happening (*wanwu*),

While that which is named is their mother.

Thus, to be really objectless in one's desires (*wuyu*) is how one observes the mysteries of all things,

While really having desires is how one observes their boundaries.

These two—the nameless and what is named—emerge from the same source yet are referred to differently.

Together they are called obscure.

The obscurest of the obscure,

They are the swinging gate of the manifold mysteries.

万物之母也。

故恒无欲也，以观其妙；恒有欲也，以观其所徼。

两者同出，异名同谓，玄之又玄，众妙之门。

Chapter 2

As soon as everyone in the world knows that the beautiful are beautiful,

There is already ugliness.

As soon as everyone knows the able,

There is ineptness.

Determinacy (*you*) and indeterminacy (*wu*) give rise to each other,

Difficult and easy complement each other,

Long and short set each other off,

High and low complete each other,

Refined notes and raw sounds harmonize (*he*) with each other,

And before and after lend sequence to each other—

This is really how it all works.

It is for this reason that sages keep to service that does not entail coercion (*wuwei*)

And disseminate teachings that go beyond what can be said.

In all that happens (*wanwu*),

The sages develop things but do not initiate them,

They act on behalf of things but do not lay any claim to them,

They see things through to fruition but do not take credit for them.

It is only because they do not take credit for them that things do not take their leave.

第二章

天下皆知美、为美，恶已。

皆知善，訾不善矣。

有，无之相生也。难，易之相成也。长，短之相形也。高，下之相盈也。音，声之相和也。先，后之相随，恒也。

是以圣人居无为之事，行不言之教。万物作而弗始也，为而弗持也，成功而弗居也。夫唯弗居，是以弗去。

第三章

不上贤，使民不争。不贵难得之货，使民不为盗。不见可欲，使民不乱。

是以圣人之治也，虚其心，实其腹，弱其志，强其骨。

恒使民无知无欲也，使夫智不敢。弗为而已，则无不治矣。

Chapter 3

Not promoting those of superior character
Will save the common people from becoming contentious.
Not prizing property that is hard to come by
Will save them from becoming thieves.
Not making a show of what might be desired
Will save them from becoming disgruntled.

It is for this reason that in the proper governing by the sages:
They empty the hearts-and-minds of the people and fill their stomachs,
They weaken their aspirations and strengthen their bones,

Ever teaching the common people to be unprincipled in their knowing (*wuzhi*)
And objectless in their desires (*wuyu*),
They keep the hawkers of knowledge at bay.
It is simply in doing things noncoercively (*wuwei*)
That everything is governed properly.

第五章

天地不仁，以万物为刍狗。圣人不仁，以百姓为刍狗。天地之间，其犹橐籥与！虚而不屈，动而愈出。多闻数穷，不若守于中。

Chapter 5

The heavens and the earth are not partial to institutionalized morality.
They take things (*wanwu*) and treat them all as straw dogs.
Sages too are not partial to institutionalized morality.
They treat the common people as straw dogs.
The space between the heavens and the earth—
Isn't it just like a bellows!
Even though empty it is not vacuous.
Pump it and more and more comes out.
It is better to safeguard what you have within
Than to learn a great deal that so often goes nowhere.

第七章

天长地久。天地之所以能长且久者，以其不自生也，故能长生。

是以圣人退其身而身先，

Chapter 7

The heavens are lasting and the earth enduring.
The reason the world is able to be lasting and enduring
Is because it does not live for itself.
Thus it is able to be long-lived.

It is on this model that the sages withdraw their persons from contention yet find themselves out in front,

Put their own persons out of mind yet find themselves taken care of.

Isn't it simply because they are unselfish that they can satisfy their own needs?

外其身而身存。不以其无私与？故能成其私。

Chapter 8

The highest efficacy is like water.

It is because water benefits everything

Yet vies to dwell in places loathed by the crowd

That it comes nearest to proper way-making.

In dwelling, the question is where the right place is.

In thinking and feeling, it is how deeply.

In giving, it is how much like nature's bounty.

In speaking, it is how credibly.

In governing, it is how effectively.

In serving, it is how capably.

In acting, it is how timely.

It is only because there is no contentiousness in proper way-making

That it incurs no blame.

第八章

上善治水。水善利万物而有静，居众人之所恶，故几于道矣。

居善地，心善渊，予善天，言善信，政善治，事善能，动善时。夫唯不争，故无尤。

Chapter 25

There was some process that formed spontaneously

Emerging before the heavens and the earth.

Silent and empty,

Standing alone as all that is, it does not suffer alteration.

[All pervading, it does not pause.]

It can be thought of as the mother of the heavens and the earth.

I do not yet know its name.

If I were to style it,

I would call it way-making.

And if forced to give it a name,

I would call it grand.

Being grand, it is called passing,

Passing, it is called distancing.

第二十五章

有物混成，先天地生。寂呵寥呵，独立而不改，可以为天地母。吾未知其名，字之曰道，吾强为之名曰大。

大曰逝，逝曰远，远曰反。道大，天大，地大，王亦大。

国中有四大，而王居一焉。

Distancing, it is called returning.

Way-making is grand,

The heavens (*tian*) are grand,

The earth is grand,

And the king is also grand.

Within our territories

There are four "grandees"

And the king occupies one of them.

人法地，地法天，天法道，道法自然。

Human beings emulate the earth,

The earth emulates the heavens,

The heavens emulate way-making,

And way-making emulates what is spontaneously so (*ziran*).

第二十八章

知其雄，守其雌，为天下溪。为天下溪，恒德不离。恒德不离，复归于婴儿。

Chapter 28

Know the male

Yet safeguard the female

And be a river gorge to the world.

As a river gorge to the world,

You will not lose your real potency (*de*),

And not losing your real potency,

You return to the state of the newborn babe.

知其荣，守其辱，为天下浴。为天下浴，恒德乃足。恒德乃足，复归于朴。

Know the clean

Yet safeguard the soiled

And be a valley to the world.

As a valley to the world

Your real potency will be ample,

And with ample potency,

You return to the state of unworked wood.

知其白，守其黑，为天下式。为天下式，恒德不忒。恒德不忒，复归于无极。

Know the white

Yet safeguard the black

And be a model for the world.

As a model for the world,

Your real potency will not be wanting,

And with your potency not wanting,

You return to the state of the limitless.

朴散则为器，圣人用则

When unworked wood is split,

It is made into utensils.

When the sages are employed,

They are made into head officials.

There is no cutting, however, in the very best tailoring.

为官长。夫大制无割。

Chapter 36

第三十六章

Whatever is gathered in

Must first be stretched out;

Whatever is weakened

Must first be made strong;

Whatever is abandoned

Must first be joined;

Whatever is taken away

Must first be given.

将欲翕之,必固张之。将欲弱之,必固强之。将欲去之,必固举之。将欲夺之,必固予之。是谓微明。

This is what is called the subtle within what is evident.

The soft and weak vanquish the hard and strong.

Fishes should not relinquish the depths.

The sharpest instruments of state should not be revealed to others.

柔弱胜强。鱼不可脱于渊,邦利器不可以示人。

Chapter 39

第三十九章

Of old there were certain things that realized oneness:

The heavens in realizing oneness became clear;

The earth in realizing oneness became stable;

The numinous in realizing oneness became animated;

The river valleys in realizing oneness became full;

The lords and kings in realizing oneness brought proper order to the world.

昔之得一者,天得一以清,地得一以宁,神得一以灵,浴得一以盈,侯王得一而以为正。

Following this line of thinking,

We could say that if the heavens had not become clear

They may well have fallen to pieces;

We could say that if the earth had not become stable

It may well have collapsed;

We could say that if the numinous had not become animated

It may well have faded away;

We could say that if the river valleys had not become full

They may well have dried up;

其致之也,谓天毋已清,将恐裂。谓地毋以宁,将恐发。谓神毋已灵,将恐歇。谓谷毋以盈,将恐竭。谓侯王毋已贵以高,将恐蹶。

故必贵而以贱为本，必高矣而以下为基。夫是以侯王自谓曰：孤、寡、不谷，此其贱之本与非也？故致数誉无誉。

是故不欲禄禄若玉，硌硌若石。

第四十章

反也者，道之动也。弱也者，道之用也。天下之物生于有，有生于无。

第七十六章

人之生也柔弱，其死也恒韧坚强。万物草木之生也柔脆，其死也枯槁。

故曰：坚强者死之徒也，柔弱微细生之徒也。兵强则不胜，木强则恒。强大居下，柔弱微细居上。

We could say that if the lords and kings had not brought proper order to the world

They may well have stumbled and fallen from power.

Thus for something to be noble it must take the humble as its root;

For something to be high it must take the low as its foundation.

It is for this reason that the lords and kings use "friendless," "unworthy," and "inept" as terms to refer to themselves.

This is a clear case of taking the humble as the root, is it not?

The highest renown is to be without renown.

They do not want to be precious like jade,

But common like stone.

Chapter 40

"Returning" is how way-making (*dao*) moves,

And "weakening" is how it functions.

The events of the world arise from the determinate (*you*),

And the determinate arises from the indeterminate (*wu*).

Chapter 76

While living, people are supple and soft,

But once dead, they become hard and rigid cadavers.

While living, the things of this world and its grasses and trees are pliant and fragile,

But once dead, they become withered and dry.

Thus it is said: Things that are hard and rigid are the companions of death;

Things that are supple and soft are the companions of life.

For this reason,

If a weapon is rigid it will not prevail;

If a tree is rigid it will snap.

Thus, the rigid and great dwell below,

While the supple and soft abide above.

Chapter Three
Philosophical Daoism: Its Enduring Legacy and Contemporary Relevance

Selections from *Chuang Tzu* [1]

《庄子》选篇 [2]

I. Enjoyment in Untroubled Ease

1. Is azure the proper colour of the sky?

In the Northern Ocean there is a fish, the name of which is Kun — I do not know how many li [1 li = ca. 500 m] in size. It changes into a bird with the name of Peng, the back of which is (also) — I do not know how many li in extent. When this bird rouses itself and flies, its wings are like clouds all around the sky. When the sea is moved (so as to bear it along), it prepares to remove to the Southern Ocean [darkness]. The Southern Ocean is the Lake of Heaven.

There is the (book called) *The Universal Harmony*, — a record of marvels. We have in it these words: "When the Peng journeys to the Southern Ocean it flaps (its wings) on the water for 3000 li. Then it ascends on a whirlwind 90,000 li, and it rests only at the end of six months." (But similar to this is the movement of the breezes which we call) the horses of the fields, of the dust (which quivers in the sunbeams), and of living things as they are blown against one another by the air. Is its azure the proper colour of the sky? Or is it occasioned by its distance and illimitable extent? If one were looking down (from above), the very same appearance would just meet his view.

2. The mushroom of the morning: Return to a third meal

If water is not heaped up deep enough, it will not have the strength to support a big boat. Upset a cup of water in a cavity, and a straw will float on it as if it were a boat. Place a cup in it, and it will stick fast; — the water is shallow and the boat is large. (So it is with) the accumulation of wind; if it be not great, it will not have strength to support great wings. Therefore (the Peng ascended to) the height of 90,000 li, and there was such a mass of wind beneath it; thenceforth the accumulation of wind was sufficient. As

一、逍遥游

北冥有鱼，其名为鲲。鲲之大，不知其几千里也。化而为鸟，其名为鹏。鹏之背，不知其几千里也。怒而飞，其翼若垂天之云。是鸟也，海运则将徙于南冥。南冥者，天池也。

《齐谐》者，志怪者也。《谐》之言曰："鹏之徙于南冥也，水击三千里，抟扶摇而上者九万里，去以六月息者也。"野马也，尘埃也，生物之以息相吹也。天之苍苍，其正色邪？其远而无所至极邪？其视下也，亦若是则已矣。

且夫水之积也不厚，则其负大舟也无力。覆杯水于坳堂之上，则芥为之舟。置杯焉则胶，水浅而舟大也。风之积也不厚，则其负大翼也无力。故九万里则风斯在下矣，而后乃今培风；背负青天而莫之夭阏者，而后乃

---

① Excerpted from *Chuang Tzu*, translated by James Legge, http://oaks.nvg.org/chuang.html.
② 选自孙通海译注：《庄子》，北京：中华书局，2007 年。

今将图南。

蜩与学鸠笑之曰："我决起而飞，抢榆枋，时则不至而控于地而已矣，奚以之九万里而南为？"适莽苍者，三飡而反，腹犹果然；适百里者，宿舂粮；适千里者，三月聚粮。之二虫又何知！

小知不及大知，小年不及大年。奚以知其然也？朝菌不知晦朔，蟪蛄不知春秋，此小年也。楚之南有冥灵者，以五百岁为春，五百岁为秋；上古有大椿者，以八千岁为春，八千岁为秋，此大年也。而彭祖乃今以久特闻，众人匹之，不亦悲乎？

汤之问棘也是已："穷发之北，有冥海者，天池也。有鱼焉，其广数千里，未有知其修者，其名为鲲。有鸟焉，其名为鹏，背若太山，翼若垂天之云；抟扶摇羊角而上者九万里，绝云气，负青天，然后图南，且适南冥也。斥鷃笑之曰：'彼且奚适也？

it seemed to bear the blue sky on its back, and there was nothing to obstruct or arrest its course, it could pursue its way to the South.

A cicada and a little dove laughed at it, saying, "We make an effort and fly towards an elm or sapan-wood tree; and sometimes before we reach it, we can do no more but drop to the ground. Of what use is it for this (creature) to rise 90,000 li, and make for the South?"

He who goes to the grassy suburbs, returning to the third meal (of the day), will have his belly as full as when he set out; he who goes to a distance of 100 li will have to pound his grain where he stops for the night; he who goes a thousand li, will have to carry with him provisions for three months. What should these two small creatures know about the matter? The knowledge of that which is small does not reach to that which is great; (the experience of) a few years does not reach to that of many. How do we know that it is so? The mushroom of a morning does not know (what takes place between) the beginning and end of a month; the short-lived cicada does not know (what takes place between) the spring and autumn. These are instances of a short term of life. In the south of Ku, there is the (tree) called Ming-ling, whose spring is 500 years, and its autumn the same; in high antiquity there was that called Ta Khun, whose spring was 8000 years, and its autumn the same. And Master Peng is the one man renowned to the present day for his length of life: if all men were (to wish) to match him, would they not be miserable?

3. Judgement energies

In the questions put by Tang to Ki we have similar statements: "In the bare and barren north there is the dark and vast ocean, — the Pool of Heaven. In it there is a fish, several thousand li in breadth, while no one knows its length. Its name is the Kun. There is (also) a bird named the Peng; its back is like the Tai mountain, while its wings are like clouds all round the sky. On a whirlwind it mounts upwards as on the whorls of a goat's horn for 90,000 li, till, far removed from the cloudy vapours, it bears on its back the blue sky, and then it shapes its course for the South, and proceeds to the

Chapter Three
Philosophical Daoism: Its Enduring Legacy and Contemporary Relevance

ocean there." A quail by the side of a marsh laughed at it, and said, "Where is it going to? I spring up with a bound, and come down again when I have reached but a few fathoms, and then fly about among the brushwood and bushes; and this is the perfection of flying. Where is that creature going to?"

This shows the difference between the small and the great.

Thus it is that men, whose wisdom is sufficient for the duties of some one office, or whose conduct will secure harmony in some one district, or whose virtue is befitting a ruler so that they could efficiently govern some one state, are sure to look on themselves in this manner (like the quail), and yet Master Jung of Sung would have smiled and laughed at them. (This Master Jung), though the whole world should have praised him, would not for that have stimulated himself to greater endeavour, and though the whole world should have condemned him, would not have exercised any more repression of his course; so fixed was he in the difference between the internal (judgement of himself) and the external (judgement of others), so distinctly had he marked out the bounding limit of glory and disgrace. Here, however, he stopped. His place in the world indeed had become indifferent to him, but still he had not planted himself firmly (in the right position).

There was Master Lieh (Lieh Tzu), who rode on the wind and pursued his way with an admirable indifference (to all external things), returning, however, after fifteen days, (to his place). In regard to the things that (are supposed to) contribute to happiness, he was free from all endeavours to obtain them; but though he had not to walk, there was still something for which he had to wait. But suppose one who mounts on (the ether of) heaven and earth in its normal operation, and drives along the six elemental energies of the changing (seasons), thus enjoying himself in the illimitable, — what has he to wait for? Therefore it is said, "The Perfect man has no (thought of) self; the Spirit-like man, none of merit; the Sagely-minded man, none of fame."

4. Names are like guests of reality

Yao, proposing to resign the throne to Hsü Yu, said, "When

我腾跃而上，不过数仞而下，翱翔蓬蒿之间，此亦飞之至也！而彼且奚适也？'"此小大之辩也。

故夫知效一官，行比一乡，德合一君而征一国者，其自视也，亦若此矣。而宋荣子犹然笑之。且举世而誉之而不加劝，举世而非之而不加沮，定乎内外之分，辩乎荣辱之境，斯已矣。彼其于世，未数数然也。虽然，犹有未树也。

夫列子御风而行，泠然善也，旬有五日而后反。彼于致福者，未数数然也。此虽免乎行，犹有所待者也。

若夫乘天地之正，而御六气之辩，以游无穷者，彼且恶乎待哉！故曰：至人无己，神人无功，圣人无名。

尧让天下于许由，曰："日

月出矣，而爝火不息，其于光也，不亦难乎！时雨降矣，而犹浸灌，其于泽也，不亦劳乎！夫子立而天下治，而我犹尸之，吾自视缺然。请致天下。"

许由曰："子治天下，天下既已治也，而我犹代子，吾将为名乎？名者，实之宾也，吾将为宾乎？鹪鹩巢于深林，不过一枝；偃鼠饮河，不过满腹。归休乎君！予无所用天下为。<u>庖人虽不治庖，尸祝不越樽俎而代之矣</u>。"

肩吾问于连叔曰："吾闻言于接舆，大而无当，往而不返。吾惊怖其言，犹河汉而无极也，大有径庭，不近人情焉。"

连叔曰："其言谓何哉？"
"曰'藐姑射之山，有神人居焉。肌肤若冰雪，绰约若处子；不食五谷，吸风饮露；乘云气，御飞龙，而游乎四海之外；其神凝，使物不疵疠而年谷熟。'吾以是狂而不信也。"

the sun and moon have come forth, if the torches have not been put out, would it not be difficult for them to give light? When the seasonal rains are coming down, if we still keep watering the ground, will not our toil be labour lost for all the good it will do? Do you, Master, stand forth (as sovereign), and the kingdom will (at once) be well governed. If I still (continue to) preside over it, I must look on myself as vainly occupying the place; — I beg to resign the throne to you."

Hsü Yu said, "You, Sir, govern the kingdom, and the kingdom is well governed. If I in these circumstances take your place, shall I not be doing so for the sake of the name? But the name is but the guest of the reality; — shall I be playing the part of the guest? The tailor-bird makes its nest in the deep forest, but only uses a single branch; the mole drinks from the Ho, but only takes what fills its belly. Return and rest in being ruler, — I will have nothing to do with the throne. Though the cook were not attending to his kitchen, the representative of the dead and the officer of prayer would not leave their cups and stands to take his place."

5. Far away on a hill there lived someone who preserved a plentiful harvest

Kien Wu asked Lien Shu, saying, "I heard Khieh-yu talking words which were great, but had nothing corresponding to them (in reality); —once gone, they could not be brought back. I was frightened by them; —they were like the Milky Way which cannot be traced to its beginning or end. They had no connexion with one another, and were not akin to the experiences of men."

"What were his words?" asked Lien Shu, and the other replied, "(He said) that 'Far away on the hill of Ku She there dwelt a Spirit-like man whose flesh and skin were (smooth) as ice and (white) as snow; that his manner was elegant and delicate as that of a virgin; that he did not eat any of the five grains, but inhaled the wind and drank the dew; that he mounted on the clouds, drove along the flying dragons, rambling and enjoying himself beyond the four seas; that by the concentration of his spirit-like powers he could save men from disease and pestilence, and secure every year a plentiful harvest.' These words appeared to me wild and incoherent and I did not believe them."

"So it is," said Lien Shu. "The blind have no perception of the beauty of elegant figures, nor the deaf of the sound of bells and drums. But is it only the bodily senses of which deafness and blindness can be predicated? There is also a similar defect in the intelligence; and of this your words supply an illustration in yourself. That man, with those attributes, though all things were one mass of confusion, and he heard in that condition the whole world crying out to him to be rectified, would not have to address himself laboriously to the task, as if it were his business to rectify the world. Nothing could hurt that man; the greatest floods, reaching to the sky, could not drown him, nor would he feel the fervour of the greatest heats melting metals and stones till they flowed, and scorching all the ground and hills. From the dust and chaff of himself, he could still mould and fashion Yaos and Shuns; how should he be willing to occupy himself with things?"

连叔曰:"然,瞽者无以与乎文章之观,聋者无以与乎钟鼓之声。岂唯形骸有聋盲哉?夫知亦有之。是其言也,犹时女也。之人也,之德也,将旁礴万物以为一,世蕲乎乱,孰弊弊焉以天下为事!之人也,物莫之伤,大浸稽天而不溺,大旱金石流、土山焦而不热。是其尘垢秕糠,将犹陶铸尧舜者也,孰肯以物为事?"

6. Oblivious eyes indicate lack of interest in ruling the people

A man of Sung, who dealt in the ceremonial caps (of Yin), went with them to Yüeh, the people of which cut off their hair and tattooed their bodies, so that they had no use for them. Yao ruled the people of the kingdom, and maintained a perfect government within the four seas. Having gone to see the four (Perfect) Ones on the distant hill of Ku She, when (he returned to his capital) on the south of the Fen water, his throne appeared no more to his deep-sunk oblivious eyes.

宋人资章甫而适诸越,越人断发文身,无所用之。

尧治天下之民,平海内之政,往见四子藐姑射之山,汾水之阳,窅然丧其天下焉。

7. Considering the good uses of many things

Master Hui told Master Chuang, saying, "The king of Wei sent me some seeds of a large calabash, which I sowed. The fruit, when fully grown, could contain five piculs (of anything). I used it to contain water, but it was so heavy that I could not lift it by myself. I cut it in two to make the parts into drinking vessels; but the dried shells were too wide and unstable and would not hold (the liquor); nothing but large useless things! Because of their uselessness I

惠子谓庄子曰:"魏王贻我大瓠之种,我树之成而实五石。以盛水浆,其坚不能自举也;剖之以为瓢,则瓠落无所容。非不呺然大也,吾为其无用而掊之。"

knocked them to pieces."

庄子曰:"夫子固拙于用大矣。宋人有善为不龟手之药者,世世以洴澼絖为事。客闻之,请买其方百金。聚族而谋之曰:'我世世为洴澼絖,不过数金。今一朝而鬻技百金,请与之。'客得之,以说吴王。越有难,吴王使之将。冬,与越人水战,大败越人,裂地而封之。能不龟手一也,或以封,或不免于洴澼絖,则所用之异也。今子有五石之瓠,何不虑以为大樽而浮乎江湖,而忧其瓠落无所容?则夫子犹有蓬之心也夫!"

Master Chuang replied, "You were indeed stupid in the use of what was large. There was a man of Sung who was skillful at making a salve which kept the hands from getting chapped; and (his family) for generations had made the bleaching of cocoon-silk their business. A stranger heard of it, and proposed to buy the art of the preparation for a hundred ounces of silver. The kindred all came together, and considered the proposal. 'We have,' said they, 'been bleaching cocoon-silk for generations, and have only gained a little money. Now in one morning we can sell to this man our art for a hundred ounces; — let him have it.' The stranger accordingly got it and went away with it to give counsel to the king of Wu, who was then engaged in hostilities with Yüeh. The king gave him the command of his fleet, and in the winter he had an engagement with that of Yüeh, on which he inflicted a great defeat, and was invested with a portion of territory taken from Yüeh. The keeping the hands from getting chapped was the same in both cases; but in the one case it led to the investiture (of the possessor of the salve), and in the other it had only enabled its owners to continue their bleaching. The difference of result was owing to the different use made of the art. Now you, Sir, had calabashes large enough to hold five piculs; — why did you not think of making large bottle-gourds of them, by means of which you could have floated over rivers and lakes, instead of giving yourself the sorrow of finding that they were useless for holding anything. Your mind, my master, would seem to have been closed against all intelligence!"

8. The useless tree

惠子谓庄子曰:"吾有大树,人谓之樗。其大本拥肿而不中绳墨,其小枝卷曲而不中规矩。立之涂,匠者不顾。今子之言,大而无用,众所同去也。"

Master Hui said to Master Chuang, "I have a large tree, which men call the Ailantus. Its trunk swells out to a large size, but is not fit for a carpenter to apply his line to it; its smaller branches are knotted and crooked, so that the disk and square cannot be used on them. Though planted on the wayside, a builder would not turn his head to look at it. Now your words, Sir, are great, but of no use; — all unite in putting them away from them."

庄子曰:"子独不见狸

Master Chuang replied, "Have you never seen a wildcat

or a weasel? There it lies, crouching and low, till the wanderer approaches; east and west it leaps about, avoiding neither what is high nor what is low, till it is caught in a trap, or dies in a net. Again there is the Yak, so large that it is like a cloud hanging in the sky. It is large indeed, but it cannot catch mice. You, Sir, have a large tree and are troubled because it is of no use; — why do you not plant it in a tract where there is nothing else, or in a wide and barren wild? There you might saunter idly by its side, or in the enjoyment of untroubled ease sleep beneath it. Neither bill nor axe would shorten its existence; there would be nothing to injure it. What is there in its uselessness to cause you distress?"

II. The Adjustment of Controversies

1. Heavenly music

Tzu Ki was seated, leaning forward on his stool. He was looking up to heaven and breathed gently, seeming to be in a trance, and to have lost all consciousness of any companion. (His disciple), Yen Master Keng Yu, who was in attendance and standing before him, said, "What is this? Can the body be made to become thus like a withered tree, and the mind to become like slaked lime? His appearance as he leans forward on the stool today is such as I never saw him have before in the same position."

Tzu Ki said, "Yen, you do well to ask such a question, I had just now lost myself; but how should you understand it? You may have heard the notes of Man, but have not heard those of Earth; you may have heard the notes of Earth, but have not heard those of Heaven."

Tzu Yu said, "I venture to ask from you a description of all these."

The reply was, "When the breath of the Great Mass (of nature) comes strongly, it is called Wind. Sometimes it does not come so; but when it does, then from a myriad apertures there issues its excited noise; — have you not heard it in a prolonged gale? Take the projecting bluff of a mountain forest; — in the great trees, a hundred spans round, the apertures and cavities are like the nostrils,

狌乎？卑身而伏，以候敖者；东西跳梁，不避高下；中于机辟，死于罔罟。今夫斄牛，其大若垂天之云，此能为大矣，而不能执鼠。今子有大树，患其无用，何不树之于无何有之乡，广莫之野，彷徨乎无为其侧，逍遥乎寝卧其下？不夭斤斧，物无害者，无所可用，安所困苦哉！"

二、齐物论

南郭子綦隐机而坐，仰天而嘘，苔焉似丧其耦。颜成子游立侍乎前，曰："何居乎？形固可使如槁木，而心固可使如死灰乎？今之隐机者，非昔之隐机者也。"

子綦曰："偃，不亦善乎，而问之也！今者吾丧我，汝知之乎？女闻人籁而未闻地籁，女闻地籁而未闻天籁夫！"

子游曰："敢问其方。"

子綦曰："夫大块噫气，其名为风。是唯无作，作则万窍怒呺。而独不闻之翏翏乎？山林之畏佳，大木百围之窍穴，似鼻，似口，似耳，似枅，似圈，似臼，似洼者，似洼者。激者、谪者、叱者、吸者、叫者、谯者、宎者、咬者。前者唱于而随者唱喁，泠风则小和，飘风则大和，厉风济则众窍为虚。而独不见之调调之刁刁乎？"

子游曰："地籁则众窍是已，人籁则比竹是已，敢问天籁。"

子綦曰："夫吹万不同，而使其自己也。咸其自取，怒者其谁邪？"

大知闲闲，小知间间；大言炎炎，小言詹詹。其寐也魂交，其觉也形开。与接为构，日以心斗。缦者、窖者、密者。小恐惴惴，大恐缦缦。其发若机栝，其司是非之谓也；其留如诅盟，其守胜之谓也；其杀如秋冬，以言其日消也；其溺之所为之，不可使复之也；其厌也如缄，以言其老洫也；近死之心，莫使复阳也。喜怒哀乐，虑叹变慹，姚佚启态。乐出虚，蒸成菌。日夜相代乎前，而莫知其所萌。已乎，已乎！

or the mouth, or the ears; now square, now round like a cup or a mortar; here like a wet footprint, and there like a large puddle. (The sounds issuing from them are like) those of fretted water, of the arrowy whizz, of the stern command, of the inhaling of the breath, of the shout, of the gruff note, of the deep wail, of the sad and piping note. The first notes are slight, and those that follow deeper, but in harmony with them. Gentle winds produce a small response; violent winds a great one. When the fierce gusts have passed away, all the apertures are empty (and still); — have you not seen this in the bending and quivering of the branches and leaves?"

Tzu Yu said, "The notes of Earth then are simply those which come from its myriad apertures; and the notes of Man may just be compared to those which (are brought from the tubes of) bamboo; — allow me to ask about the notes of Heaven."

Tzu Ki replied, "When (the wind) blows, (the sounds from) the myriad apertures are different, and (its cessation) makes them stop of themselves. Both of these things arise from (the wind and the apertures) themselves: should there be any other agency that excites them?"

2. The world of changes

Great knowledge is wide and comprehensive; small knowledge is partial and restricted. Great speech is exact and complete; small speech is (merely) so much talk. When we sleep, the soul communicates with (what is external to us); when we awake, the body is set free. Our intercourse with others then leads to various activity, and daily there is the striving of mind with mind. There are hesitancies; deep difficulties; reservations; small apprehensions causing restless distress, and great apprehensions producing endless fears. Where their utterances are like arrows from a bow, we have those who feel it their charge to pronounce what is right and what is wrong. Where they are given out like the conditions of a covenant, we have those who maintain their views, determined to overcome. (The weakness of their arguments), like the decay (of things) in autumn and winter, shows the failing (of the minds of some) from day to day; or it is like their water which, once voided, cannot be gathered up again. Then their ideas seem as if fast bound with cords, showing that the mind is [has] become like an old and dry moat, and that it is nigh to death, and cannot be restored to vigour and brightness.

Joy and anger, sadness and pleasure, anticipation and regret, fickleness and fixedness, vehemence and indolence, eagerness and tardiness; — (all these moods), like music from an empty tube, or mushrooms from the warm moisture, day and night succeed to one another and come before us, and we do not know whence they sprout. Let us stop! Let us stop! Can we expect to find out suddenly how they are produced?

旦暮得此，其所由以生乎！

If there were not (the views of) another, I should not have mine; if there were not I (with my views), his would be uncalled for: this is nearly a true, statement of the case, but we do not know what it is that makes it be so. It might seem as if there would be a true Governor concerned in it, but we do not find any trace (of his presence and acting). That such an One could act so I believe; but we do not see His form. He has affections, but He has no form.

非彼无我，非我无所取。是亦近矣，而不知其所为使。若有真宰，而特不得其朕。可行己信，而不见其形，有情而无形。

3. The true Ruler inside

Given the body, with its hundred parts, its nine openings, and its six viscera, all complete in their places, which do I love the most? Do you love them all equally? or do you love some more than others? Is it not the case that they all perform the part of your servants and waiting women? All of them being such, are they not incompetent to rule one another? or do they take it in turns to be now ruler and now servants? There must be a true Ruler (among them) whether by searching you can find out His character or not, there is neither advantage nor hurt, so far as the truth of His operation is concerned. When once we have received the bodily form complete, its parts do not fail to perform their functions till the end comes. In conflict with things or in harmony with them, they pursue their course to the end, with the speed of a galloping horse which cannot be stopped; — is it not sad? To be constantly toiling all one's lifetime, without seeing the fruit of one's labour, and to be weary and worn out with his labour, without knowing

百骸、九窍、六藏、赅而存焉，吾谁与为亲？汝皆说之乎？其有私焉？如是皆有为臣妾乎？其臣妾不足以相治乎？其递相为君臣乎？其有真君存焉！如求得其情与不得，无益损乎其真。

一受其成形，不亡以待尽。与物相刃相靡，其行尽如驰而莫之能止，不亦悲乎！终身役役而不见其成功，茶然疲役而不知其所归，可不哀邪！人谓之不死，奚益！其形化，其心与之然，可不谓大哀乎？人之生也，固若是芒乎？其我独芒，而人亦有不芒者乎？

夫随其成心而师之，谁独且无师乎？奚必知代而心自取者有之？愚者与有焉！未成乎心而有是非，是今日适越而昔至也。是以无有为有。无有为有，虽有神禹且不能知，吾独且奈何哉！

夫言非吹也。言者有言，其所言者特未定也。果有言邪？其未尝有言邪？其以为异于鷇音，亦有辩乎？其无辩乎？

道恶乎隐而有真伪？言恶乎隐而有是非？道恶乎往而不存？言恶乎存而不可？道隐于小成，言隐于荣华。故有儒墨之是非，以是其所非而非其所是。欲是其所非而非其所是，则莫若以明。

物无非彼，物无非是。

where he is going to: is it not a deplorable case? Men may say, "But it is not death; yet of what advantage is this? When the body is decomposed, the mind will be the same along with it: must not the case be pronounced very deplorable? Is the life of man indeed enveloped in such darkness? Is it I alone to whom it appears so? And does it not appear to be so to other men?"

If we were to follow the judgements of the predetermined mind, who would be left alone and without a teacher? Not only would it be so with those who know the sequences (of knowledge and feeling) and make their own selection among them, but it would be so as well with the stupid and unthinking. For one who has not this determined mind, to have his affirmations and negations is like the case described in the saying, "He went to Yüeh today, and arrived at it yesterday."

It would be making what was not a fact to be a fact. But even the spirit-like Yü could not have known how to do this, and how should one like me be able to do it?

4. Sub specie aeternitatis

But speech is not like the blowing (of the wind) the speaker has (a meaning in) his words. If, however, what he says, is indeterminate (as from a mind not made up), does he then really speak or not? He thinks that his words are different from the chirpings of fledgelings; but is there any distinction between them or not? But how can the Tao be so obscured? That there should be "a True" and "a False" in it? How can speech be so obscured that there should be 'the Right' and 'the Wrong' about them? Where shall the Tao go to that it will not be found? Where shall speech be found that it will be inappropriate? Tao becomes obscured through the small comprehension (of the mind), and speech comes to be obscure through the vain-gloriousness (of the speaker). <u>So it is that we have the contentions between the Literati and the Mohists, the one side affirming what the other denies, and vice versa. If we would decide on their several affirmations and denials, no plan is like bringing the (proper) light (of the mind) to bear on them.</u>

All subjects may be looked at from (two points of view), —

Chapter Three
Philosophical Daoism: Its Enduring Legacy and Contemporary Relevance

from that and from this. If I look at a thing from another's point of view, I do not see it; only as I know it myself, do I know it. Hence it is said, "That view comes from this; and this view is a consequence of that:" — which is the theory that that view and this — (the opposite view) — produce each other. Although it be so, there is affirmed now life and now death; now death and now life; now the admissibility of a thing and now its inadmissibility; now its inadmissibility and now its admissibility. (The disputants) now affirm and now deny; now deny and now affirm. Therefore the sagely man does not pursue this method, but views things in the light of (his) Heaven (-ly nature), and hence forms his judgement of what is right.

自彼则不见，自是则知之。故曰：彼出于是，是亦因彼。彼是方生之说也。虽然，方生方死，方死方生；方可方不可，方不可方可；因是因非，因非因是。是以圣人不由而照之于天，亦因是也。是亦彼也，彼亦是也。彼亦一是非，此亦一是非。果且有彼是乎哉？果且无彼是乎哉？彼是莫得其偶，谓之道枢。枢始得其环中，以应无穷。是亦一无穷，非亦一无穷也。故曰：莫若以明。

5. There is nothing like the one who stands in the centre of thoughts

This view is the same as that, and that view is the same as this. But that view involves both a right and a wrong; and this view involves also a right and a wrong: are there indeed, or are there not the two views, that and this? They have not found their point of correspondence which is called the pivot of the Tao. As soon as one finds this pivot, he stands in the centre of the ring (of thought), where he can respond without end to the changing views; — without end to those affirming, and without end to those denying. Therefore I said, "There is nothing like the proper light (of the mind)."

6. Let a path be formed according to proper capability

By means of a finger (of my own) to illustrate that the finger (of another) is not a finger is not so good a plan as to illustrate that it is not so by means of what is (acknowledged to be) not a finger; and by means of (what I call) a horse to illustrate that (what another calls) a horse is not so, is not so good a plan as to illustrate that it is not a horse, by means of what is (acknowledged to be) not a horse. (All things in) heaven and earth may be (dealt with as) a finger; (each of) their myriads may be (dealt with as) a horse. Does a thing seem so to me? (I say that) it is so. Does it seem not so to me? (I say that) it is not so. A path is formed by (constant) treading

以指喻指之非指，不若以非指喻指之非指也；以马喻马之非马，不若以非马喻马之非马也。天地一指也，万物一马也。

可乎可，不可乎不可。道行之而成，物谓之而然。恶乎然？然于然。恶乎不然？

— 135 —

不然于不然。物固有所然，物固有所可。无物不然，无物不可。故为是举莛与楹，厉与西施，恢恑憰怪，道通为一。

其分也，成也；其成也，毁也。凡物无成与毁，复通为一。唯达者知通为一，为是不用而寓诸庸。庸也者，用也。用也者，通也。通也者，得也。适得而几矣。因是已。已而不知其然，谓之道。劳神明为一而不知其同也，谓之"朝三"。何谓"朝三"？狙公赋芧，曰："朝三而暮四。"众狙皆怒。曰："然则朝四而暮三。"众狙皆悦。名实未亏，而喜怒为用，亦因是也。是以圣人和之以是非，而休乎天钧，是之谓两行。

on the ground. A thing is called by its name through the (constant) application of the name to it. How is it so? It is so because it is so. How is it not so? It is not so, because it is not so. Everything has its inherent character and its proper capability. There is nothing which has not these. Therefore, this being so, if we take a stalk of grain and a (large) pillar, a loathsome (leper) and (a beauty like) Hsi Shih, things large) and things insecure, things crafty and things strange; — they may in the light of the Tao all be reduced to the same category (of opinion about them).

It was separation that led to completion; from completion ensued dissolution. But all things, without regard to their completion and dissolution, may again be comprehended in their unity; — it is only the far reaching in thought who know how to comprehend them in this unity. This being so, let us give up our devotion to our own views, and occupy ourselves with the ordinary views. These ordinary views are grounded on the use of things. (The study of that) use leads to the comprehensive judgement, and that judgement secures the success (of the inquiry). That success gained, we are near (to the object of our search), and there we stop. When we stop, and yet we do not know how it is so, we have what is called the Tao.

When we toil our spirits and intelligence, obstinately determined (to establish our own view), and do not know the agreement (which underlies it and the views of others), we have what is called "In the morning three."

What is meant by that "In the morning three?"

A keeper of monkeys, in giving them out their acorns, (once) said, "In the morning I will give you three (measures) and in the evening four."

This made them all angry, and he said, "Very well. In the morning I will give you four and in the evening three."

His two proposals were substantially the same, but the result of the one was to make the creatures angry, and of the other to make them pleased: an illustration of the point I am insisting on. Therefore the sagely man brings together a dispute in its

Chapter Three
Philosophical Daoism: Its Enduring Legacy and Contemporary Relevance

affirmations and denials, and rests in the equal fashioning of Heaven. Both sides of the question are admissible.

7. Opinions go on as ordinary or different, or both

Among the men of old their knowledge reached the extreme point. What was that extreme point? Some held that at first there was not anything. This is the extreme point, the utmost point to which nothing can be added. A second class held that there was something, but without any responsive recognition of it (on the part of men).

A third class held that there was such recognition, but there had not begun to be any expression of different opinions about it. It was through the definite expression of different opinions about it that there ensued injury to (the doctrine of) the Tao. It was this injury to the (doctrine of the) Tao which led to the formation of (partial) preferences. Was it indeed after such preferences were formed that the injury came? or did the injury precede the rise of such preferences? If the injury arose after their formation, Kâo's method of playing on the lute was natural. If the injury arose before their formation, there would have been no such playing on the lute as Kâo's.

Kâo Wän's playing on the lute, Shih Kwang's indicating time with his staff, and Master Hui's (giving his views), while leaning against a dryandra tree (were all extraordinary). The knowledge of the three men (in their several arts) was nearly perfect, and therefore they practised them to the end of their lives. They loved them because they were different from those of others. They loved them and wished to make them known to others. But as they could not be made clear, though they tried to make them so, they ended with the obscure (discussions) about "the hard" and "the White."

And their sons, moreover, with all the threads of their fathers' compositions, yet to the end of their lives accomplished nothing. If they, proceeding in this way, could be said to have succeeded, then am I also successful; if they cannot be pronounced successful, neither I nor any other can succeed.

Therefore the scintillations of light from the midst of

古之人，其知有所至矣。恶乎至？有以为未始有物者，至矣，尽矣，不可以加矣！其次以为有物矣，而未始有封也。其次以为有封焉，而未始有是非也。是非之彰也，道之所以亏也。道之所以亏，爱之所以成。果且有成与亏乎哉？果且无成与亏乎哉？有成与亏，故昭氏之鼓琴也；无成与亏，故昭氏之不鼓琴也。昭文之鼓琴也，师旷之枝策也，惠子之据梧也，三子之知几乎皆其盛者也，故载之末年。唯其好之也以异于彼，其好之也欲以明之。彼非所明而明之，故以坚白之昧终。而其子又以文之纶终，终身无成。若是而可谓成乎，虽我亦成也；若是而不可谓成乎，物与我无成也。是故滑疑之耀，圣人之所图也。为是不用而寓诸庸，此之谓"以明"。

confusion and perplexity are indeed valued by the sagely man; but not to use one's own views and to take his position on the ordinary views is what is called using the (proper) light.

8. Let there be room for the concepts of "existing Heaven and a reachable Earth"

今且有言于此，不知其与是类乎？其与是不类乎？类与不类，相与为类，则与彼无以异矣。虽然，请尝言之。有始也者，有未始有始也者，有未始有夫未始有始也者。有有也者，有无也者，有未始有无也者，有未始有夫未始有无也者。俄而有无矣，而未知有无之果孰有孰无也。今我则已有谓矣，而未知吾所谓之其果有谓乎？其果无谓乎？

But here now are some other sayings: I do not know whether they are of the same character as those which I have already given, or of a different character. Whether they are of the same character or not when looked at along with them, they have a character of their own, which cannot be distinguished from the others. But though this be the case, let me try to explain myself.

There was a beginning. There was a beginning before that beginning. There was a beginning previous to that beginning before there was the beginning.

There was existence; there had been no existence. There was no existence before the beginning of that no existence. There was no existence previous to the no existence before there was the beginning of the no existence. If suddenly there was nonexistence, we do not know whether it was really anything existing, or really not existing. Now I have said what I have said, but I do not know whether what I have said be really anything to the point or not.

天下莫大于秋豪之末，而大山为小；莫寿于殇子，而彭祖为夭。天地与我并生，而万物与我为一。既已为一矣，且得有言乎？既已谓之一矣，且得无言乎？一与言为二，二与一为三。自此以往，巧历不能得，而况其凡乎！故自无适有，以至于三，而况自有适有乎！无适焉，因是已！

Under heaven there is nothing greater than the tip of an autumn down, and the Tai mountain is small. There is no one more long-lived than a child which dies prematurely, and Master Peng did not live out his time. Heaven, Earth, and I were produced together, and all things and I are one. Since they are one, can there be speech about them? But since they are spoken of as one, must there not be room for speech? One and Speech are two; two and one are three. Going on from this (in our enumeration), the most skillful reckoner cannot reach (the end of the necessary numbers), and how much less can ordinary people do so! Therefore from non-existence we proceed to existence till we arrive at three; proceeding from existence to existence, to how many should we reach? Let us abjure such procedure, and simply rest here.

Chapter Three
Philosophical Daoism: Its Enduring Legacy and Contemporary Relevance

9. A judgement is not really an argument, and the heavenly treasure-house is found by purity

The Tao at first met with no responsive recognition. Speech at first had no constant forms of expression. Because of this there came the demarcations (of different views). Let me describe those demarcations: they are the Left and the Right; the Relations and their Obligations; Classifications and their Distinctions; Emulations and Contentions. These are what are called "the Eight Qualities."

Outside the limits of the world of men, the sage occupies his thoughts, but does not discuss anything; inside those limits he occupies his thoughts, but does not pass any judgements. In the Khun Khiu, which embraces the history of the former kings, the sage indicates his judgements, but does not argue (in vindication of them). Thus it is that he separates his characters from one another without appearing to do so, and argues without the form of argument. How does he do so? The sage cherishes his views in his own breast, while men generally state theirs argumentatively, to show them to others. Hence we have the saying, "Disputation is a proof of not seeing clearly."

<u>The Great Tao does not admit of being praised. The Great Argument does not require words. Great Benevolence is not (officiously) benevolent. Great Disinterestedness does not vaunt its humility. Great Courage is not seen in stubborn bravery.</u>

The Tao that is displayed is not the Tao. Words that are argumentative do not reach the point. Benevolence that is constantly exercised does not accomplish its object. Disinterestedness that vaunts its purity is not genuine. Courage that is most stubborn is ineffectual. These five seem to be round (and complete), but they tend to become square (and immovable). Therefore the knowledge that stops at what it does not know is the greatest. Who knows the argument that needs no words, and the Way that is not to be trodden?

He who is able to know this has what is called "The Heavenly Treasure-house."

He may pour into it without its being filled; he may pour from

夫道未始有封，言未始有常，为是而有畛也。请言其畛。有左有右，有伦有义，有分有辩，有竞有争，此之谓八德。六合之外，圣人存而不论；六合之内，圣人论而不议；春秋经世先王之志，圣人议而不辩。故分也者，有不分也；辩也者，有不辩也。曰：何也？圣人怀之，众人辩之以相示也。故曰：辩也者，有不见也。

夫大道不称，大辩不言，大仁不仁，大廉不嗛，大勇不忮。道昭而不道，言辩而不及，仁常而不成，廉清而不信，勇忮而不成。五者无弃而几向方矣！故知止其所不知，至矣。孰知不言之辩，不道之道？若有能知，此之谓天府。注焉而不满，酌焉而不竭，而不知其所由来，此之谓葆光。

故昔者尧问于舜曰："我欲伐宗、脍、胥敖，南面而不释然。其故何也？"

舜曰："夫三子者，犹存乎蓬艾之间。若不释然，何哉？昔者十日并出，万物皆照，而况德之进乎日者乎！"

啮缺问乎王倪曰："子知物之所同是乎？"

曰："吾恶乎知之！"

"子知子之所不知邪？"

曰："吾恶乎知之！"

"然则物无知邪？"

曰："吾恶乎知之！虽然，尝试言之：庸讵知吾所谓知之非不知邪？庸讵知吾所谓不知之非知邪？且吾尝试问乎女：民湿寝则腰疾偏死，鳅然乎哉？木处则惴栗恂惧，猿猴然乎哉？三者孰知正处？民食刍豢，麋鹿食荐，蝍蛆甘带，鸱鸦耆鼠，四者孰知正味？猨猵狙以为雌，麋与鹿交，鳅与鱼游。毛嫱丽姬，人之所美也；鱼见之深入，鸟见之高飞，麋鹿见之决骤，四者孰知天下之正色哉？自我观之，仁义之端，是非之涂，樊然淆乱，吾恶能知其辩！"

it without its being exhausted; and all the while he does not know whence (the supply) comes. This is what is called "The Store of Light."

Therefore of old Yao asked Shun, saying, "I wish to smite (the rulers of) Zung, Kwei, and Hsü-âo. Even when standing in my court, I cannot get them out of my mind. How is it so?"

Shun replied, "Those three rulers live (in their little states) as if they were among the mugwort and other brushwood; — how is it that you cannot get them out of your mind? Formerly, ten suns came out together, and all things were illuminated by them; — how much should (your) virtue exceed (all) suns!"

10. Tall tales of the perfect man and some proper principles

Nieh Khüeh asked Wang Î, saying, "Do you know, Sir, what all creatures agree in approving and affirming?"

"How should I know it?" was the reply.

"Do you know what it is that you do not know?" asked the other again, and he got the same reply. He asked a third time, — "Then are all creatures thus without knowledge?" and Wang Î answered as before, (adding however), "Notwithstanding, I will try and explain my meaning. How do you know that when I say 'I know it,' I really (am showing that) I do not know it, and that when I say 'I do not know it,' I really am showing that I do know it."

And let me ask you some questions: "If a man sleep in a damp place, he will have a pain in his loins, and half his body will be as if it were dead; but will it be so with an eel? If he be living in a tree, he will be frightened and all in a tremble; but will it be so with a monkey? And does any one of the three know his right place? Men eat animals that have been fed on grain and grass; deer feed on the thickset grass; centipedes enjoy small snakes; owls and crows delight in mice; but does any one of the four know the right taste? The dog-headed monkey finds its mate in the female gibbon; the elk and the axis deer cohabit; and the eel enjoys itself with other fishes. Mâo Zhiang and Li Ki were accounted by men to be most beautiful, but when fishes saw them, they dived deep in the water from them; when birds, they flew from them aloft; and when deer saw them, they separated and fled away. But did any of these four know which in the world is the right female attraction? As I look at the matter, the first principles of benevolence and righteousness and the paths of approval and disapproval are inextricably mixed and confused together: how is it possible that I should know how to discriminate among them?"

Nieh Khüeh said (further), "Since you, Sir, do not know what is advantageous and what is hurtful, is the Perfect man also in the same way without the knowledge of them?"

啮缺曰："子不知利害，则至人固不知利害乎？"

Wang Î replied, "The Perfect man is spirit-like. Great lakes might be boiling about him, and he would not feel their heat; the Ho and the Han might be frozen up, and he would not feel the cold; the hurrying thunderbolts might split the mountains, and the wind shake the ocean, without being able to make him afraid. Being such, he mounts on the clouds of the air, rides on the sun and moon, and rambles at ease beyond the four seas. Neither death nor life makes any change in him, and how much less should the considerations of advantage and injury do so!"

王倪曰："至人神矣！大泽焚而不能热，河汉冱而不能寒，疾雷破山、飘风振海而不能惊。若然者，乘云气，骑日月，而游乎四海之外，死生无变于己，而况利害之端乎！"

11. Is the love of life a shared delusion of grooms and others?

Master Khü Zhiâo asked Master Khang-wu, saying, "I heard the Master (speaking of such language as the following): 'The sagely man does not occupy himself with worldly affairs. He does not put himself in the way of what is profitable, nor does he try to avoid what is hurtful; he has no pleasure in seeking (for anything from anyone); he does not care to be found in (any established) Way; he speaks without speaking; he does not speak when he speaks; thus finding his enjoyment outside the dust and dirt (of the world).' The Master considered all this to be a shoreless flow of mere words, and I consider it to describe the course of the Mysterious Way. — What do you, Sir, think of it?"

瞿鹊子问乎长梧子曰："吾闻诸夫子，圣人不从事于务，不就利，不违害，不喜求，不缘道，无谓有谓，有谓无谓，而游乎尘垢之外。夫子以为孟浪之言，而我以为妙道之行也。吾子以为奚若？"

Khang-wu dze replied, "The hearing of such words would have perplexed even Hwang-Ti, and how should Khiu be competent to understand them? And you, moreover, are too hasty in forming your estimate (of their meaning). You see the egg, and

长梧子曰："是黄帝之所听荧也，而丘也何足以知之！且女亦大早计，见卵而求时夜，见弹而求鸮炙。予尝为女妄言之，女以妄听之。奚旁日月，挟宇宙，为其吻合，置其滑涽，以隶相尊？众人役役，圣人愚芚，参万岁而一成纯。万物尽然，而以是相蕴。予恶乎知说生之非惑邪！予恶乎知恶死之非弱丧而不知归者邪！

"丽之姬，艾封人之子也。晋国之始得之也，涕泣沾襟。及其至于王所，与王同筐床，食刍豢，而后悔其泣也。予恶乎知夫死者不悔其始之蕲生乎？梦饮酒者，旦而哭泣；梦哭泣者，旦而田猎。方其梦也，不知其梦也。梦之中又占其梦焉，觉而后知其梦也。且有大觉而后知此其大梦也。而愚者自以为觉，窃窃然知之。君乎！牧乎！固哉丘也！与女皆梦也！予谓女梦，亦梦也。是其言也，其名为吊诡。万世之后，而一遇大圣，知其解者，是旦暮遇之也。"

(at once) look out for the cock (that is to be hatched from it); you see the bow, and (at once) look out for for the dove (that is to be brought down by it) being roasted. I will try to explain the thing to you in a rough way; do you in the same way listen to me.

"How could anyone stand by the side of the sun and moon, and hold under his arm all space and all time? (Such language only means that the sagely man) keeps his mouth shut, and puts aside questions that are uncertain and dark; making his inferior capacities unite with him in honouring (the One Lord). Men in general bustle about and toil; the sagely man seems stupid and knows nothing. He blends ten thousand years together in the one (conception of time); the myriad things all pursue their spontaneous course, and they are all before him as doing so.

"How do I know that the love of life is not a delusion? and that the dislike of death is not like a young person's losing his way, and not knowing that he is (really) going home? Li Ki was a daughter of the border Warden of Ai. When (the ruler of) the state of Zin first got possession of her, she wept till the tears wetted all the front of her dress. But when she came to the place of the king, shared with him his luxurious couch, and ate his grain-and-grass-fed meat, then she regretted that she had wept. How do I know that the dead do not repent of their former craving for life?

"Those who dream of (the pleasures of) drinking may in the morning wail and weep; those who dream of wailing and weeping may in the morning be going out to hunt. When they were dreaming they did not know it was a dream; in their dream they may even have tried to interpret it; but when they awoke they knew that it was a dream. And there is the great awaking, after which we shall know that this life was a great dream. All the while, the stupid think they are awake, and with nice discrimination insist on their knowledge; now playing the part of rulers, and now of grooms. Bigoted was that Khiu! He and you are both dreaming. I who say that you are dreaming am dreaming myself. These words seem very strange; but if after ten thousand ages we once meet with a great sage who knows how to explain them, it will be as if we met him (unexpectedly) some morning or evening."

12. Heaven's operations go on in secret also

"Since you made me enter into this discussion with you, if you have got the better of me and not I of you, are you indeed right, and I indeed wrong? If I have got the better of you and not you of me, am I indeed right and you indeed wrong? Is the one of us right and the other wrong? are we both right or both wrong? Since we cannot come to a mutual and common understanding, men will certainly continue in darkness on the subject.

"Whom shall I employ to adjudicate in the matter? If I employ one who agrees with you, how can he, agreeing with you, do so correctly? And the same may be said, if I employ one who agrees with me. It will be the same if I employ one who differs from us both or one who agrees with us both. In this way I and you and those others would all not be able to come to a mutual understanding; and shall we then wait for that (great sage)? (We need not do so.) To wait on others to learn how conflicting opinions are changed is simply like not so waiting at all. The harmonizing of them is to be found in the invisible operation of Heaven, and by following this on into the unlimited past. It is by this method that we can complete our years (without our minds being disturbed)."

"What is meant by harmonizing (conflicting opinions) in the invisible operation of Heaven? There is the affirmation and the denial of it; and there is the assertion of an opinion and the rejection of it. If the affirmation be according to the reality of the fact, it is certainly different from the denial of it: there can be no dispute about that. If the assertion of an opinion be correct, it is certainly different from its rejection: neither can there be any dispute about that. Let us forget the lapse of time; let us forget the conflict of opinions. Let us make our appeal to the Infinite, and take up our position there."

13. The psyche butterfly that is understood as something else

The Penumbra asked the Shadow, saying, "Formerly you were walking on, and now you have stopped; formerly you were sitting, and

"既使我与若辩矣，若胜我，我不若胜，若果是也，我果非也邪？我胜若，若不吾胜，我果是也，而果非也邪？其或是也，其或非也邪？其俱是也，其俱非也邪？我与若不能相知也，则人固受其黮暗，吾谁使正之？使同乎若者正之，既与若同矣，恶能正之？使同乎我者正之，既同乎我矣，恶能正之？使异乎我与若者正之，既异乎我与若矣，恶能正之？使同乎我与若者正之，既同乎我与若矣，恶能正之？然则我与若与人俱不能相知也，而待彼也邪？"

"何谓和之以天倪？"

曰："是不是，然不然。是若果是也，则是之异乎不是也亦无辩；然若果然也，则然之异乎不然也亦无辩。化声之相待，若其不相待，和之以天倪，因之以曼衍，所以穷年也。忘年忘义，振于无竟，故寓诸无竟。"

罔两问景曰："曩子行，今子止；曩子坐，今子起。

何其无特操与？"

景曰："吾有待而然者邪？吾所待又有待而然者邪？吾待蛇蚹蜩翼邪？恶识所以然？恶识所以不然？"

昔者庄周梦为胡蝶，栩栩然胡蝶也。自喻适志与，不知周也。俄然觉，则蘧蘧然周也。不知周之梦为胡蝶与？胡蝶之梦为周与？周与胡蝶则必有分矣。此之谓物化。

now you have risen up: how is it that you are so without stability?"

The Shadow replied, "I wait for the movements of something else to do what I do, and that something else on which I wait waits further on another to do as it does. My waiting, —is it for the scales of a snake, or the wings of a cicada? How should I know why I do one thing, or do not do another?

"Formerly, I, Chuang Chou, dreamt that I was a butterfly, a butterfly flying about, feeling that it was enjoying itself. I did not know that it was Chou. Suddenly I awoke, and was myself again, the veritable Chou. I did not know whether it had formerly been Chou dreaming that he was a butterfly, or it was now a butterfly dreaming that it was Chou. But between Chou and a butterfly there must be a difference. This is a case of what is called the Transformation of Things."

Extensive Readings

A. Daoist Correlative Cosmology[①]
道家关联宇宙学

Roger T. Ames and David L. Hall
安乐哲、郝大维

1. Daoist Cosmology: An Interpretive Context[②]

We begin our argument for translating *Daodejing* as "Making This Life Significant" from Daoist cosmology. Taking a closer look at the interpretation of both the title and the content of the *Daodejing* as "The Classic of This Focus" (*de* 德) and "Its Field (*dao* 道)," we might first ask what the expression "this focus" means? The Daoist correlative cosmology begins from the assumption that the endless stream of always novel yet still continuous situations we encounter are real, and hence, that there is ontological parity among the things and events that constitute our lives. As a

---

① Excerpted from *Dao De Jing "Making This Life Significant"—A Philosophical Translation*, translated by Roger T. Ames and David L. Hall, Ballantine Books, 2003. The original title of this chapter is "Philosophical Introduction: Correlative Cosmology—An Interpretive Context."

② Ibid., pp. 24-33.

parody on Parmenides, who claimed that "only Being is," we might say that for the Daoist, "only *beings* are," or taking one step further in underscoring the reality of the process of change itself, "only *becomings* are." That is, the Daoist does not posit the existence of some permanent reality behind appearances, some unchanging substratum, some essential defining aspect behind the accidents of change. Rather, there is just the ceaseless and usually cadenced flow of experience.

……

The Daoist understanding of "cosmos" as the "ten thousand things" means that, in effect, the Daoist has no concept of cosmos at all insofar as that notion entails a coherent, single-ordered world which is in any sense enclosed or defined. The Daoists are, therefore, primarily, "acosmotic" thinkers.

One implication of this distinction between a "cosmotic" and an "acosmotic" worldview is that, in the absence of some overarching arche or "beginning" as an explanation of the creative process, and under conditions which are thus "an-archic" in the philosophic sense of this term, although the "nature" of something might indeed refer to "kinds," such "natural kinds" would be no more than generalizations made by analogizing among similar phenomena. That is, difference is prior to identifiable similarities.

The Chinese binomial most frequently translated as *kosmos* is *yuzhou* 宇宙, a term that overtly expresses the interdependence between time and space. The "world" as *shijie* 世界 is likewise expressed literally as the "boundaries between one's generation and the tradition." For ancient China, time pervades everything and is not to be denied. Time is not independent of things, but a fundamental aspect of them. Unlike traditions that devalue both time and change in pursuit of the timeless and eternal, in classical China things are always transforming (wuhua 物化). In fact, in the absence of some claim to objectivity that "objectifies" and thus makes "objects of phenomena," the Chinese tradition does not have the separation between time and entities that would allow for either time without entities, or entities without time—there is no possibility of either an empty temporal corridor or an eternal anything (in the sense of being timeless).

What encourages us within a Western metaphysical tradition to separate time and space is our inclination, inherited from the Greeks, to see things in the world as fixed in their formal aspect, and thus as bounded and limited. If instead of giving ontological privilege to the formal aspect of phenomena, we were to regard them as having parity in their formal and changing aspects, we might be more like classical China in temporalizing them in light of their ceaseless transformation, and conceive of them more as "events" than as "things." In this processual worldview, each phenomenon is some unique current or impulse within a temporal flow. In fact, it is the pervasive and collective capacity of the events of the world to transform continuously that is the actual meaning of time.

A second assumption of Daoist "cosmology" (now using this term "cosmology" under advisement) that follows from this acknowledgment of the reality of both change and the uniqueness that follows from it is that particular "things" are in fact processual events, and are thus *intrinsically* related to the other "things" that provide them context. Said another way, these procedural events are porous, flowing into each other in the ongoing transformations we call experience. Formation and function—the shape of things and what they do to whom—are interdependent and mutually determining characteristics of these events. It is for this reason that things resist "definition" in the literal sense of *finis*—a practice that delineates some ostensibly discrete boundary around them, and thus reduces all relations to external, extrinsic transactions. With fluid and shifting boundaries among things, integrity for any particular thing does not mean *being* or *staying* whole, or even actualizing its own internal potential. Rather, integrity is something *becoming whole in its co-creative relationships with other things*. Integrity is consummatory relatedness.

……

In the received Judeo-Christian tradition, the all-powerful God *determines* things, *makes* things. God, as Omnipotent Other who commands the world into being, is *Maker* of the world, not its *Creator*. In the presence of the perfection that is God, nothing can be added or taken away. There can be no novelty or spontaneity. Thus, all subsequent acts of "creativity" are in fact secondary and derivative exercises of power. Creativity can make sense only in a processual world that admits of ontological parity among its constitutive events and of the spontaneous emergence of novelty.

Power is to be construed as the production of intended effects determined by external causation. Real creativity, on the other hand, entails the spontaneous production of novelty, irreducible through causal analysis. Power is exercised with respect to and over others. Creativity is always reflexive and is exercised over and with respect to "self". And since self in a processive world is always communal, creativity is contextual, transactional, and multidimensional. Thus creativity is both *self*-creativity and *co*-creativity. Either everything shares in creativity, or there is no creativity. Indeed, it is this transactional, co-creative character of all creative processes that precludes the project of self-cultivation and self-creation from being egoistic.

One further point can be made with respect to the creativity that the spontaneous emergence of novelty makes possible. The radical sense of creativity that we associate with "bringing into being" in a *creatio ex nihilo* sensibility is too isolated and extreme for this idea within the Daoist tradition. The term *dao*, like the terms "building," "learning," and "work," entails both the process and the created product. It is the locus and the time frame within which the always contextualized creativity takes place.

When the *Zhuangzi* observes that "we are one with all things 万物与我为一," this

Chapter Three
Philosophical Daoism: Its Enduring Legacy and Contemporary Relevance

insight is a recognition that each and every unique phenomenon is continuous with every other phenomenon within one's field of experience. But is this an exhaustive claim: are we talking about all phenomena in the continuing present? Because the world is processional and because its creativity is *ab initio* rather than *ex nihilo*—a contextual creativity expressed across the careers of its constitutive phenomena—any answer to this question would have to be provisional. Phenomena are never either atomistically discrete or complete. The *Zhuangzi* recounts:

> *With the ancients, understanding had gotten somewhere. Where was that? Its height, its extreme, that to which no more could be added, was this: Some of these ancients thought that there had never begun to be things. The next lot thought that there were things, but that there had never begun to be boundaries among them. ...*①

A third assumption in the Daoist "cosmology" is that life broadly construed is entertained through and only through these same phenomena that constitute our experience. The field of experience is always construed from one perspective or another. There is no view from nowhere, no external perspective, no decontextualized vantage point. We are all in the soup. The intrinsic, constitutive relations that obtain among things make them reflexive and mutually implicating, residing together within the flux and flow.

This mutuality does not in any way negate the uniqueness of the particular perspective. Although any and all members of a family have implicated within them and thus present (rather than represent) the entire family, all members constitute and experience the family from their own particular point of view. And members in making the family their own quite appropriately have a distinctive proper name.

A corollary to this radical perspectivism is that each particular element in our experience is holographic in the sense that it has implicated within it the entire field of experience. This single flower has leaves and roots that take their nourishment from the environing soil and air. And the soil contains the distilled nutrients of past growth and decay that constitute the living ecological system in which all of its participants are organically interdependent. The sun enables the flower to process these nutrients, while the atmosphere that caresses the flower also nourishes and protects it. By the time we have "cashed out" the complex of conditions that conspire to produce and conserve this particular flower, one ripple after another in an ever-extending series of radical circles, we have implicated the entire cosmos within it without remainder. For the Daoist, there is an intoxicating bottomlessness to any particular event in our experience. The entire cosmos

---

① See *Zhuangzi* 5.2.40 and commentary on it in 63.23.58; compare A. C. Graham, "The Origins of the Legend of Lao Tan." In *Studies in Chinese Philosophy and Philosophical Literature*. State University of New York Press, 1990, p.54, p. 104. and Burton Watson, trans. *The Complete Works of Chuang Tzu*. Columbia University Press, 1968, p. 41, p.257.

resides happily in the smile on the dirty face of this one little child.

If the insistent particular (*de* 德) is holographic, how does differentiation occur among particular things? In the human community, for example, what does it mean for a person to become distinguished and an object of deference?

First, this holographic sensibility is not simply Daoist, but a shared commitment of classical Chinese natural cosmology. The Confucian Mencius, for example, is also articulating this classical Chinese common sense when he interprets the field of *qi* in terms of moral energy and offers his advice on the attainment of human excellence. He speaks of his ability to nourish his "flood-like *qi* (*haoran zhi qi* 浩然之气)," describing this *qi* as that which is "most vast (*zhida* 至大)" and "most firm (*zhigang* 至刚)."① Restated in the language of focus and field, Mencius is saying that his "flood-like *qi*" has the greatest "extensive" and "intensive" magnitudes. This language of extensive field and intensive focus suggests that one nourishes one's *qi* most successfully by making of oneself the most integral focus of the most extensive field of *qi*. In this manner, one gains greatest virtue (excellence, potency) in relation to the most far-reaching elements of one's environs. As we read in the *Mencius*:

> *Everything is here in me. There is no joy greater than to discover creativity (cheng 诚) in one's person and nothing easier in striving to be authoritative in one's conduct (ren 仁) than committing oneself to treating others as one would oneself be treated.*

Our argument for translating *cheng* 诚 as "creativity" in this *Mencius* passage is that its more familiar translations as "sincerity" and "integrity" in fact reference a creative process. "Sincerity" as affective tone is the ground of growth in mutual relationships, and "integrity" is the "becoming one" that occurs as we become intimate. The deepening of these relationships that in sum constitute us as a person is a profoundly co-creative process of "doing and undergoing," of shaping and being shaped.

The Daoist variation on the efficacy of one's "flood-like *qi*" is the way in which the intensive focus of one's insistent particularity (*de* 德) provides the most extensive range of influence or potency in shaping one's world. Said simply, persons who "have their stuff together" change the world around them. In chapter 54 of the *Daodejing*, the cultivation of personal excellence is described as the starting point in world-making and in enhancing the ethos of the cosmos:

---

① *Mencius* 2A2. 出自《孟子·公孙丑章句上·第二节》:"敢问夫子恶乎长?"曰:"我知言,我善养吾浩然之气。""敢问何谓浩然之气?"曰:"难言也。其为气也,至大至刚,以直养而无害,则塞于天地之间。其为气也,配义与道;无是,馁也。是集义所生者,非义袭而取之也。行有不慊于心,则馁矣。我故曰,告子未尝知义,以其外之也。必有事焉而勿正,心勿忘,勿助长也。无若宋人然:宋人有闵其苗之不长而揠之者,芒芒然归。谓其人曰:'今日病矣,予助苗长矣。'其子趋而往视之,苗则槁矣。天下之不助苗长者寡矣。以为无益而舍之者,不耘苗者也;助之长者,揠苗者也。非徒无益,而又害之。"

Chapter Three
Philosophical Daoism: Its Enduring Legacy and Contemporary Relevance

> *Cultivate it in your person,*
> *And the character you develop will be genuine;*
> *Cultivate it in your family,*
> *And its character will be abundant;*
> *Cultivate it in your village,*
> *And its character will be enduring;*
> *Cultivate it in the state,*
> *And its character will flourish;*
> *Cultivate it in the world,*
> *And its character will be all-pervading.* [①]

This relationship between intensive resolution and extensive influence is also captured in chapter 23:

> *Thus, those who are committed to way-making in what they do*
> *Are on their way.*
> *Those who are committed to character in what they do*
> *Achieve this character.*
> *While those who lose it*
> *Are themselves lost.*
> *Way-making is moreover enhanced by those who express character,*
> *Just as it is diminished by those who themselves have lost it.* [②]

Optimizing experience by getting the most out of it requires a kind of "husbanding" of one's resources, where "husbanding" is understood as a combination of cultivation and frugality. High resolution in one's character elevates one as a focal presence and as an enduring influence on the extended community through the patterns of deference that have come to define one's person. This achieved character provides the world with a resource for resolving its problems as they arise. Such is the import of chapter 59:

> *For bringing proper order to the people and in serving tian,*
> *Nothing is as good as husbandry.*
> *It is only through husbandry that you come early to accept the way,*

---

① 修之于身，其德乃真；修之于家，其德乃余；修之于乡，其德乃长；修之于邦，其德乃丰；修之于天下，其德乃普。
② 故从事于道者同于道；德者同于德；失者同于失。同于道者，道亦乐得之；同于德者，德亦乐得之；同于失者，失亦乐得之。

And coming early to accept the way is what is called redoubling your accumulation of character.

> *If you redouble your accumulation of character, all obstacles can be overcome,*
> *And if all obstacles can be overcome, none can discern your limit.*
> *Where none can discern your limit,*
> *You can preside over the realm.*
> *In presiding over the mother of the realm*
> *You can be long-enduring.*

In this processual Daoist cosmology, continuity is prior to individuality, and the particular character or disposition of each event is thus an ongoing distinctive achievement. That is, each event distinguishes itself by developing its own uniqueness within the totality. And freedom is neither the absence of constraint nor some isolable originality, but the full contribution of this achieved uniqueness to a shared community.

A fourth presumption of Daoist cosmology is that we are not passive participants in our experience. The energy of transformation lies within the world itself as an integral characteristic of the events that constitute it. There is no appeal to some efficient cause: no Creator God or primordial determinative principle. In the absence of any preordained design associated with such an external cause, this energy of transformation is evidenced in the mutual accommodation and co-creativity that is expressed in relations that obtain among things. When turned to proper effect, this energy can make the most of the creative possibilities of any given situation. This kind of responsive participation we have characterized elsewhere as *ars contextualis*[①]: the art of contextualizing. *Ars contextualis* is a way of living and relating to a world that quite simply seeks to get the most out of the diversity of experience.

2. The Mutual Entailing of Opposites

In the *Book of Changes*, experience itself is defined simply as a succession of *yin* and *yang* phrases: 一阴一阳之谓道. This description is an abstract way of making the empirical observation that all predicates give way to their opposites: order and disorder succeed each other, and so on. This characteristic of experience is ascribed to the natural cyclical movement of *qi* rather than some supernatural force, and is captured and made explicit in the metaphorical language of *yinyang* 阴阳 and the five phases 五行 cosmology.

As chapter 40 of the *Daodejing* observes, the mutual entailing of opposites means that

---

① See David L. Hall, *Thinking Through Confucius*. State University of New York Press, 1987 and David L. Hall and Roger T. Ames, *Thinking from the Han: Self, Truth, and Transcendence in Chinese and Western Culture*. State University of New York Press, 1998, pp.39-43, pp.111-112.

whatever "goes out" and becomes consummately distinct, also "returns":

> "Returning" is how way-making moves,
> And "weakening" is how it functions.
> The events of the world arise from the determinate,
> And the determinate arises from the indeterminate.①

The most basic meaning of "returning" restates what has been said above. As Tang Junyi reports, cosmology is not simply a linear zerosum victory of order over chaos driven by some external cause, but rather is the endless alternation between rising and falling, emerging and collapsing, moving and attaining equilibrium that is occasioned by its own internal energy of transformation. This cosmic unfolding is not "cyclical" in the sense of reversibility and replication, but is rather a continuing spiral that is always coming back upon itself and yet is ever new.

It is the disposition of all things that their present condition entails their opposite. The *Daodejing* observes in chapter 58:

> *It is upon misfortune that good fortune leans,*
> *It is within good fortune itself that misfortune crouches in an ambush,*
> *And where does it all end?*②

This insight into the mutuality of opposites has several implications. Perhaps most obviously, young is "young-becoming-old"; dark is "dark-becoming-light"; soft is "soft-becoming-hard." In the fullness of time, any and all of the qualities that define each event will yield themselves up to their opposites. Those who are born into the world and live to grow old will eventually die. Anything that embarks upon this journey toward fruition has in its first few steps set off on the long road home. And it is at the moment of setting out as a newborn infant that a person has maximum potency. Thus, the journey can fairly be characterized both as a returning and a gradual weakening of one's initial promise. And it is by effectively husbanding this potency over one's career that one is able to make the most of one's experience.

By anticipating the changes in your conditions, and by remaining focused despite the unavoidable vicissitudes that are visited upon you as you move along the continuum from beginning to end, you are able to optimize the possibilities at each moment and thus enjoy joy the ride to its fullest. Cultivating a proper disposition and being prepared for the seasons through which you pass from birth to death will enable you to consistently get the most out of

---

① 反者道之动，弱者道之用。天下万物生于有，有生于无。
② 祸兮，福之所倚；福兮，祸之所伏。孰知其极……

your circumstances. It is your resolution—the intensity found at the center—that will keep your life experience in focus, establish you as an object of deference, and enable you to enjoy both a productive life and a healthy death.

Said another way, to lose focus and stray off course along the way while on this journey will precipitate reversion. Squandered energy while young will age you prematurely. As it says in chapter 55:

> *For something to be old while in its prime.*
> *Is called a departure from the way of things.*
> *And whatever departs from the way of things will come to an untimely end.* ①

Aggression directed at others will, like Monsieur Guillotine's guillotine, come back to shorten your own life. Again, as in chapter 74:

> *To stand in for the executioner in killing people*
> *Is to stand in for the master carpenter in cutting his lumber.*
> *Of those who would thus stand in for the master carpenter,*
> *Few get away without injuring their own hands.* ②

The world around us is always an interface between persistent form and novelty, the familiar honeycombed by the unexpected. The new emerges within the context and the security of the ordinary, and in the due course, what was new overtakes and supplants the ordinary, and what was ordinary becomes an in increasingly fragile memory for those who can still remember. In time, the new becomes the newly ordinary, and the ordinary returns whence it came.

B. The Early Modern European (Non) Reception of the Zhuangzi Text③
早期现代欧洲对《庄子》文本的（不）接受

Elizabeth Harper
伊丽莎白·哈珀

There exists a notable neglect of the *Zhuangzi* 庄子 text (a body of work attributed at least

---

① 物壮则老，是谓不道，不道早已。
② 夫代司杀者杀，是谓代大匠斫。夫代大匠斫者，希有不伤其手者矣。
③ Elizabeth Harper, "The Early Modern European (Non) Reception of the Zhuangzi Text," in *Journal of East-West Thought*, 2019(4): 23-27.

Chapter Three
Philosophical Daoism: Its Enduring Legacy and Contemporary Relevance

in part to the Warring States philosopher Zhuang Zhou 庄周 (ca. 369-286 BCE)① in early modern European receptions (roughly 1580-1880) of Chinese thought and philosophy. Of the two native thought systems of China, namely Confucianism and Daoism, it took centuries of European contact and the arrival of Romanticism before serious engagement (with one or two exceptions) with the great Daoist texts: the *Laozi* 老子 or *Daodejing* 道德经 and particularly, the *Zhuangzi* took place. In the early centuries of Jesuit contact with China, much interest was taken in the *Yijing* 易经 (the *Changes*) that great mystical text of divination, and of course, in the Confucian Four Books (*Lunyu* 论语 "the Analects," *Mengzi* 孟子 "the Mencius," *Daxue* 大学 "the Great Learning" and the *Zhongyong* 中庸 "the Doctrine of the Mean"). These texts were seemingly unproblematic for those early Catholic humanists eager to hold a mirror up to Chinese culture and see reflected there their own Judeo-Christian symbolic universe. The foundational Daoist texts, the *Laozi* and the *Zhuangzi* were, however, much more difficult to accommodate to universal Christian truth. As the first Jesuit accounts of the early modern period provided the intellectual foundations for the future field of Sinology, the gap on the *Zhuangzi* as Daoist traditions were sidelined and downgraded by the early missionaries (in line with contemporary Chinese judgement) is highly significant.

What I explore here, then, is the problematic of how European thought missed out on the early discovery and appreciation of Daoist philosophical texts.② I focus on the *Zhuangzi* as

---

① Scholarly consensus generally agrees that only the so called "Inner Chapters" (nei pian 内篇), which are seven in number, are homogenous in thought and style and thought to be substantially the work of Zhuangzi himself. The rest of the thirty-three chapter edition that has been passed down to us from the time of Guo Xiang (郭象, 252–312) is separated into the "Outer Chapters" (wai pian 外篇) and "Miscellaneous Chapters" (za pian 杂篇), chapters 8–22 and 23–33 respectively. The collection of scrolls containing the *Zhuangzi* did not achieve a standard form until the collation efforts of Liu Xiang 刘向 (77–6 BCE) who edited them for the Imperial Library of the Han. According to the bibliographical chapter of the *Han Shu* 汉书 , the Imperial copy originally had 52 chapters. See Livia Kohn, *Zhuangzi: Text and Context* (Honolulu: Three Pines Press, 2004, pp.1-10) for a detailed summary on the *Zhuangzi*'s textual history.

② I am not unaware of the debate within the academy on the relative merits or pitfalls of separating religious Daoism (dao jiao 道教) from the foundational texts of philosophical Daoism (dao jia 道家). The French scholar Isabelle Robinet is probably the most stringent representative of the no separation camp writing in her *Taoism: Growth of a Religion* (Stanford: Stanford University Press, 1997) that any apparent differences are due merely to those between "self-discipline (techniques, training etc.) and ... the speculations that can accompany or crown it." (Robinet, *Taoism*, 3.) As I am interested here less in the history of Daoism in China and more in how the *Zhuangzi* was read by Europeans, I use the distinction to avoid having to deal with the immensely complex mass of esoteric texts epitomized by the Daozang 道藏 or collected sacred texts of Daoism, canonized in 1444 and still largely untranslated into English. For the sectarian differences in the practice of Daoism brought about by these thousands of texts, see Robinet, *Taoism*, pp.196-197. On the other side, the Chinese scholar Feng Youlan 冯友兰 suggests the difference between "Taoism as a philosophy [which] teaches the doctrine of following nature, and Taoism the religion [which] teaches the doctrine of working against nature." (1948, 3) The semantic problem of mapping "philosophical Daoism" onto the Chinese dao jia "family of the Dao" and "religious Daoism" onto dao jiao "teachings of the Dao" is itself a form of hermeneutics involving translation and mediation.

the *Laozi* was somewhat taken up as a mystical text in the *philosophia perennis* vein①. It was also translated and commented upon much earlier in Europe and had a number of high-profile champions in the eighteenth century. Today the *Daodejing* is the most translated Chinese work, indeed after the *Bible* it is thought to be the most translated work in the world.② The other texts sometimes included as part of the Daoist corpus around the central Lao-Zhuang tradition are the syncretic *Huainanzi* 淮南子 (circa 140 BC) and the *Guanzi* 管子 (Xinshu 心术, Baixin 白心, Neiye 内业) and the *Liezi* 列子 from the Jin period 晋 (265–420), written by Lie Yukou 列御寇. I leave these texts aside to focus on the *Zhuangzi* because it is the *Zhuangzi*, I think, that is most interestingly implicated both in the early missionary reluctance to appreciate the complexity of Daoist philosophical thought and in the (post) modern European "discovery" of Daoism by philosophers and literary critics. It is the case of an absence followed by an explosive discovery. From Ricci's establishment of a missionary residence in Beijing in 1601 and the proliferation of works engaging with the Confucian Classics, the *Yijing* and latterly the *Laozi* that follow, it will not be until the end of the nineteenth century that a full scholarly translation of the *Zhuangzi* will appear and a serious discussion of the text in Europe can begin.③

…As Lach writes in his epilogue to *Asia in the Making of Europe: The Age of Discovery*: "perhaps what is most significant of all is the dawning realization in the West that not all truth and virtue were contained within its own cultural and religious traditions" (Lach 1965, 835). This

---

① The term *philosophia perennis* is often associated with the philosopher and sinophile Leibniz who uses the term in an oft-quoted letter to Remond dated August 26, 1714. In his article "Perennial Philosophy: From Agostino, Steuco to Leibniz" (*Journal of the History of the Ideas* 27 (1966), pp. 505-532), Schmitt points out that the first use of the term indeed precedes Leibniz and is used as a title to a treatise by the Italian Augustinian Agostino Steuco (1497–1548). Steuco believed that all religious traditions drew from a universal source and he drew on a well-developed philosophical tradition to create his own synthesis of philosophy, religion and history which he labelled philosophia perennis. This syncretic tradition was the intellectual heritage of the first missionaries in China. Although they posited the end of philosophy as piety and the contemplation of God, many of the Jesuits were still open to the truths of the ancient Chinese philosophical tradition as conversant with and in some cases typologies for Christian Revelation. The concept of *philosophia perennis* continued to influence intellectuals well into the twentieth century: C.G Jung and Mircea Eliade and their work on archetypes are two famous examples.

② It is also one of the most misappropriated and misunderstood of the Chinese Classics; harnessed to western spiritual capitalism in the 1960s the marketization of Daoism as self-help has nothing to do with its Classical Chinese context. See Louis Komjathy, *Daoism: A Guide for the Perplexed,* 2014. A professor of Chinese and an ordained Daoist priest, Komjathy successfully shows how "much of what goes by in the name of 'Daoism' in the modern world is fabrication, fiction and fantasy" (Louis Komjathy, "Daoist Texts in Translation." www.daoistcenter.org/advanced.html. Posted online 15 September 2003.).

③ The earliest partial translation of the *Zhuangzi* can be found in an eighteenth century translation of the short story "Zhuang Zhou Drums on a Bowl and Attains the Great Dao" by the late Ming writer Feng Menglong. For complete translations we must wait for those of Frederic Balfour, Herbert Giles and James Legge (all into English) in 1881, 1889 and 1891 respectively. Giles' English translation of 1889 was based on the first German partial edition of *Zhuangzi* by Martin Buber (1910). For Buber's final edition he then drew in turn on the complete translations of Giles and Legge in 1891.

Chapter Three
Philosophical Daoism: Its Enduring Legacy and Contemporary Relevance

collision of religious faith with alternative credos was of course not new to these Catholic voyagers in distant lands: as Jesuit scholars steeped in Humanist learning, the accommodation of pagan wisdom to Christian truths had already been subsumed into Jesuit practice. The early story as to how a philosophico-religious foundational Daoist text influenced those currents of intellectual thought in Europe before the end of the nineteenth century remains something of a mystery.

......

In his path-breaking book *China and the Christian Impact*[①], Jacques Gernet points to the early seventeenth century as a particularly amenable time for the Jesuits to be propagating the Catholic faith thanks to the amalgamation and accommodation of European and Chinese science, technology, philosophy and ethics. He writes:

> *There happened at that time to be a happy conjunction between the teaching of the Jesuits and the tendencies of the period. An orthodox reaction, hostile to the Buddhist influences which had deeply penetrated literate circles, had been developing ever since the last years of the seventeenth century. [...] Along with Buddhism itself, the Buddhist-inspired deviations, originating in the school of Wang Yangming (Wang Shouren, 1472–1529) were being condemned. The egoistical quest for wisdom by the men of the fifteenth and sixteenth centuries was rejected as vain and immoral at the point when, faced with a general decline of society and its institutions, the elite circles were rediscovering the importance of their social responsibilities. (Gernet, 1985, 23)*

Though Gernet discusses the lack of appeal of Buddhist practices and belief to the ruling elites, Daoist texts are simply lumped together with Buddhist ones as sources of selfishness and idolatry. Ricci's reply to a letter from a Chinese contemporary urging him not to attack Buddhism before reading the Buddhist texts is indicative of the missionary attitude to anything that was not state Confucianism. Ricci writes: "Since entering China, I have learned only of Yao, Shun, the Duke of Zhou and Confucius and I do not intend to change." (Quoted in Gernet 1985, 214) This willful turning away from other textual traditions was indicative of the way early Jesuits selected their encounters with Chinese classical texts and rejected the syncretic nature of Chinese belief systems. Riding a wave of internal power struggles to undermine Buddhist monks at court and Daoist folk practices amongst the populace, the early missionaries aligned themselves with the *ru* scholars to create a civic-centered theology.

There was, of course, early Chinese opposition to the Jesuits' denunciations of Buddhism and Daoism and their preaching of Christianity. In 1623, a Wang Qiyuan writes:

---

① First French edition. Paris: Gallimard, 1982; English translation. Cambridge: Cambridge University Press, 1985.

> The barbarians began by attacking Buddhism. Next, they attacked Taoism, next the later Confucianism [hou ru 后儒]. If they have not yet attacked Confucius, that is because they wish to remain on good terms with the literate elite and the mandarins, in order to spread their doctrine. But they are simply chafing at the bit in secret, and have not yet declared themselves. (Gernet, 1985, 52)

In truth, the Jesuits were often received by the Chinese elites with an adverse mixture of admiration, disdain, indignation and bemusement. Though the Mission did achieve some noteworthy conversions and won the toleration of both the Wanli and Kangxi emperors, the predominant mood in China remained one of bafflement at the central concept of 天主 *tianzhu* and horror at the crucifixion. Ricci in particular, was very aware of the essential absurdity of his task and believed that his goal "was not to multiply baptisms, but to win for Christianity an accepted place in Chinese life." (Leys 1983, 46) This suave modo approach ultimately meant that although the Jesuits had sought to use the prestige of European science to reinforce the authority of the Catholic religion, the Chinese rejected that religion wishing to keep only the scientific knowledge.① In his understanding of how difficult Christian doctrine was to convey to those not already sufficiently primed for it, Ricci had turned to philosophy to sugar the pill because, as Feng Youlan puts it: "The Chinese people take even their religion philosophically." (Feng 1948, 2) That Ricci wasn't quite persuasive enough is testimony to the strength and sophistication of China's native ethical philosophy and its skepticism towards the more mystical elements of Christianity (the Virgin Birth, the Incarnation, the Resurrection and the Trinity).

In one letter, Ricci seeks to make Confucius intelligible to those European humanists back home similarly with an appeal to ethics, on how to live, rather than to religious doctrine. He describes the Chinese sage as "un altro Seneca" (a second Seneca) intuiting the shared mission despite the difference in form of the philosophical works of Plato, Aristotle and Seneca, and the Chinese Masters. He writes: "At the very time when, if I calculate correctly, Plato and Aristotle flourished among us, there also flourished [amongst the Chinese] certain literati of good life who produced books dealing with moral matters, not in a scientific way, but in the form of maxims." (Standaert, 2003, 375) The identification of ethics as the heart of philosophy both east and west allowed Ricci to consolidate his accommodationist line. Just as Renaissance authors were aware of the important distinctions between Christianity and Stoicism but ultimately deemed them

---

① Works written by missionaries in Classical Chinese were included in the great compilation commissioned by the Qianlong emperor 乾隆 (r. 1735–1795) in 1773. In the 1781 special guide to the collection, the Siku quanshu zongmu tiyao 四库全书总目提要 there was the following note appended to the section dealing with missionary works: "The superiority of the Western teaching (xixue) lies in their calculations; their inferiority lies in their veneration of a Master of Heaven of a kind to upset men's minds." Quoted in Jacques Gernet, *China and the Christian Impact: A Conflict of Cultures*. Cambridge University Press, 1985, p.59.

Chapter Three
Philosophical Daoism: Its Enduring Legacy and Contemporary Relevance

compatible, so did Ricci merge Stoicism and Confucianism as a way of clearing the intellectual pathways for Christianity. The Jesuits also tried and failed to have Aristotelian philosophy introduced as the basis of the Chinese education system.

The reason for the missionaries not attacking Confucianism was, then, in some senses purely tactical. In a letter of 15 February 1609, Ricci acknowledges this utilitarian aspect of championing the Confucian Classics despite any personal affinities he may or may not have had with Daoist texts. He writes:

> *In the books that I have written, I begin by singing their praises [i.e. Those of the Confucian men of letters] and by using them to confound the others [the Buddhists and the Taoists], not refuting them directly but interpreting the points on which they are in disagreement with our faith.... A most distinguished person who belongs to the sect of idols has even called me an adulator of the literate elite.... And I am very keen that others should regard me in that light, for we should have much more to do if we were obliged to fight against all three sects. (Gernet 1985, 52)*

The ambiguity surrounding Ricci and the Jesuits' intentions, the extent to which their views changed on encounter with Chinese texts and customs, and how the Chinese themselves understood the Jesuit mission is born out in this passage. Here Ricci pictures the Jesuits as engaging in a fight against the *san jiao* 三教 using a divide and conquer mentality. However, in a letter by the infamous "maverick thinker and intellectual provocateur" (Handler Spitz, 2017, 3) Li Zhi 李贽 (1527–1602), it would seem that the literati had no clue what to make of Ricci's intentions. In an oft-cited passage Li Zhi writes:

> *Now he is perfectly able to speak our language, he can write our characters, he follows the customs and ceremonies in use here, he is an unusually accomplished man...But I still don't know what he has come here for. I have already met him three times, and I still don't know what he is here to do.*

今尽能言我此间之言，作此间之文字，行此间之仪礼，是一极标致人也……但不知到此何为，我已经三度相合，毕竟不知道此何干也。(Li Zhi, 2016, 256-7)

The enigmatic quality of Ricci in particular as he was perceived by the Chinese reminds us of what a feat it was for the Jesuits to master the language, culture and mores of China sufficiently to become prominent members of society at the highest level. That Ricci was not known as a proselytizer of the Catholic faith is testimony to his roles as an outstanding cultural mediator and a Humanist scholar at home with ambiguity and ambivalence.

……

When we leave the rather exceptional figure of Ricci and return to the Jesuit China mission as a whole, we see that the textual culmination of the Jesuit proposal to create a Confucian Christian synthesis was the translation (completed by hundreds of Jesuit collaborators) of the first three of the Confucian① *Four Books Sishu* 四书 into Latin. This mammoth project was completed in 1687 and edited by Philippe Couplet in Paris. Published under the rather revealing title *Confucius Sinarum Philosophus*② *(Confucius, the Philosopher of China)*, this was the book that successfully launched Confucianism in Europe and represented it as the eastern counterpart to the European Renaissance at the expense of Daoist texts. The *Four Books* had been used as Chinese language primers for newly arrived missionaries in China, and now they were to be selectively disseminated in Europe as the very spirit and essence of native Chinese thought. Ricci and his collaborators were content to treat the *Great Learning*, the *Doctrine on the Mean* and the *Analects* as serious philosophical texts and exemplary models of enlightened deism: sections of translations were entitled *"Scientiae Sinicae" (Learning of the Chinese)*, *"Sapientia Sinica" (Chinese Wisdom)*, and *"Sinarum scientia politico moralis" (The Politico Moral Learning of the Chinese)*. When it comes to the key Daoist texts, however, the *Laozi* receives only a cursory and dismissive mention, and the *Zhuangzi* no mention at all.

……

The compilers of the *Confucius Sinarum Philosophus* would have a lasting influence on how philosophical Daoism would be received (i.e. constructed) in Europe. The great sinologist and (not inconsequentially) Protestant missionary James Legge writes at the end of the nineteenth century: "The brilliant pages of Kwang tze [Zhuangzi] contain little more than his ingenious defense of his master's [Laozi's] speculations, and an aggregate of illustrative narratives…in themselves for the most part unbelievable, often grotesque and absurd" (Legge 1962a [1891], 39). Legge's Protestant paradigm of a pure master text, namely the *Daodejing* opposed to the later "popish" contamination with ritualistic and magical practices left little room for a deep and

---

① This appellation is always somewhat problematic given that what the Jesuits promulgated as the essence of Confucius' teaching was in fact the selections made by the much later Song neo-Confucian Zhu Xi 朱熹 (1130-1200). For example, the *Daxue* 大学 and *Zhongyong* 中庸 were separate chapters drawn from the traditional classic the *Liji* 礼记 *The Book of Rites*. Zhu Xi, following up on an earlier trend among his Song predecessors, chose these passages because they provided a brief, compact formulation of the basics of all learning, capable of serving as a guide to one's reading of the other classics. Indeed, Zhu Xi's concise selection was so succinct and focused that it readily became the heart of a Neo-Confucian education. First adopted on the local level in Song private academies, next in the curriculum of the Imperial College, then in the civil-service examination system, ultimately it reached beyond the borders of China into the schools of Korea, Japan, and Vietnam. See De Bary, "Thomas Merton and Confucianism: Why the Contemplative Never Got the Religion Quite Right." *First Things: A Monthly Journal of Religion & Public Life*, 2011.

② *Confucius sinarum philosophus, sive scientia sinensis: latine exposita …; adjecta est tabula chronologica sinicae monarchiae…*(Parisiis: apud Danielem Horthemels… 1687)

meaningful appreciation of the *Zhuangzi* as a composite philosophical text.

Western philosophers up until the twentieth century continued to dismiss Daoism as the very infancy of philosophy, a nihilistic reductive credo in which the goal of perpetual tranquility and the erasure of all distinctions was seen as anathema to western philosophical systems built upon logical rigor. In Hegel's *Lectures on The History of Philosophy*, delivered in 1825–1826 he famously described the Chinese master texts as uninteresting manifestations of an early stage in the evolution of Spirit or Geist. If each civilization represents a stage of development which for Hegel culminates in nineteenth century Germany, China is characterised by Stillstand a marmoreal, static civilization ruled by a despotic emperor over a people characterized by passivity and conformity. For the Jesuits, while Daoism was deemed an obstacle to their accommodationist mission, Confucius at least was revered as a moral philosopher. For Hegel the *whole* of masters' literature in early China is understood as lacking the speculative thinking and systematicity he deemed essential to "philosophy." He describes Confucius as "merely a practical statesman" whose reflections "never rise above the conventional views." Though Hegel finds the *Yijing* intriguing, he still deems it overly concerned with the external ordering rather than the inner nature of reality. He discusses Laozi and the *Daodejing* but finds the Dao too obscure for any substantial commentary and he makes no reference to the *Zhuangzi* at all. Ignored by the Jesuits and the Enlightenment philosophies, it will not be until the early twentieth century that the efforts of Richard Wilhelm and Martin Buber will create a Dao fever (*Dao-fiebers*) in Germany, Giles' *Zhuangzi* and Legge's *The Texts of Taoism* will do the same in England, and in 1823 in France Abel Rémusat, the first European chair of Chinese language and literature at the Collège de France will publish *Mémoire sur la vie et les opinions de Lao Tseu*, one of the earliest European works on Lao-tzu and classical Daoism.

The *Zhuangzi* has now been rehabilitated as a linguistically playful philosophical text that offers complex perspectives on alternative ways to live. It is also an extraordinary literary text; Victor Mair describes it as "primarily a work of literature than a work of philosophy." Herbert Giles' English translation was rapturously received by Oscar Wilde who penned a review of it in *The Speaker* in 1890 under the title "A Chinese Sage." Deeply appreciative of Zhuangzi's contrarian spirit, Wilde praised the rejection of instrumental morality and "the idealist's contempt for utilitarian systems." Cribbing from the Oxford theologian Aubrey Moore's introduction to Giles' translation, Wilde writes: "Chuang Tsŭ may be said to have summed up in himself almost every mood of European metaphysical or mystical thought, from Heracleitus down to Hegel."[1] In this he publicizes a new appreciation of East West understanding in Europe. Though Wilde was

---

[1] Review "Chuang Tsŭ, translated from the Chinese by Herbert A. Giles," *The Speaker* 1:6 (8 February 1890), pp. 144-146, reprinted in Richard Ellman, ed. *The Artist As Critic: Critical Writings of Oscar Wilde* (University of Chicago Press, 1982) as "A Chinese Sage (Confucius)," pp. 221-228.

no sinologist and he uses Daoist ideas impressionistically and to suit his own purposes, it is hard not to appreciate the kindred spiritual ethos that Wilde captures in his reading of Giles' *Zhuangzi*. Speaking very much of his own day, Wilde goes on:

> *But Chuang Tsŭ was something more than a metaphysician and an illuminist. He sought to destroy society, as we know it, as the middle classes know it. ...There is nothing of the sentimentalist in him. He pities the rich more than the poor, if he ever pities at all, and prosperity seems to him as tragic a thing as suffering. He has nothing of the modern sympathy with failures, nor does he propose that the prizes should always be given on moral grounds to those who come in last in the race. It is the race itself that he objects to; and as for active sympathy, which has become the profession of so many worthy people in our own day, he thinks that trying to make others good is as silly an occupation as 'beating a drum in a forest in order to find a fugitive.'... While as for a thoroughly sympathetic man, he is, in the eyes of Chuang Tsŭ, simply a man who is always trying to be someone else, and so misses the only possible excuse for his own existence.*

If the *Zhuangzi*'s joyful abstention from the will to rule and serve had been what set it apart from the *Laozi* and from what Wiebke Denecke calls "the Huanglao version of a cosmic administration of the universe through the 'law' of the Way" (2010: 233), now that abstention was celebrated as a source of radical freedom from bourgeois society. If the text's incongruity with ordered hierarchical government had sealed its fate in oblivion for so long, by the late nineteenth century *Zhuangzi* was poised to become the Chinese philosopher of choice for an atheistic and world weary Europe seeking a break with conformism.

Connections now being made between Zhuangzi and Heidegger, Zhuangzi and Derrida, Zhuangzi and Spinoza, Zhuangzi and the philosophy of language, etc. reflect the text's celebration of the unstable nature of the self and the world: the function of life becomes an exhilarating process of spontaneous self-creation. It also insists repeatedly that death and life are just the same and that neither should be sought or feared.① Profoundly anti-dogma, anti-government and anti-otherworld at the expense of this one it is clear why the Jesuits did not quite know what to do with Zhuangzi's chutzpah②. That the text was ignored for so long is a reminder of the extent to which

---

① It is, of course, paradoxical that the Zhuangzi would be linked with immortality cults and the concept of *yang sheng* 养生 when the text rejects both the possibility and desirability of immortality.

② Chutzpah is the quality of audacity, for good or for bad. A close English equivalent is sometimes "hubris." The word derives from the Hebrew ḥuṣpāh (חֻצְפָּה), meaning "insolence," "cheek" or "audacity." Thus, the original Yiddish word has a strongly negative connotation, but the form which entered English as a Yiddishism in American English has taken on a broader meaning, having been popularized through vernacular use in film, literature, and television. In American English the word is sometimes interpreted—particularly in business parlance—as meaning the amount of courage, mettle or ardor that an individual has.

the early European reception of Chinese texts were entirely reliant upon the missionary accounts filtered through a Catholic agenda. The missionaries decided what got read and how because they were the only Europeans equipped with the skills to read and interpret Classical Chinese texts. The *Zhuangzi*, however, has always floated free of the traditions that have surrounded it. Neither a prescriptive text nor a coherent system of belief, the *Zhuangzi* still might be deemed a quasi-religious text that offers a different (and for its European readers, competing) vision of revelation. In this sense, it has been thoroughly rediscovered by modernity. The story of that modernity as a gradual detachment from monotheism and from a faith in overarching, hierarchical structures is reflected in the neglect and subsequent feverish interest in the *Zhuangzi* in the West.

C. A Chinese Sage[①]
一位中国圣人

Oscar Wild
奥斯卡·王尔德

An eminent Oxford theologian once remarked that his only objection to modern progress was that it progressed forward instead of backward—a view that so fascinated a certain artistic undergraduate that he promptly wrote an essay upon some unnoticed analogies between the development of ideas and the movements of the common sea-crab. I feel sure THE SPEAKER will not be suspected of holding this dangerous heresy of retrogression even by its most enthusiastic friends. But I must candidly admit that I have come to the conclusion that the most caustic criticism of modern life I have met with for some time is that contained in the writings of the learned Chuang Tsŭ, recently translated into the vulgar tongue by Mr. Herbert Giles, Her Majesty's Consul at Tamsui.

......

Chuang Tsŭ, whose name must carefully be pronounced as it is not written, was born in the fourth century before Christ, by the banks of the Yellow River, in the Flowery Land; and portraits of the wonderful sage seated on the flying dragon of contemplation may still be found on the simple tea-trays and pleasing screens of many of our most respectable suburban households. The honest ratepayer and his healthy family have no doubt often mocked at the dome-like forehead of the philosopher, and laughed over the strange perspective of the landscape that lies beneath him. If they really knew who he was, they would tremble. For Chuang Tsŭ spent his life in preaching the great creed of Inaction,

---

① Excerpted from "Review of *Chuang Tsŭ*", translated from the Chinese by Herbert A. Giles, Speaker I: 6 (8 February 1890), pp. 144-146.

and in pointing out the uselessness of all useful things. "Do nothing, and everything will be done," was the doctrine which he inherited from his great master Lao Tsŭ. To resolve action into thought, and thought into abstraction, was his wicked transcendental aim. Like the obscure philosopher of early Greek speculation, he believed in the identity of contraries; like Plato, he was an idealist, and had all the idealist's contempt for utilitarian systems; he was a mystic like Dionysius, and Scotus Erigena[①], and Jacob Böhme[②], and held, with them and with Philo[③], that the object of life was to get rid of self-consciousness, and to become the unconscious vehicle of a higher illumination. In fact, Chuang Tsŭ may be said to have summed up in himself almost every mood of European metaphysical or mystical thought, from Heraclitus down to Hegel. There was something in him of the Quietist[④] also; and in his worship of Nothing he may be said to have in some measure anticipated those strange dreamers of medieval days who, like Tauler[⑤] and Master Eckhart, adored the *purum nihil* [⑥] and the Abyss. The great middle classes of this country, to whom, as we all know, our prosperity, if not our civilization, is entirely due, may shrug their shoulders over all this, and ask, with a certain amount of reason, what is the identity of contraries to them, and why they should get rid of that self-consciousness which is their chief characteristic. But Chuang Tsŭ was something more than a metaphysician and an illuminist. He sought to destroy society, as we know it, as the middle classes know it; and the sad thing is that he combines with the passionate eloquence of a Rousseau the scientific reasoning of a Herbert Spencer[⑦].

---

① Also known as Johannes Scotus Erigena, John the Scot, or John the Irish-born (c.800–c.877) was an Irish Neoplatonist philosopher, theologian and poet of the Early Middle Ages.

② Jacob Böhme (24 April 1575–17 November 1624) was a German philosopher, Christian mystic, and Lutheran Protestant theologian.

③ Philo of Alexandria (c.20 BCE–c.50 CE), also called Philō Judæus, was a Hellenistic Jewish philosopher who lived in Alexandria, in the Roman province of Egypt.

④ Quietism (静默主义) is the name given (especially in Catholic theology) to a set of contemplative practices that rose in popularity in France, Italy, and Spain during the late 1670s and 1680s, particularly associated with the writings of the Spanish mystic Miguel de Molinos (and subsequently François Malaval and Madame Guyon), and which were condemned as heresy by Pope Innocent XI in the papal bull Coelestis Pastor of 1687. "Quietism" was seen by critics as holding that man's highest perfection consists in a sort of psychical self-annihilation and a consequent absorption of the soul into the Divine Essence even during the present life.

⑤ Johannes Tauler OP (c.1300–16 June 1361) was a German mystic, a Roman Catholic priest and a theologian. A disciple of Meister Eckhart, he belonged to the Dominican order. Tauler was known as one of the most important Rhineland mystics. He promoted a certain neo-platonist dimension in the Dominican spirituality of his time.

⑥ "Purum nihil" is a Latin phrase that translates to "pure nothing" or "absolute nothingness" in English. It is often used to describe a state of complete non-existence or the absence of anything.

⑦ Herbert Spencer (27 April 1820–8 December 1903) was an English polymath active as a philosopher, psychologist, biologist, sociologist, and anthropologist. Spencer originated the expression "survival of the fittest," which he coined in *Principles of Biology* (1864) after reading Charles Darwin's 1859 book *On the Origin of Species*. The term strongly suggests natural selection, yet Spencer saw evolution as extending into realms of sociology and ethics.

Chapter Three
Philosophical Daoism: Its Enduring Legacy and Contemporary Relevance

There is nothing of the sentimentalist in him. He pities the rich more than the poor, if he ever pities at all, and prosperity seems to him as tragic a thing as suffering. He has nothing of the modern sympathy with failures, nor does he propose that the prizes should always be given on moral grounds to those who come in last in the race. It is the race itself that he objects to; and as for active sympathy, which has become the profession of so many worthy people in our own day, he thinks that trying to make others good is as silly an occupation as "beating a drum in a forest in order to find a fugitive." It is a mere waste of energy. That is all. While as for a thoroughly sympathetic man, he is, in the eyes of Chuang Tsŭ, simply a man who is always trying to be somebody else, and so misses the only possible excuse for his own existence.

Yes; incredible as it may seem, this curious thinker looked back with a sigh of regret to a certain Golden Age when there were no competitive examinations, no wearisome educational systems, no missionaries, no penny dinners for the people, no Established Churches, no Humanitarian Societies, no dull lectures about one's duty to one's neighbour, and no tedious sermons about any subject at all. <u>In those ideal days, he tells us, people loved each other without being conscious of charity, or writing to the newspapers about it. They were upright, and yet they never published books upon Altruism. As every man kept his knowledge to himself, the world escaped the curse of scepticism; and as every man kept his virtues to himself, nobody meddled in other people's business. They lived simple and peaceful lives, and were contented with such food and raiment as they could get. Neighbouring districts were in sight, and "the cocks and dogs of one could be heard in the other," yet the people grew old and died without ever interchanging visits. There was no chattering about clever men, and no laudation of good men. The intolerable sense of obligation was unknown. The deeds of humanity left no trace, and their affairs were not made a burden for posterity by foolish historians.</u>

......

The economic question, also, is discussed by this almond-eyed sage at great length, and he writes about the curse of capital as eloquently as Mr. Hyndman. The accumulation of wealth is to him the origin of evil. It makes the strong violent, and the weak dishonest. It creates the petty thief, and puts him in a bamboo cage. It creates the big thief, and sets him on a throne of white jade. It is the father of competition, and competition is the waste, as well as the destruction, of energy. The order of nature is rest, repetition, and peace. Weariness and war are the results of an artificial society based upon capital; and the richer this society gets, the more thoroughly bankrupt it really is, for it has neither sufficient rewards for the good nor sufficient punishments for the wicked. There is also this to be remembered—that the prizes of the world degrade a man as much as the world's punishments. The age is rotten with its worship of success. As for education, true wisdom can neither be learnt nor taught. It is a spiritual state, to which he who lives in harmony with nature attains. Knowledge is shallow if we compare it with the extent of the unknown, and only the unknowable is of value. Society produces rogues, and education makes one rogue cleverer than another. …

Who, then, according to Chuang Tsŭ, is the perfect man? And what is his manner of life? The perfect man does nothing beyond gazing at the universe. He adopts no absolute position. "In motion, he is like water. At rest, he is like a mirror. And, like Echo, he only answers when he is called upon." He lets externals take care of themselves. Nothing material injures him; nothing spiritual punishes him. His mental equilibrium gives him the empire of the world. He is never the slave of objective existences. He knows that, "just as the best language is that which is never spoken, so the best action is that which is never done." He is passive, and accepts the laws of life. He rests in inactivity, and sees the world become virtuous of itself. He does not try to "bring about his own good deeds." He never wastes himself on effort. He is not troubled about moral distinctions. He knows that things are what they are, and that their consequences will be what they will be. His mind is the "speculum of creation," and he is ever at peace.

All this is of course excessively dangerous, but we must remember that Chuang Tsŭ lived more than two thousand years ago, and never had the opportunity of seeing our unrivalled civilisation. And yet it is possible that, were he to come back to earth and visit us, he might have something to say to Mr. Balfour① about his coercion and active misgovernment in Ireland; he might smile at some of our philanthropic ardours, and shake his head over many of our organised charities; the School Board might not impress him, nor our race for wealth stir his admiration; he might wonder at our ideals, and grow sad over what we have realised. Perhaps it is well that Chuang Tsŭ cannot return.

Meanwhile, thanks to Mr. Giles and Mr. Quaritch, we have his book to console us, and certainly it is a most fascinating and delightful volume. Chuang Tsŭ is one of the Darwinians before Darwin. He traces man from the germ, and sees his unity with nature. As an anthropologist he is excessively interesting, and he describes our primitive arboreal ancestor living in trees through his terror of animals stronger than himself, and knowing only one parent, the mother, with all the accuracy of a lecturer at the Royal Society. Like Plato, he adopts the dialogue as his mode of expression, "putting words into other people's mouths," he tells us, "in order to gain

---

① Arthur James Balfour, 1st Earl of Balfour (25 July 1848–19 March 1930) was a British statesman and Conservative politician who was Prime Minister of the United Kingdom from 1902 to 1905. As foreign secretary in the Lloyd George ministry, he issued the Balfour Declaration of 1917 on behalf of the cabinet, which supported a "home for the Jewish people" in Palestine. Entering Parliament in 1874, Balfour achieved prominence as Chief Secretary for Ireland, in which position he suppressed agrarian unrest whilst taking measures against absentee landlords. He opposed Irish Home Rule, saying there could be no half-way house between Ireland remaining within the United Kingdom or becoming independent.

breadth of view." As a story-teller he is charming. The account of the visit of the respectable Confucius to the great Robber Chê is most vivid and brilliant, and it is impossible not to laugh over the ultimate discomfiture of the sage, the barrenness of whose moral platitudes is ruthlessly exposed by the successful brigand. Even in his metaphysics, Chuang Tsǔ is intensely humorous. He personifies his abstractions, and makes them act out plays before us. The Spirit of the Clouds, when passing eastward through the expanse of air, happened to fall in with the Vital Principle. The latter was slapping his ribs and hopping about: whereupon the Spirit of the Clouds said, "Who are you, old man, and what are you doing?" "Strolling!" replied the Vital Principle, without stopping, for all activities are ceaseless. "I want to know something," continued the Spirit of the Clouds. "Ah!" cried the Vital Principle, in a tone of disapprobation, and a marvellous conversation follows, that is not unlike the dialogue between the Sphinx and the Chimæra in Flaubert's curious drama. Talking animals, also, have their place in Chuang Tsǔ's parables and stories, and through myth and poetry and fancy his strange philosophy finds musical utterance.

Of course it is sad to be told that it is immoral to be consciously good, and that doing anything is the worst form of idleness. Thousands of excellent and really earnest philanthropists would be absolutely thrown upon the rates if we adopted the view that nobody should be allowed to meddle in what does not concern them. The doctrine of the uselessness of all useful things would not merely endanger our commercial supremacy as a nation, but might bring discredit upon many prosperous and serious-minded members of the shop-keeping classes. What would become of our popular preachers, our Exeter Hall orators, our drawing-room evangelists, if we said to them, in the words of Chuang Tsǔ, "Mosquitoes will keep a man awake all night with their biting, and just in the same way this talk of charity and duty to one's neighbour drives us nearly crazy. Sirs, strive to keep the world to its own original simplicity, and, as the wind bloweth where it listeth, so let Virtue establish itself. Wherefore this undue energy?" And what would be the fate of governments and professional politicians if we came to the conclusion that there is no such thing as governing mankind at all? It is clear that Chuang Tsǔ is a very dangerous writer, and the publication of his book in English, two thousand years after his death, is obviously premature, and may cause a great deal of pain to many thoroughly respectable and industrious persons. It may be true that the ideal of self-culture and self-development, which is the aim of his scheme of life, and the basis of his scheme of philosophy, is an ideal somewhat needed by an age like ours, in which most people are so anxious to educate their neighbours that they have actually no time left in which to educate themselves. But would it be wise to say so? It seems to me that if we once admitted the force of any one of Chuang Tsǔ's destructive criticisms we should have to put some check on our national habit of self-glorification; and the only thing that ever consoles man for the stupid things he does is the praise he always gives himself for doing them. There may, however, be a few who have grown wearied of that strange modern tendency that sets enthusiasm to do the work of the intellect. To these, and such as these, Chuang Tsŭ will be welcome. But let them only read him. Let them not talk about him. He would be disturbing at dinner-parties, and impossible at afternoon teas, and his whole life was a protest against platform speaking. "The perfect man ignores self; the divine man ignores action; the true sage ignores reputation." These are the principles of Chuang Tsŭ.

Exercises

I. Vocabulary Practice

Define the following terms taken from the Daoist texts and use each term in a sentence that reflects its philosophical meaning:

1. Dao (道)
2. Wu Wei (无为)
3. Ziran (自然)
4. De (德)
5. Tianni (天倪)

II. Comprehension

A. Read the excerpts from *Dao De Jing* and answer the following questions:

6. What is the significance of the statement "The nameless is the beginning of heaven and earth"?
7. How does the concept of "Wu Wei" relate to the idea of natural order and effortless action?

B. Analyze the teachings in Chapter 25 of *Dao De Jing* and discuss:

8. What is the nature of the process that "formed spontaneously, emerging before the heavens and the earth"?
9. How does the Dao emulate what is spontaneously so (ziran)?

C. Reflect on the themes of perception and knowledge in Zhuangzi's philosophy. Discuss the following:

10. How does the story of the cicada, the little dove, and the Peng bird illustrate the limitations of perspective and knowledge?
11. What does Zhuangzi suggest about the nature of truth and the relativity of our understanding of the world?

D. Analyze the concept of "uselessness" as presented in Zhuangzi's teachings:

12. What is Zhuangzi's response when Master Hui complains about the uselessness of the

calabash fruit?

13. How does Zhuangzi use the metaphor of the tree to convey a deeper philosophical message about the value of things and the nature of utility?

E. Consider Zhuangzi's views on life, death, and the nature of existence:

14. How does Zhuangzi describe the state of being alive and the process of dying as stated in Chapter 76 of *Dao De Jing*?

F. Examine Zhuangzi's approach to governance and societal roles:

15. How does Zhuangzi critique the conventional ideas of governance and societal order?
16. What alternative vision of society does Zhuangzi propose, and what are the implications of this vision for our understanding of power and leadership?

G. Discuss Zhuangzi's perspective on the nature of reality:

17. What is the famous butterfly dream parable, and what philosophical questions does it raise?
18. How does Zhuangzi use the concept of dreams to challenge our perceptions of reality and the distinction between waking life and dreams?

H. Reflect on Zhuangzi's views on language and communication:

19. How does Zhuangzi approach the limitations and potential of language in conveying truth and understanding?
20. What does Zhuangzi suggest about the relationship between language, thought, and reality?

III. Application and Interpretation

A. Translate the underlined sections from the "Philosophical Introduction: Correlative Cosmology—An Interpretive Context" and discuss how the Daoist view of reality as a continuous process of change contrasts with Western metaphysical traditions. Write an essay exploring the implications of this contrast for understanding the nature of existence and time.

B. Consider Zhuangzi's perspective on the parity and unity of all things and write an essay on how this view can offer insights into modern environmental ethics and the human relationship with nature.

C. Reflect on Zhuangzi's challenge to conventional morality and societal norms as highlighted in Oscar Wilde's review. Write an essay discussing the relevance of Zhuangzi's thought to contemporary social and political issues, such as the critique of consumerism and the pursuit of simplicity and authenticity in life.

Chapter Four

Essential Sutras and Chan Teachings—Exploring the Heart of Buddhist Wisdom

导读

本章课文节选了《心经》全文、《金刚经》（第三至十品）和《坛经》（行由品第一）。拓展性阅读材料的A篇为赤松所著的《〈心经〉的历史背景》；B篇为现象学学者长友繁法所著的《〈金刚经〉的逻辑：A则非A》；C篇为马克瑞所著的《审视法脉：理解禅宗的新视角》。

Introduction

1. *The Heart Sutra*

The Heart Sutra is perhaps the most famous Buddhist scripture which has exercised a fascination over the minds of Buddhist thinkers in India, China, Japan, Korea, and Central Asia. It covers more of the Buddha's teachings in a shorter span than any other scripture. Whoever the author was, he begins by calling upon Avalokiteshvara 观世音, Buddhism's most revered bodhisattva, to introduce the teaching of Prajnaparamita 般若, the Perfection of Wisdom, to the Buddha's wisest disciple, Shariputra 舍利子.

Avalokiteshvara explains the fundamental emptiness of all phenomena, known through and as the five aggregates of human existence, then shines the light of this radical wisdom on the major approaches to reality used by the Sarvastivadins 说一切有部, and finally provides a famous and oft-recited Buddhist mantra, a mantra that occurs not in a tantric text, but in a sutra.

The Heart Sutra has evoked commentaries from many of the pivotal figures in the history of Buddhist thought, including Kamalasila 莲花戒, Atisa 阿底峡, Kuiji 窥基, Kukai 空海. It has also enlightened some western philosophers to develop their thoughts, including Schopenhauer. In his *The World as Will and Representation*, Schopenhauer wrote: "for everyone who is still filled with the will, what remains after it is completely abolished is certainly nothing. But conversely, for those in whom the will has turned and negated itself, this world of ours which is so very real with all its suns and galaxies is — nothing." To this, he appended the following note: "This is precisely the Pradschna-Paramita of the Buddhists, the 'beyond of all knowledge', i.e. the point where subject and object are no more."[①]

2. *The Diamond Sutra*

Another mainstay of the Mahayana prajnaparamita literature is *The Diamond Sutra*. Scholars believe the original text was written in India sometime in the 2nd century C.E. It has evoked commentaries from many great thinkers such as Asanga 无著 and Vasubandhu 世亲. Kumarajiva 鸠摩罗什 is believed to have made the first translation into Chinese in 401 C.E. Prince Zhaoming 昭明太子(501–531) divided the sutra into 32 chapters and gave each chapter a title. A complete woodblock printed scroll, dated 868 C.E., was discovered in Dunhuang in 1900.

Most of the text takes the form of a dialogue between the Buddha and a disciple named Subhuti 须菩提. Through their dialogue, there are the core tenets of Mahayana Buddhism, such as emptiness, the concept of no-self, and what true enlightenment means. Unlike Theravada 上座部 which places much emphasis on individual enlightenment, *The Diamond Sutra* represents an important milestone in the development of Mahayana, which stresses the ideal of bodhisattva, a being who seeks enlightenment not for his or her own benefit, but for the benefit of all sentient beings.

3. *Sutra Spoken by the Sixth Patriarch*

The Platform Sutra of the Sixth Patriarch is the fundamental text of Mahayana Chan 禅 Buddhism. The earliest extant version of the sutra was written around the year 780 and was preserved among the treasures of Dunhuang. It relates the life and teachings of Master Hui-Neng 惠能, the last of the officially designated patriarchs in direct lineage from the days of the Buddha. As such, these are the only teachings of a Chinese high monk which are regarded by Buddhists as a sutra. With the spread of Chan in Asia and beyond, it has been regarded as the greatest contribution that Chinese Buddhism has ever made to the world.

Sutra Spoken by the Sixth Patriarch is not a statement of an undifferentiated perennial philosophy. But the narratives of the primacy of the buddha-nature, the identity of meditation and wisdom, the "formless" approach to repentance and the precepts, and the *samadhi* of the single practice—all these are religious principles that are valid beyond the limits of its literary genre.

---

① Schopenhauer, *The World as Will and Representation*, translated and edited by Judith Norman et al., in *The Cambridge Edition to the Works of Schopenhauer*, Vol. I, Christopher Janaway (ed). Cambridge: Cambridge University Press, 2010, p.439.

《心经》[①] The Heart Sutra[①]

观自在菩萨，行深般若波罗密多时，照见五蕴皆空，度一切苦厄。

The noble Avalokiteshvara Bodhisattva,
while practicing the deep practice of Prajnaparamita,
looked upon the Five Skandhas
and seeing they were empty of self-existence,
said, "Here, Shariputra,

舍利子，色不异空，空不异色，色即是空，空即是色，受、想、行、识，亦复如是。

form is emptiness, emptiness is form;
emptiness is not separate from form, form is not separate from emptiness;
whatever is form is emptiness, whatever is emptiness is form.
The same holds for sensation and perception, memory and consciousness.

舍利子，是诸法空相，不生不灭，不垢不净，不增不减。

Here, Shariputra, all dharmas are defined by emptiness
not birth or destruction, purity or defilement, completeness or deficiency.

是故，空中无色，无受、想、行、识；无眼、耳、鼻、舌、身、意；无色、声、香、味、触、法；无眼界，乃至无意识界；无无明，亦无无明尽；乃至无老死，亦无老死尽；无苦、集、灭、道，无智亦无得。

Therefore, Shariputra, in emptiness there is no form,
no sensation, no perception, no memory and no consciousness;
no eye, no ear, no nose, no tongue, no body and no mind;
no shape, no sound, no smell, no taste, no feeling and no thought;
no element of perception, from eye to conceptual consciousness;
no causal link, from ignorance to old age and death,
and no end of causal link, from ignorance to old age and death;
no suffering, no source, no relief, no path;
no knowledge, no attainment and no non-attainment.

以无所得故，菩提萨埵，依般若波罗密多故，心无挂碍。无挂碍故，无有恐怖。远离颠倒梦想，究竟涅槃。

Therefore, Shariputra, without attainment,
bodhisattvas take refuge in Prajnaparamita
and live without walls of the mind.
Without walls of the mind and thus without fears,

---

① 选自陈秋平译注：《金刚经·心经》，北京：中华书局，2010年，第125–139页。

② Excerpted from *The Heart Sutra, The Womb of Buddhas*, translation and commentary by Red Pine, Washington D.C.: Shoemaker & Hoard, 2004, pp.2-3.

they see through delusions and finally nirvana.
All buddhas past, present and future
also take refuge in Prajnaparamita
and realize unexcelled, perfect enlightenment.
You should therefore know the great mantra of Prajnaparamita,
the mantra of great magic,
the unexcelled mantra,
the mantra equal to the unequalled,
which heals all suffering and is true, not false,
the mantra in Prajnaparamita spoken thus:
'Gate gate, paragate, parasangate, bodhi svaha.'"

三世诸佛，依般若波罗密多故，得阿耨多罗三藐三菩提。

故知般若波罗密多，是大神咒，是大明咒，是无上咒，是无等等咒，能除一切苦，真实不虚。

故说般若波罗密多咒，即说咒曰：

揭谛揭谛，波罗揭谛，波罗僧揭谛，菩提萨婆诃。

Selections from *The Diamond Sutra*①

《金刚经》选篇②

大乘正宗分第三

佛告须菩提："诸菩萨摩诃萨应如是降伏其心：所有一切众生之类，若卵生，若胎生，若湿生，若化生；若有色，若无色；若有想，若无想，若非有想非无想，我皆令入无余涅槃而灭度之。如是灭度无量无数无边众生，实无众生得灭度者。何以故？须菩提，若菩萨有我相、人相、众生相、寿者相，即非菩萨。"

The Buddha said to Subhuti, "All the bodhisattva-mahasattvas, who undertake the practice of meditation, should cherish one thought only: 'When I attain perfect wisdom, I will liberate all sentient beings in every realm of the universe, whether they be egg-born, womb-born, moisture-born, or miraculously born; those with form, those without form, those with perception, those without perception, and those with neither perception nor non-perception. So long as any form of being is conceived, I must allow it to pass into the eternal peace of nirvana, into that realm of nirvana that leaves nothing behind, and to attain final awakening.'

"And yet although immeasurable, innumerable, and unlimited beings have been liberated, truly no being has been liberated. Why? Because no bodhisattva who is a true bodhisattva entertains such concepts as a self, a person, a being, or a living soul. Thus, there

---

① Excerpted from *The Diamond Sutra: Transforming the Way We Perceive the World*. Mu Soeng trans. Boston: Wisdom Publications, 2000, pp.141-155.

② 选自陈秋平译注：《金刚经·心经》，北京：中华书局，2010 年，第 23—47 页。

are no sentient beings to be liberated and no self to attain perfect wisdom.

妙行无住分第四

"复次，须菩提，菩萨于法应无所住，行于布施。所谓不住色布施，不住声、香、味、触、法布施。须菩提，菩萨应如是布施，不住于相。何以故？若菩萨不住相布施，其福德不可思量。须菩提。于意云何？东方虚空可思量不？"

"不也，世尊。"

"须菩提。南、西、北方、四维、上下虚空可思量不？"

"不也，世尊。"

"须菩提，菩萨无住相布施福德，亦复如是不可思量。须菩提，菩萨但应如所教住。"

如理实见分第五

"须菩提，于意云何？可以身相见如来不？"

"不也，世尊。不可以身相得见如来。何以故？如来所说身相即非身相。"

佛告须菩提："凡所有相皆是虚妄。若见诸相非相，即见如来。"

正信希有分第六

须菩提白佛言："世尊，颇有众生得闻如是言说章句，生实信不？"

佛告须菩提："莫作是说。如来灭后，后五百岁，有持戒修福者，于此章句能生信

"Furthermore, Subhuti, in the practice of generosity a bodhisattva should be unsupported. He or she should practice generosity without regard to sight, sound, touch, flavor, smell, or any thought that arises in it. Subhuti, thus should a bodhisattva practice generosity without being supported by any notion of a sign. Why? When a bodhisattva practices generosity without being supported by any notion of a sign, his or her merit will be beyond conception. Subhuti, what do you think? Can you measure the space extending eastward?"

"No, World-Honored One, I cannot."

"Subhuti, can you measure the space extending toward the south, or west, or north, or above, or below?"

"No, World-Honored One, I cannot."

"Subhuti, so it is with the merit of a bodhisattva who practices generosity without cherishing any notion of a sign; it is beyond measure like space. Subhuti, a bodhisattva should persevere one-pointedly in this instruction.

"Subhuti, what do you think? Is it possible to recognize the Tathagata by means of bodily marks?"

"No, World-Honored One. And why? When the Tathagata speaks of the bodily marks, he speaks of the no-possession of no marks."

The Buddha said to Subhuti, "All that has a form is an illusory existence. When the illusory nature of form is perceived, the Tathagata is recognized."

Subhuti said to the Buddha, "World-Honored One, in times to come, will there be beings who, when they hear these teachings, have real faith and confidence in them?"

The Buddha said, "Subhuti, do not utter such words. Five hundred years after the passing of the Tathagata, there will be

Chapter Four
Essential Sutras and Chan Teachings—Exploring the Heart of Buddhist Wisdom

beings who, having practiced rules of morality and being thus possessed of merit, happen to hear of these statements and will understand their truth. Such beings, you should know, have planted their root of merit not only under one, two, three, four, or five Buddhas, but under countless Buddhas. When such beings, upon hearing these statements, arouse even one moment of pure and clear confidence, the Tathagata will see them and recognize their immeasurable amount of merit. Why? Because all these beings are free from the idea of a self, a person, a being, or a living soul; they are free from the idea of a dharma as well as a no-dharma. Why? Because if they cherish the idea of a dharma, they are still attached to a self, a person, a being, or a living soul. If they cherish the idea of a no-dharma, they are attached to a self, a person, a being, or a living soul. Therefore, do not cherish the idea of a dharma nor that of a no-dharma. For this reason, the Tathagata always preaches thus: 'O you bhikshus, know that my teaching is to be likened unto a raft. Even a dharma is cast aside, much more a no-dharma.'"

"Subhuti, what do you think? Has the Tathagata attained the supreme awakening? Has he something he can preach?"

Subhuti said, "World-Honored One, as I understand the teaching of the Buddha, the Buddha has no doctrine to convey. The truth is ungraspable and inexpressible. It neither is nor is not. How is it so? Because all noble teachers are exalted by the unconditioned."

"Subhuti, what do you think? If a son or daughter of a good family should fill the three thousand chiliocosms with the seven precious treasures and give them all as a gift to the Tathagatas, would not the merit thus obtained be great?"

Subhuti said, "Very great, indeed, World-Honored One. Why? Because their merit is characterized with the quality of not being merit. Therefore, the Tathagata speaks of the merit as being great."

The Buddha: "If there is a person who, memorizing even four lines from this sutra, preaches it to others, his merit will be superior

心，以此为实。当知是人不于一佛、二佛、三、四、五佛而种善根，已于无量千万佛所种诸善根。闻是章句乃至一念生净信者。须菩提，如来悉知悉见，是诸众生得如是无量福德。何以故？是诸众生无复我相、人相、众生相、寿者相，无法相亦无非法相。何以故？是诸众生，若心取相，则为著我、人、众生、寿者；若取法相，即著我、人、众生、寿者。何以故？若取非法相，即著我、人、众生、寿者，是故不应取法，不应取非法。以是义故，如来常说汝等比丘知我说法如筏喻者。法尚应舍，何况非法。"

无得无说分第七
"须菩提，于意云何？如来得阿耨多罗三藐三菩提耶？如来有所说法耶？"
须菩提言："如我解佛所说义，无有定法名阿耨多罗三藐三菩提，亦无有定法如来可说。何以故？如来所说法皆不可取，不可说，非法、非非法。所以者何？一切圣贤皆以无为法而有差别。"

依法出生分第八
"须菩提，于意云何？若人满三千大千世界七宝，以用布施，是人所得福德宁为多不？"

须菩提言："甚多，世尊。何以故？是福德即非福德性，是故如来说福德多。"

"若复有人于此经中，受持乃至四句偈等，为他人说，其福胜彼。何以故？须菩提，一切诸佛及诸佛阿耨多罗三藐三菩提法皆从此经出。须菩提,所谓佛法者即非佛法。"

一相无相分第九

"须菩提,于意云何?须陀洹能作是念,我得须陀洹果不?"

须菩提言:"不也,世尊。何以故?须陀洹名为入流,而无所入,不入色、声、香、味、触、法,是名须陀洹。"

"须菩提,于意云何?斯陀含能作是念,我得斯陀含果不?"

须菩提言:"不也,世尊。何以故?斯陀含名一往来,而实无往来,是名斯陀含。"

"须菩提,于意云何?阿那含能作是念,我得阿那含果不?"

须菩提言:"不也,世尊。何以故?阿那含名为不来,而实无不来,是故名阿那含。"

"须菩提,于意云何?阿罗汉能作是念,我得阿罗汉道不?"

须菩提言:"不也,世尊。何以故?实无有法名阿罗汉。世尊,若阿罗汉作是念,我得阿罗汉道,即为著我、人、众生、寿者。世尊,佛说我得无诤三昧,人中最为第一,是第一离欲阿罗汉。世尊,我不作是念,我是离欲阿罗汉。世尊,我若作是念,我得阿罗汉道,世尊则不说须菩提是乐阿兰那行者。以须菩提实无所行,而名须菩提,是乐阿兰那行。"

to the one just mentioned. Why? Because, Subhuti, all the Buddhas and their supreme awakening issue from this sutra. Subhuti, what is known as the teaching of the Buddha is not the teaching of the Buddha."

"Subhuti, what do you think? Does a srotapanna think, 'I have obtained the fruit of srotapatti'?"

Subhuti said, "No, World-Honored One, he does not. Why? Because while srotapanna means 'entering the stream,' there is no entering here. A true srotapanna is one who does not enter sound, odor, flavor, touch, or any thought that arises."

"Subhuti, what do you think? Does a sakridagamin think, 'I have obtained the fruit of a sakridagamin'?"

Subhuti said, "No, World-Honored One, he does not. Why? Because while sakridagamin means 'going and coming for once,' one who understands that there is really no going-and-coming, he or she is a true sakridagamin."

"Subhuti, what do you think? Does an anagamin think, 'I have obtained the fruit of an ana-gamin'?"

Subhuti said, "No, World-Honored One, he does not. Why? Because while anagamin means 'not coming,' there is really no not-coming; therefore the one who realizes this is called an anagamin."

"Subhuti, what do you think? Does an arhat think, 'I have obtained arhatship'?"

Subhuti said, "No, World-Honored One, he does not. Why? Because there is no dharma to be called arhat. If, World-Honored One, an arhat thinks, 'I have obtained arhatship,' this means that he has the idea of an ego-self, a person, a living being, or a soul.

"Although the Buddha has said that I am the foremost of those who have obtained aranasamadhi, that I am the foremost of those arhats who are liberated from unwholesome desires, World-Honored One, I cherish no thought that I have attained arhatship. World-Honored One, [if I did] you would not have declared of me, 'Subhuti, who is the foremost of those who dwell in peaceful abiding, does not dwell anywhere; that is why he is called a dweller in peace.'"

Chapter Four
Essential Sutras and Chan Teachings—Exploring the Heart of Buddhist Wisdom

The Buddha asked Subhuti, "What do you think? When the Tathagata practiced in ancient times under Dipankara Buddha, did he attain any Dharma?"

"No, World-Honored One, he did not attain any Dharma while practicing with the Dipankara Buddha."

"Subhuti, what do you think? Does a bodhisattva create any harmonious buddha fields?"

"No, World-Honored One, he does not. Why? Because to create a harmonious buddha field is not to create a harmonious buddha field, and therefore it is known as creating a harmonious buddha field."

"So, Subhuti, all bodhisattvas should develop a pure, lucid mind that doesn't depend upon sight, sound, touch, flavor, smell, or any thought that arises in it. A bodhisattva should develop a mind that functions freely, without depending on anything whatsoever."

The Buddha continued, "Subhuti, what do you think? If someone were to have a body as large as Mount Sumeru, would not this body be very large?"

Subhuti said, "Very large indeed, World-Honored One. Why? Because the Buddha teaches that that which is no-body is known as a large body."

Selections from *Sutra Spoken by the Sixth Patriarch*[①]

Chapter 1
Autobiography of Hui-Neng

...

After arrangements had been made for my mother's support, I left for Wong-mui which took me about thirty days to reach.

I paid homage to the Patriarch and was asked where I came

庄严净土分第十

佛告须菩提："于意云何？如来昔在燃灯佛所，于法有所得不？"

"不也，世尊。如来在然灯佛所，于法实无所得。"

"须菩提，于意云何？菩萨庄严佛土不？"

"不也，世尊。何以故？庄严佛土者则非庄严，是名庄严。"

"是故，须菩提，诸菩萨摩诃萨应如是生清净心，不应住色生心，不应住声、香、味、触、法生心，应无所住而生其心。须菩提。譬如有人身如须弥山王，于意云何？是身为大不？"

须菩提言："甚大，世尊。何以故？佛说非身是名大身。"

《坛经》选篇[②]

行由品第一

……

惠能安置母毕，即便辞违，不经三十余日，便至黄梅，礼拜五祖。

[①] Excerpted from Wong Mou-lam trans. "Sutra Spoken by the Sixth Patriach," *A Buddhist Bible*, Dwight Goddard ed., New York: E.P. Dutton & Co. Inc., 1952, pp.497-507.

[②] 选自赖永海主编，陈秋平译注：《坛经》，北京：中华书局，2010年，第1-38页。

祖问曰:"汝何方人,欲求何物?"

惠能对曰:"弟子是岭南新州百姓,远来礼师,惟求作佛,不求余物。"

祖言:"汝是岭南人,又是獦獠,若为堪作佛?"

惠能曰:"人虽有南北,佛性本无南北,獦獠身与和尚不同,佛性有何差别?"五祖更欲与语,且见徒众总在左右,乃令随众作务。

惠能曰:"惠能启和尚,弟子自心常生智慧,不离自性,即是福田。未审和尚教作何务?"

祖云:"这獦獠根性大利,汝更勿言,著槽厂去。"

惠能退至后院,有一行者,差惠能破柴踏碓。

经八月余,祖一日忽见惠能,曰:"吾思汝之见可用,恐有恶人害汝,遂不与汝言,汝知之否?"

惠能曰:"弟子亦知师意,不敢行至堂前,令人不觉。"

祖一日唤诸门人总来:"吾向汝说,世人生死事大,汝等终日只求福田,不求出离生死苦海。自性若迷,福

from and what I expected to get from him. I replied that I was a commoner from Sun-chow in Kwang-tung and had travelled far to pay my respects to him, and then said, "I ask for nothing but Buddhahood."

The Patriarch replied: "So you are a native of Kwang-tung, are you? You evidently belong to the aborigines; how can you expect to become a Buddha?"

I replied: "Although there are Northern men and Southern men, but North or South make no difference in their Buddha-nature. An aborigine is different from your Eminence physically, but there is no difference in our Buddha-nature."

He was going to speak further to me but the presence of other disciples made him hesitate and he told me to join the other laborers at their tasks.

"May I tell Your Eminence," I urged, "that Prajna (transcendental Wisdom) constantly rises in my mind. As one cannot go astray from his own nature one may be rightly called, 'a field of merit' (this is a title of honor given to monks as a monk affords the best of opportunities to others, 'to sow the seed of merit'). I do not know what work Your Eminence would ask me to do."

"This aborigine is very witty," he remarked, "Go to the work-rooms and say no more." I then withdrew to the rear where the work of the monastery was carried on and was told by a lay brother to split firewood and hull rice.

More than eight months after, the Patriarch met me one day and said, "I know that your knowledge of Buddhism is very sound, but I have to refrain from speaking with you lest evil men should harm you. Do you understand?" "Yes, Sir, I understand," I replied. "And I will not go near your hall, lest people take notice of me."

One day the Patriarch assembled all his disciples and said to them: "The question of incessant rebirth is a very momentous one, but instead of trying to free yourselves from that bitter sea of life and death, you men, day after day, seem to be going after tainted merits only. Merit will be of no help to you if your essence of mind

Chapter Four
Essential Sutras and Chan Teachings—Exploring the Heart of Buddhist Wisdom

is polluted and clouded. Go now and seek for the transcendental wisdom that is within your own minds and then write me a stanza about it. He who gets the clearest idea of what Mind-essence is will be given the insignia of the Patriarch; I will give him the secret teaching of the Dharma, and will appoint him to be the Sixth Patriarch. Go away quickly, now, and do not delay in writing the stanza; deliberation is quite unnecessary and will be of no use, The one who has realised Essence of Mind can testify to it at once as soon as he is spoken to about it. He cannot lose sight of it, even if he were engaged in a battle."

Having received this instruction, the disciples withdrew and said to one another, "There is no use of our making an effort to write a stanza and submit it to His Eminence; the Patriarchship is bound to go to Elder Shin-shau, our Master, anyway. Why go through the form of writing, it will only be a waste of energy." Hearing this they decided to write nothing, saying, "Why should we take the trouble to do it? Hereafter we will simply follow our Master Shin-shau wherever he goes and will look to him for guidance."

Shin-shau reasoned within himself, "Considering that I am their Master, none of them will take part in competition. I wonder whether I should write a stanza and submit it to His Eminence, or not. If I do not, how can the Patriarch know how deep or how superficial my knowledge is? If my object is to get the Dharma, my motive is pure. If it is to get the Patriarchship, then it is bad; my mind would be that of a worldling and my action would amount to a theft of the Patriarch's holy seat. But if I do not submit the stanza, I will lose my chance of getting the Dharma. It is very difficult to know what to do."

In front of the Patriarch's hall there were three corridors the walls of which were to be painted by a court artist named Lo-chun, with pictures suggested by the Lankavatara Sutra depicting the transfiguration of the assembly, and with scenes showing the genealogy of the five Patriarchs, for the information and veneration of the public. When Shin-shau had composed his stanza he made

何可救？汝等各去，自看智慧，取自本心般若之性，各作一偈，来呈吾看，若悟大意，付汝衣法，为第六代祖。火急速去，不得迟滞。思量即不中用，见性之人，言下须见。若如此者，轮刀上阵，亦得见之。"

众得处分，退而递相谓曰："我等众人，不须澄心用意作偈，将呈和尚，有何所益？神秀上座，现为教授师，必是他得；我辈谩作偈颂，枉用心力。"余人闻语，总皆息心，咸言："我等已后依止秀师，何烦作偈。"

神秀思惟：诸人不呈偈者，为我与他为教授师，我须作偈，将呈和尚。若不呈偈，和尚如何知我心中见解深浅。我呈偈意，求法即善，觅祖即恶，却同凡心夺其圣位奚别？若不呈偈，终不待法。大难大难。

五祖堂前，有步廊三间，拟请供奉卢珍画《楞伽经变相》及《五祖血脉图》，流传供养。神秀作偈成已，数度欲呈，行至堂前，心中恍惚，遍身汗流，拟呈不得。前后经四日,一十三度,呈偈不得。

秀乃思惟:不如向廊下书著,从他和尚看见,忽若道好,即出礼拜,云是秀作。若道不堪,枉向山中数年,受人礼拜,更修何道?"

是夜三更,不使人知,自执灯,书偈于南廊壁间,呈心所见。偈曰:

身是菩提树,心如明镜台。
时时勤拂拭,勿使惹尘埃。

秀书偈了,便却归房,人总不知。秀复思惟:五祖明日见偈欢喜,即我与法有缘,若言不堪,自是我迷,宿业障重,不合得法,圣意难测。房中思想,坐卧不安,直至五更。

祖已知神秀入门未得,不见自性。天明,祖唤卢供奉来,向南廊壁间绘画图相,忽见其偈。报言:"供奉却不用画,劳尔远来。经云:凡所有相,皆是虚妄。但留此偈,与人诵持。依此偈修,免堕恶道。依此偈修,有大

several attempts to submit it, but his mind was so perturbed that he was prevented from doing it.

Then he suggested to himself, "It would be better for me to write it on the wall of the corridor and let the Patriarch find it himself, If he approves it, then I will go to pay him homage and tell him that it was done by me; but if he disapproves it,—well, then I have wasted several years' time in this mountain receiving homage which I did not deserve, If I fail, what progress have I made in learning Buddhism?"

At midnight of that night, he went secretly to write his stanza on the wall of the south corridor, so that the Patriarch might know to what spiritual insight he had attained. The stanza read:—

"Our body may be compared to the Bodhi-tree;
While our mind is a mirror bright.
Carefully we cleanse and watch them hour by hour,
And let no dust collect upon them."

As soon as he had written it, he returned at once to his room, so no one knew what he had done. In the quiet of his room he pondered: "When the Patriarch sees my stanza tomorrow, if he is pleased with it, it will show that I am (spiritually) ready for the Dharma; but if he disapproves of it, then it will mean that I am unfit for the Dharma owing to misdeeds in previous lives and karmic accumulations that so thickly becloud my mind. What will the Patriarch say about it? How difficult it is to speculate." He could neither sleep nor sit at ease; and so in this vein he kept on thinking until dawn.

In the morning the Patriarch sent for Lo, the court artist, to have the walls painted with pictures and went with him to the south corridor. The Patriarch noticed the stanza and said to the artist, "I am sorry to have troubled you to come so far, but the walls do not need to be painted now. The Sutra says, 'All forms and phenomena are transient and illusive'; we will leave the stanza here so that people may study the stanza and recite it. If they put its teachings into actual practice, they will be saved from the misery of being

Chapter Four
Essential Sutras and Chan Teachings—Exploring the Heart of Buddhist Wisdom

born in evil realms of existence. Any one who practices it will gain great merit." The Patriarch ordered incense to be burnt before it, and instructed all his disciples to pay homage to it and recite it, so that they might realise Essence of Mind.

After his disciples had recited it, they all exclaimed, "Well done!"

That midnight the Patriarch sent for Shin-shau and asked if he had written the stanza. Shin-shau admitted that he had written it and then added: "I am not so vain as to expect to get the Patriarchship, but I wish Your Eminence would kindly tell me whether my stanza shows the least grain of wisdom."

"To attain supreme enlightenment," replied the Patriarch, "one must be able to know spontaneously one's own self-nature which is neither created nor can it be annihilated. From one momentary sensation to another, one should always be able to realise Essence of Mind; then all conceptions of the mind will be free of any graspings by the mind. As one thing is being realized as to its reality, so the mind will reflect all circumstances and conditions as being a state of naturalness. This means that the mind in its pure state is truthful. For if the mind is able to see things truthfully in their pure state it sees them to be the same as its own essential nature of Supreme Enlightenment. You had better return now and think it over for a couple of days and then submit another stanza. In case the new stanza shows that you have entered 'the door of enlightenment,' I will transmit to you the robe and the Dharma."

Shin-shau made obeisance to the Patriarch and went away. For several days he tried in vain to write another stanza, which upset his mind so much that he was as ill at ease as though he was in a nightmare; he could find comfort neither in sitting nor walking.

Two days after, it happened that a boy who was passing by the room where l was hulling rice, was loudly reciting the stanza written by Shin-shau. As soon as I heard it I knew at once that its composer had not yet realised Essence of Mind. Although at that time I never had had instruction about it, I already had a general idea of it. "What stanza is this," I asked the boy.

利益。"令门人炷香礼敬，尽诵此偈，即得见性。

门人诵偈，皆叹善哉。

祖三更唤秀入堂，问曰："偈是汝作否？"

秀言："实是秀作，不敢妄求祖位。望和尚慈悲，看弟子有少智慧否？"

祖曰："汝作此偈，未见本性，只到门外，未入门内。如此见解，觅无上菩提，了不可得。无上菩提，须得言下识自本心，见自本性。不生不灭，於一切时中，念念自见，万法无滞，一真一切真，万境自如如。如如之心，即是真实。若如是见，即是无上菩提之自性也。汝且去一两日思惟，更作一偈，将来吾看汝偈，若入得门，付汝衣法。"

神秀作礼而出。又经数日，作偈不成，心中恍惚，神思不安，犹如梦中，行坐不乐。

复两日，有一童子，于碓坊过，唱诵其偈。惠能一闻，便知此偈未见本性。虽未蒙教授，早识大意。遂问童子曰："诵者何偈？"

童子曰："尔这獦獠不知。大师言：'世人生死事大。'欲得传付衣法，令门人作偈来看。若悟大意，即付衣法，为第六祖。神秀上座，于南廊壁上，书无相偈，大师令人皆诵，依此偈修，免堕恶道。依此偈修，有大利益。"

惠能曰："我亦要诵此，结来生缘。上人，我此踏碓，八个余月，未曾行到堂前，望上人引至偈前礼拜。"

童子引至偈前礼拜。惠能曰："惠能不识字，请上人为读。"

时有江州别驾，姓张，名日用，便高声读。惠能闻已，遂言："亦有一偈，望别驾为书。"

别驾言："汝亦作偈，其事希有。"

惠能向别驾言："欲学无上菩提，不得轻于初学。下下人有上上智，上上人有没意智。若轻人，即有无量无边罪。"

别驾言："汝但诵偈，吾为汝书。汝若得法，先须度吾，勿忘此言。"

惠能偈曰：
菩提本无树，明镜亦非台。
本来无一物，何处惹尘埃。

书此偈已，徒众总惊，无不嗟讶，各相谓言："奇哉，不得以貌取人，何得多时使他肉身菩萨。"①

"You aborigine," he said, "don't you know about it? The Patriarch told his disciples that the question of rebirth was a momentous one, and those who wished to inherit his robe and the Dharma should write him a stanza and the one who had the true idea of Mind-essence would get them and become the Sixth Patriarch. Elder Shin-shau wrote this 'formless' stanza on the wall of the south corridor and the Patriarch told us to recite it. He also said that those who put its teachings into actual practice would attain great merit and be saved from being born in the evil realms of existence."

I told the boy that I wished to learn the stanza also, so that I might have the benefit of it in future life. Although I had been hulling rice for eight months, l had never been to the hall, so l asked the boy to show me where the stanza was written, so that I might make obeisance to it.

The boy took me there and as I was illiterate, I asked him to read it to me. A petty officer of the Kong-chow District, named Chang Fat-yung, who happened to be there, then read it clearly. When he had finished reading, I told him that I also, had composed a stanza and asked him to write it for me. "Extraordinary," he exclaimed, "that you, also, can compose a stanza."

"If you are a seeker of supreme enlightenment, you will not despise a beginner," I said.

"Please recite your stanza," said he, "l will write it down for you, but if you should succeed in getting the Dharma, do not forget to deliver me."

My stanza read as follows:

By no means is Bodhi a kind of tree,
Nor is the bright reflecting mind, a case of mirrors.
Since mind is emptiness,
Where can dust collect?

---

① 此处有部分文字并未在英文中译出。为确保中英文基本对应，故此处未译出文字用斜体表示。

Chapter Four
Essential Sutras and Chan Teachings—Exploring the Heart of Buddhist Wisdom

Later on, seeing that a crowd was collecting, the Patriarch came out and erased the stanza with his shoe lest jealous ones should do me injury. Judging by this, the crowd took it for granted that the author of it had also not yet realised Mind-essence.

Next day the Patriarch came secretly to the room where the rice was being hulled and seeing me at work with the stone pestle, said, "A seeker of the Path risks his life for the Dharma. Should he do so?"

Then he asked, "Is the rice ready?" "Ready long ago," I replied, "only waiting for the sieve." He knocked the mortar thrice with his stick and went away.

Knowing what his signal meant, in the third watch of the night, I went to his room.

Using his robe as a screen so that no one would see us, he expounded the Diamond Sutra to me. When he came to the sentence, "One should use one's mind in such a way that it will be free from any attachment," I suddenly became thoroughly enlightened and realised that all things in the universe are Mind-essence itself.

I said to the Patriarch, "Who could have conceived that Mind-essence is intrinsically pure! Who could have conceived that Mind-essence is intrinsically free from becoming and annihilation! That Mind-essence is intrinsically self-sufficient, and free from change! Who could have conceived that all things are manifestations of Mind-essence!"

Thus at midnight, to the knowledge of no one, was the Dharma transmitted to me, and I consequently became the inheritor of the teachings of the "Sudden" School, and the possessor of the robe and the begging-bowl.

"You are now the Sixth Patriarch," said His Eminence. "Take good care of yourself and deliver as many sentient beings as possible. Spread the teaching; keep the teaching alive; do not let it come to an end. Listen to my stanza:

祖见众人惊怪，恐人损害，遂将鞋擦了偈，曰："亦未见性。"众以为然。

次日祖潜至碓坊，见能腰石舂米，语曰："求道之人，为法忘躯，当如是乎！"

乃问曰："米熟也未？"
惠能曰："米熟久矣，犹欠筛在。"

祖以杖击碓三下而去。惠能即会祖意。三鼓入室。

祖以袈裟遮围，不令人见。为说《金刚经》，至"应无所住而生其心"，惠能言下大悟"一切万法不离自性"。遂启祖言："何期自性，本自清净；何期自性，本不生灭；何期自性，本自具足；何期自性，本无动摇；何期自性，能生万法。"

祖知悟本性，谓惠能曰：*"不识本心，学法无益。若识自本心，见自本性，即名丈夫、天人师、佛。"*[①]

三更受法，人尽不知，便传顿教及衣钵。云："汝为第六代祖，善自护念，广度有情，流布将来，无令断绝。听吾偈。"曰：

---

① 此处有部分文字并未在英文中译出。为确保中英文基本对应，故此处未译出文字用斜体表示。

有情来下种，因地果还生，
无情既无种，无性亦无生。

祖复曰："昔达磨大师，初来此土，人未之信，故传此衣，以为信体，代代相承。法则以心传心，皆令自悟自解。自古佛佛惟传本体，师师密付本心。衣为争端，止汝勿传，若传此衣，命如悬丝，汝须速去，恐人害汝。"

惠能启曰："向甚处去？"
祖云："逢怀则止，遇会则藏。"
惠能三更领得衣钵，云："能本是南中人，素不知此山路，如何出得江口？"
五祖言："汝不须忧，吾自送汝。"
祖相送直至九江驿。祖令上船，五祖把橹自摇。惠能言："请和尚坐，弟子合摇橹。"祖云："合是吾渡汝。"
惠能云："迷时师度，悟了自度，度名虽一，用处不同。惠能生在边方，语音不正，蒙师传法，今已得悟，只合自性自度。"祖云："如是如是。以后佛法，由汝大行，

'Sentient beings who sow seed of Enlightenment
In the field of causation, will reap the fruit of Buddhahood.
Inanimate objects which are void of Buddha-nature
Sow not and reap not.'"

His Eminence further said: "When Patriarch Bodhidharma first came to China, few Chinese had confidence in him and so this robe has been handed down as a testimony from one Patriarch to another. As to the Dharma, as a rule it is transmitted from heart to heart and the recipient is expected to understand it and to realise it by his own efforts. From time immemorial, it has been the practice for one Buddha to pass on to his successor the quintessence of the Dharma, and for one Patriarch to transmit to another, from mind to mind, the esoteric teaching. As the robe may give cause for dispute, you will be the last one to inherit it. If you should again hand it down to a successor, your life would be in imminent danger. You must now leave this place as quickly as you can, lest some one should harm you."

I asked him, "Where shall I go?" and he replied, "Stop at Wei and seclude yourself at Wui."

As it was the middle of the night when I thus received the begging-bowl and the robe, I told the Patriarch that as I was a Southerner I did not know the mountain trails and it would be impossible for me to get down to the river. "You need not worry," he replied, "I will go with you." He then accompanied me to the Kiu-kiang landing where we got a boat. As he started to do the rowing himself, I asked him to be seated and let me handle the oar. He replied, "It is only right for me to get you across" (This is an illusion to the sea of birth and death which one has to cross before the shore of Nirvana can be reached.)

To this I replied,"(So long as I was) under illusion, I was dependent on you to get me across, but now it is different. It was my fortune to be born on the frontier and my education is very deficient, but I have had the honor to inherit the Dharma from you; since I am now enlightened, it is only right for me to cross the sea of birth and death by my own effort to realise my own Essence of

Chapter Four
Essential Sutras and Chan Teachings—Exploring the Heart of Buddhist Wisdom

Mind."

"Quite so, quite so," he agreed. "Beginning with you (Ch'an) Buddhism will become very widespread. Three years from your leaving me I shall pass from this world. You may start on your journey now; go as fast as you can toward the South. Do not begin preaching too soon; (Ch'an) Buddhism is not to be easily spread."

After saying good-bye, I left him and walked toward the South. In about two months I reached the Tai-yu Mountain where I noticed several hundred men were in pursuit of me with the intention of recovering the robe and begging-bowl. Among them, the most vigilant was a monk of the name of Wei-ming whose surname was Chen. In lay-life he had been a general of the fourth rank. His manner was rough and his temper hot. When he overtook me, I threw the robe and the begging-bowl on a rock, saying, "This robe is nothing but a testimonial; what is the use of taking it away by force?" When he reached the rock, he tried to pick them up but could not. Then in astonishment he shouted, "Lay Brother, Lay Brother, (Hui-neng, although appointed the Sixth Patriarch, had not yet formally been admitted to the Order), I have come for the Dharma; I do not care for the robe." Whereupon I came from my hiding place and took the position on the rock of a Patriarch. He made obeisance and said, "Lay Brother, l beg you to teach me."

Since the object of your coming is for the Dharma," said I, "please refrain from thinking about anything and try to keep your mind perfectly empty and receptive. I will then teach you." When he had done this for a considerable time, l said, "Venerable Sir, at the particular moment when you are thinking of neither good nor evil, what is your real self-nature (the word is, physiognomy)?"

As soon as he heard this he at once became enlightened, but he asked, "Apart from these sayings and ideas handed down by the Patriarchs from generation to generation, are there still any esoteric teachings?"

"What I can tell you is not esoteric," I replied, "If you turn your light inward, you will find what is esoteric within your own mind."

汝去三年，吾方逝世。汝今好去，努力向南，不宜速说，佛法难起。"

惠能辞违祖已，发足南行。两月中间，至大庾岭，逐后数百人来，欲夺衣钵。

一僧俗姓陈，名惠明。先是四品将军，性行粗糙，极意参寻，为众人先，趋及惠能。惠能掷下衣钵于石上，曰："此衣表信，可力争耶。"

能隐草莽中，惠明至，提掇不动。乃唤云："行者行者，我为法来，不为衣来！"

惠能遂出，盘坐石上。惠明作礼云："望行者为我说法。"惠能云："汝既为法而来，可屏息诸缘，勿生一念，吾为汝说。"

明良久。惠能云："不思善，不思恶，正与么时，那个是明上座本来面目。"

惠明言下大悟。复问云："上来密语密意外，还更有密意否？"

惠能云："与汝说者，即非密也。汝若反照，密在汝边。"

明曰:"惠明虽在黄梅,实未省自己面目。今蒙指示,如人饮水,冷暖自知。今行者即惠明师也。"

惠能曰:"汝若如是,吾与汝同师黄梅。善自护持。"

明又问:"惠明今后向甚处去?"

惠能曰:"逢袁则止,遇蒙则居。"

明礼辞。

惠能后至曹溪,又被恶人寻逐。乃于四会,避难猎人队中,凡经一十五载。时与猎人随宜说法。猎人常令守网,每见生命,尽放之。每至饭时,以菜寄煮肉锅。或问,则对曰:但吃肉边菜。

一日思惟:时当弘法,不可终遁。遂出至广州法性寺,值印宗法师讲《涅槃经》。时有风吹幡动,一僧曰风动,一僧曰幡动,议论不已。

惠能进曰:"不是风动,不是幡动,仁者心动。"

一众骇然。印宗延至上席,征诘奥义。见惠能言简理当,不由文字。宗云:"行者定非常人。久闻黄梅衣法南来,莫是行者否?"

惠能曰:"不敢。"

宗于是作礼,告请传来衣钵,出示大众。宗复问曰:

"In spite of my stay in Wong-mui," said he, "I did not realise my own self-nature. Now, thanks to your guidance, I realise it in the same way a water-drinker knows how hot and how cold the water is. Lay Brother, I am now your disciple." I replied, "If this is the case, then you and I are fellow disciples of the Fifth Patriarch. Please take good care of yourself." He paid homage and departed.

Some time after I reached Tso-kai, but as evil-doers were again persecuting me, I took refuge in Sze-wui where l staid with a party of hunters for fifteen years. They used to put me to watch their nets, but when I found living creatures entangled in them I would set them free. At meal time l would put vegetables in the same pan in which they cooked their meat. Some of them questioned me and l explained to them that I could only eat vegetables. Occasionally I talked to them in a way that befitted their understanding. One day I bethought myself that I ought not to pass so secluded a life all the time; I felt that the time had come for me to propagate the Dharma. Accordingly I left there and went to the Fatshin Temple in Canton.

At the time I reached that temple, the monk Yen-chung, Master of Dharma, was lecturing on the Maha Parinirvana Sutra. It happened one day when a pennant was being blown about by the wind, that two monks entered into a dispute as to what was in motion, the wind or the pennant. As they failed to settle their difference, I suggested that it was neither; that what actually moved was their own mind. The whole group was surprised by what I said and the Master Yen-chung invited me to a seat of honor and questioned me about various knotty points in the Sutra. Seeing that my answers were precise and accurate, that they inferred more than book knowledge, he said to me, "Lay Brother, you must be an extraordinary man. I was told long ago that the inheritor of the Fifth Patriarch's robe and Dharma had come to the South; very likely you are the man?"

To this l politely assented. He made obeisance and courteously asked me to show to the assembly the robe and begging-bowl which I had inherited, He further asked what instructions I had

Chapter Four
Essential Sutras and Chan Teachings—Exploring the Heart of Buddhist Wisdom

received at the time the Fifth Patriarch had transmitted the Dharma to me.

I replied, "Apart from a discussion on the realisation of Mind-essence, he gave me no other instruction, He did not refer to Dhyana nor to Emancipation." The Master asked, "Why not?" I replied, "Because that would mean two kinds of Dharmas. That is not the Buddha Dharma, for the Buddha Dharma is not dual in its nature, He then asked, "What is the Buddha Dharma that is not dual in its nature?"

I replied, "The Maha Parinirvana Sutra which you are expounding teaches that Buddha-nature is the only way. For example: in that Sutra King-ko-kwai-tak, a Bodhisattva, asked the Buddha whether those who commit the four serious sins, or the five deadly sins, or are heretics, etc., would thereby root out their 'element of goodness' and their Buddha-nature. Buddha replied, 'There are two kinds of 'goodness-elements': an eternal element, and a non-eternal. Since Buddha-nature is neither eternal nor non-eternal, therefore, the Buddha's essential nature is not to be regarded as 'eradicated,' it is to be regarded as already, 'non-duality'. There are good natures and evil natures but Buddha's essential nature belongs to neither; it is non-dual. From the point of view and prejudices of ordinary people, there is a difference between the physical sense-ingredients and the mental and conscious ingredients, but enlightened men know that they are not dual in nature. It is that nature of non-duality that is Buddha-nature."

Master Yen-chung was pleased with my answer. Putting his hands together in token of respect, he said, "My interpretation of the Sutra is as worthless as a heap of debris, while your discourse is as valuable as pure gold." Subsequently he conducted a ceremony of initiation, receiving me into the order, and then asked me to accept him as a pupil.

Thenceforth under the Bodhi-tree I have discoursed about the teachings of the Fourth and Fifth Patriarchs. Since the Dharma was transmitted to me in Tung Mountain, I have gone through

"黄梅付嘱，如何指授？"

惠能曰："指授即无，惟论见性，不论禅定解脱。"

宗曰："何不论禅定解脱？"

谓曰："为是二法，不是佛法。佛法是不二之法。"

宗又问："如何是佛法不二之法？"

惠能曰："法师讲《涅槃经》，明佛性是佛法不二之法。如高贵德王菩萨白佛言：'犯四重禁，作五逆罪，及一阐提等，当断善根佛性否？'佛言：'善根有二：一者常，二者无常。'佛性非常非无常，是故不断，名为不二；一者善，二者不善，佛性非善非不善，是名不二。蕴之与界，凡夫见二，智者了达其性无二，无二之性即是佛性。"

印宗闻说，欢喜合掌，言："某甲讲经，犹如瓦砾；仁者论义，犹如真金。"于是为惠能剃发，愿事为师。惠能遂于菩提树下，开东山法门：

"惠能于东山得法，辛苦受尽，命似悬丝。今日得与使君、官僚、僧尼、道俗同此一会，莫非累劫之缘，亦是过去生中供养诸佛，同种善根，方始得闻如上顿教、得法之因。教是先圣所传，不是惠能自智。愿闻先圣教者，各令净心，闻了各自除疑，如先代圣人无别。"

一众闻法，欢喜作礼而退。

many hardships and often my life seemed to be hanging by a thread. Today I have had the honor of meeting Your Highness, and you, officials, monks and nuns, Taoists and lay-men, in this great assembly. I must ascribe this good fortune to our happy connection in previous kalpas, as well as to our common accumulated merits in making offerings to various Buddhas in our past incarnations. Otherwise we would have had no chance of hearing the teachings of the "Sudden" School of Ch'an and thereby laying the foundation of our present success in understanding the Dharma.

This teaching is not a system of my own invention, but has been handed down by the Patriarchs. Those who wish to hear the teaching should first purify their own minds; and after hearing it, each must clear up his own doubts, even as the Sages have done in the past.

At the end of the address, the assembly felt rejoiced, made obeisance and departed.

Extensive Readings

A. Historical Background of the *Heart Sutra*[①]
《心经》的历史背景

Red Pine
赤松

The *Heart Sutra* hardly fills a page, and yet it is the best known of the thousands of scriptures in the Buddhist Canon. Its fame, though, is relatively recent in terms of Buddhist history and didn't begin until a thousand years after the Buddha's Nirvana. During the chaos that occurred in China between the collapse of the Sui (581–618) and the rise of the T'ang Dynasty (618–907), many people fled the country's twin capitals of Loyang and Ch'ang-an, and sought refuge in the southwest province of Szechuan. Among the refugees was a Buddhist novice still in his teens. One day this novice befriended a man who was impoverished and ill, and the man, in turn, taught him the words of the *Heart Sutra*. Not long afterward, the novice was ordained

---

① Excerpted from *The Heart Sutra*, translated by Red Pine, Shoemaker & Hoard, 2004.

Chapter Four
Essential Sutras and Chan Teachings—Exploring the Heart of Buddhist Wisdom

a monk, and several years later, in 629, he embarked on one of the great journeys of Chinese history.

The young monk's name was Hsuan-tsang, and he set out on the Silk Road for India in search of answers to questions concerning the Buddha's teaching that this world is nothing but mind. In the course of his journey, Hsuan-tsang is said to have traveled 10,000 miles — west across the Taklamakan Desert to Samarkand, south over the Hindu Kush to the Buddhist center of Taxila, and down the Ganges into India and back again. And time and again, he turned to the *Heart Sutra* to ward off demons, dust storms, and bandits. When he finally returned to China in 645, he was welcomed back by the emperor, and stories about the power of the *Heart Sutra* began making the rounds.

This account about how Hsuan-tsang first encountered the sutra was recorded by Hui-li (慧立) (b. 614) in his biography of Hsuan-tsang written in 688. Several decades later, the Tantric master Amoghavajra (不空) (705–774) embellished this earlier account in a preface to the *Heart Sutra* preserved on a manuscript found at Tunhuang in Northwest China. This manuscript (S2464) had been sealed in a cave shrine with thousands of other Buddhist, Taoist, and Zoroastrian scriptures in the eleventh century, and was rediscovered 900 years later in the early twentieth century. Although Amoghavajra's version was clearly fanciful and historically inaccurate, it became the seed from which sprang the series of stories about Hsuan-tsang that eventually resulted in the Ming Dynasty novel *Journey to the West*. Hsuan-tsang also produced his own translation of the *Heart Sutra* in 649, and it wasn't long afterward that the first commentaries began appearing, as his fellow monks realized that not only was this a scripture of great power, but its summary of Buddhist teaching provided the perfect platform from which to offer their own interpretations of the Dharma.

Since then, the *Heart Sutra* has become the most popular of all Buddhist scriptures, arid yet no one knows where it came from or who was responsible for its composition. Its earliest recorded appearance was in the form of a Chinese translation made by a Central Asian monk sometime between A.D. 200 and 250. The monk's name was Chih-ch'ien (支谦), and he was a disciple of Chih-liang (支亮), who was a disciple of Chih-lou-chia-ch'an (支娄伽谶) (Lokakshema). Th *Chih* (支) at the beginning of these monks' names indicated that they were not Chinese, but Yueh-chih (月支人). During the second century B.C., one branch of this nomadic tribe migrated westward from their ancestral home along China's northwest border and settled in the upper reaches of the Oxus River (Amu Darya). In the following century, they spread south across the Hindu Kush, and by A.D. 150 they controlled a territory that included all of Tajikistan, Afghanistan, Pakistan, and most of Northern India, as well as parts of Uzbekistan and Kyrgyzstan. Since their territory straddled both sides of the Hindu Kush, it was known as the

Kushan Empire, and it was one of the great empires of the ancient world.

In their conquest of this region, the Yueh-chih made use of a network of roads first created by the Mauryan Empire (321–181B.C.) of Candragupta and Ashoka and expanded by a series of short-lived dynasties ruled by Bactrian Greeks, Scythians, and Parthians. This network also served the purpose of administrative control and provided the revenue from merchants and guilds that financed the Kushan state. The same guilds and merchants also supported hundreds, if not thousands, of Buddhist monasteries along the same network of roads and towns, and Buddhism flourished under the Kushans. King Kanishka (fl. A.D. 100–125) even put the images of Shakyamuni and Maitreya Buddha on his coins.

Although Buddhist monks began arriving in China as early as the first century B.C., it wasn't until the height of the Kushan Empire, or around A.D. 150, that they began translating the texts they brought with them or that others brought to China on their behalf. The Yueh-chih monk Chih-lou-chia-ch'an is said to have begun working in the Han Dynasty capital of Loyang around this time on some of the earliest known scriptures of Mahayana Buddhism, including the *Perfection of Wisdom in Eight Thousand Lines* (《八千颂般若波罗蜜多经》). Between A.D. 200 and 250, his disciple's disciple, Chih-ch'ien, also translated a number of Mahayana scriptures, including the first translations of the *Vimalakirti Sutra* (维摩诘经) and the *Longer Sukhavativyuha Sutra* (《无量寿经》) of Pure Land Buddhism, as well as a second rendition of the *Perfection of Wisdom in Eight Thousand Lines* and the first translation of the *Heart Sutra*, which he titled the *Prajnaparamita Dharani*.

In his *Maha Prajnaparamita Shastra*《大智度论》, written at the end of the second century A.D., Nagarjuna (龙树) says the ideas and inspiration of such early Mahayana scriptures, if not the scriptures themselves, originated in Southern India and later spread west and then north. Most of Northern India was controlled by the Kushans during this period, and such teachings and scriptures would have moved easily along the trade routes under their control through what are now Pakistan and Afghanistan, then north through Uzbekistan, and finally east along the major arteries of the Silk Road to China.

Although the teachings that make up the Prajnaparamita are thought to have originated in Southern India in the first or second century B.C., the *Heart Sutra* was most likely composed during the first century A.D. further north, in the territories under the control of the Kushans: if not in Bactria (Afghanistan) or Gandhara (Pakistan) then perhaps in Sogdia (Uzbekistan) or Mathura (India's Uttar Pradesh).

Not long after Ashoka inherited the Mauryan throne in 268 B.C., he sent Sarvastivadin (说一切有部) missionaries to Gandhara. Ashoka had been governor of Gandhara during the reign of his grandfather, Candragupta, and his decision to send Sarvastivadin monks there was a sign of favor.

Chapter Four
Essential Sutras and Chan Teachings—Exploring the Heart of Buddhist Wisdom

The cities in this part of India were at the center of a network of transcontinental trade routes and among the richest in the subcontinent. Thus, it is not surprising that the Sarvastivadins soon became the dominant Buddhist sect in this region. Over the course of the next several centuries, preferential patronage by merchants and the ruling elite extended their dominance beyond Gandhara to Bactria, Sogdia, and Mathura—basically the boundaries of the Kushan Empire. And since the *Heart Sutra* was clearly organized as a response to the teachings of the Sarvastivadins, it was probably a Sarvastivadin monk (or former Sarvastivadin monk) in this region who composed the *Heart Sutra* upon realizing the limitations of the Sarvastivadin Abhidharma. This was Edward Conze's conclusion concerning other Prajnaparamita texts, and most likely it was also the case with the *Heart Sutra*.

As noted above, the *Heart Sutra*'s earliest appearance was in the form of a Chinese translation made by Chih-ch'ien sometime between A.D. 200 and 250. This was followed by a second version by Kumarajiva (鸠摩罗什) around A.D. 400. In his translations, Kumarajiva often incorporated whole sections of Chih-ch'ien's earlier work, and he may have done so on this occasion as well. We'll probably never know. Chih-ch'ien's translation was listed as missing as early as A.D. 519. Hence, it must have been Kumarajiva's version that Hsuan-tsang first learned to chant as a young novice. Later, after returning from India, he produced his own translation of the *Heart Sutra*. But except for making a few character changes peculiar to him and deleting a few phrases negating the Sarvastivadin conception of time, Hsuan-tsang followed Kumarajiva's translation word for word, which is what we would expect of a text whose spiritual efficacy Hsuan-tsang had witnessed firsthand and whose wording he was, no doubt, reluctant to alter.

……

In the years that followed the appearance of Hsuan-tsang's *Heart Sutra*, this text continued to attract the attention of translators. Fang K'uang-ch'ang (方广錩) lists twenty-one different versions in Chinese. Although the translations of Chih-ch'ien (c. 250), Bodhiruchi (菩提流志) (693), and Shikshananda (实叉难陀) (c. 700) have disappeared, those that have survived include one made around 735 by Fa-yueh (法月). His was the first translation of a longer version of the sutra that included an introduction and a conclusion. This longer version, however, was clearly an attempt to give the text the stature of a standard sutra, and few Buddhists or Buddhologists have accepted it as the sutra's original form. …

Not only has the *Heart Sutra* attracted the interest of translators, it has also been the subject of numerous commentaries. In Chinese alone, over one hundred are recorded prior to modern times, and of these more than eighty still exist. As the *Heart Sutra* was not well-known prior to Hsuan-tsang's translation of 649, no commentaries are recorded during the first four hundred years of its existence in China—though we do have a Chinese translation of one attributed to

Deva, who lived in India in the third century. Also, no commentaries prior to the eighth century have survived in Sanskrit or Tibetan. …

B. The Logic of the *Diamond Sutra*: A is not A, therefore it is A[①]
《金刚经》的逻辑：A则非A

Shigenori Nagatomo
长友繁法

I. Introduction

An early phase of Mahayana Buddhism witnessed the development of a genre of literature that Buddhologists call *prajnpramita*, which is translated in English as the "perfection of wisdom." To this genre of literature belongs a treatise that is named the *Diamond Sutra*. (Hereafter, it will be abbreviated as the *Sutra*) This paper attempts to render intelligible the logic that is used in this *Sutra* in which a seemingly contradictory assertion is made to articulate the Buddhist understanding of (human) reality. The renowned Japanese Buddhologist, Hajime Nakamura, calls it a "logic of not." The "logic of not" can be stated in propositional form as: "A is not A, therefore it is A." When this is read and interpreted in light of Aristotelean logic, the linguistic formulation of this logic is outright contradictory, and one may therefore dismiss it as nonsensical. As I think such a pronouncement is based on an un-informed and misguided judgement when it is assessed in light of Mahayana Buddhism in general, and the *Diamond Sutra* in particular, I should like to elucidate its significance by clarifying the philosophical reasoning that informs the formulation of the "logic of not." In order to do so, I will develop in this paper the position that it remains contradictory only as long as one understands the "logic of not" in light of Aristotelean logic, which assumes a dualistic, either-or egological stance, but to understand it properly, I shall argue that one must read it by effecting a perspectival shift to a non-dualistic, non-egological stance. Only then can one see that it is not contradictory, and hence that it is not nonsensical.

In order to show unequivocally that the "logic of not" does indeed appear to be contradictory, or if not that, paradoxical, it is best to cite some of the representative examples from the *Sutra*. To this end, note the following examples of the "logic of not."

(1) "The world is not the world, therefore it is the world" (section 13-c).

(2) "All *dharmas* are not all *dharmas*, therefore they are all *dharmas*" (section 17-c).

---

① Excerpted from Shigenori Nagatomo, "The Logic of the *Diamond Sutra*: A is not A, therefore it is A", *Asian Philosophy*, Vol. 10, No. 3, 2000, pp.213-244.

(3) "The perfection of wisdom [*prajnaparamita*] is not the perfection of wisdom, therefore it is the perfection of wisdom" (section 13-a).

(4) "A thought of truth [*bhutasamjna*] is not a thought of truth, therefore it is the thought of truth" (section 14-a).

Although these instances obviously do not exhaust all the occurrences of the "logic of not" in the *Sutra*, it is clear that the "logic of not" uses the form "A is not A, therefore it is A," where A stands for a linguistic sign, such as "the world," "all *dharmas*," "the perfection of wisdom," and "a thought of truth," mentioned in the above sample sentences. Each of these terms can be systematically placed into this propositional form to formalise the logic as: "A is not A, therefore it is A." ...

II. The Goal of the *Diamond Sutra*

As preparatory to making the "logic of not" intelligible, it will be helpful to have in our purview the original meaning of the sutra's Sanskrit title *Vajraccedhikapraitaparamita*...the first components *vajraccedhika* means to "cut like a diamond" or to "sunder like a thunderbolt" where "diamond" or "thunderbolt" is used metaphorically to designate the power of severing all doubts and attachments from the cognitive activity of the human being...

The second component of the title, *prajnaparamita*, as mentioned at the beginning, designates the "perfection of wisdom," where wisdom (*prajna*) operates in the form of knowledge that is non-discriminatory in nature. ... In light of the practical nature of "severing all doubts and attachments," the perfection of wisdom is an existential project aiming at achieving and embodying a non-discriminatory basis for knowledge. ...

III. The Conceptual Scheme of the Sutra: the Bodhisattva

With this understanding of the goal of the *Sutra* in mind, I will examine some of the fundamental characteristics which the *Sutra* gives to the person of the *bodhisattva*, while drawing philosophical implications from them, insofar as they are pertinent to rendering the "logic of not" intelligible. In so doing, the conceptual scheme of the *Sutra* will become evident. ...

In order to qualify as a *bodhisattva*, then, the *Sutra* maintains that one should not seize on the thoughts of a self (*atman*), a living being (*sattva-samjna*), an individual soul (*jiva-samjna),* or a person *(pudgala-samjna*), where "should not" carries a sense of negating the "foolish" thoughts that are ascribed to the "foolish, ordinary people" as their characteristic, thereby moving away from foolishness toward the perfection of wisdom. ... What distinguishes the *bodhisattva* from the "foolish, ordinary people" in regard to their conceptual schemes is whether or not there is "seizing" or "attachment" in the act-aspect of the cognition.

Now with these observations in mind, we will see a further qualification given to the idea of the *bodhisattva*, this time regarding the object of both sensory perception and mind. ... To qualify as a *bodhisattva* in search of the supreme, right and equal enlightenment, the *Sutra* stipulates in this passage that the *bodhisattva* must not dwell on material objects, objects of external sensory perception, or objects of mind. …

…the *Sutra* introduces the most comprehensive category of Buddhism, *dharma*, to subsume the idea of a self, a being, etc., and states that the ideas such as the objects of external sensory perception and the objects of mind arise in virtue of "having a thought of either *dharma* or no-*dharma*." …

To give the general, philosophical point of this passage, then, the act of "seizing on (or attaching to) either a *dharma* or a no-*dharma*" creates a one-sided attitude. For example, if a *bodhisattva* seizes on a *dharma*, it leads to the postulation of a metaphysical substance, i.e. the creation of substance ontology, when *dharma* is metaphysicalised. …On the other hand, if the *bodhisattva* seizes on a no-*dharma*, it leads to nihilism. Both of these positions are entailed by the egological act of "seizing" intrinsic to the epistemological stance of the everyday standpoint. …

When we examine the linguistic aspect that accompanies the egological constitution of the object, it entails the following consequences. Seizing on (or attaching to) either a *dharma* or a *no-dharma* translates into accepting a dichotomy of either affirmation or negation as the standard for making a judgment, which presupposes either-or logic as its *modus operandi*. Here, the either-or attitude is a logical stance that *prioritises* one over the other by dichotomising the whole, usually saving the explicit at the expense of the implicit, hence resulting in the one-sidedness of "seizing on either *dharma* or no-*dharma*." As such, it favours an imbalanced attitude that is invested by ego interest and desire. In this context, we have a clearer understanding of the term "*egological* constitution" wherein the "logical" designates the either-or logic operative in the constitution of an object when making judgements or when discerning an object. Once it is accepted as the standard of thinking, it is easy to create various kinds of dualisms. The use of the terminology, "dualistic, egological" is thus justified in such dualisms as mind *vs* body (matter), good *vs* evil, along with a host of others, for dualism of any kind is seamlessly interwoven with the epistemological structure that frames the ego-consciousness through either-or logic, i.e. it either affirms or negates a statement. In other words, the egological constitution of an object inherently involves the necessity of dichotomizing the whole, and this in turn is linked to the act of prioritising one part of the whole over the other parts. (I will examine another implication of this structure when we analyse the nature of affirmation in a subsequent section.) What is troublesome is that this process appears "natural and reasonable" to the "foolish, ordinary people," for it is propelled and guaranteed by the structure of their epistemological stance. As a consequence of prioritisation by means of either-or logic, dualism is accordingly legitimised in the mind of the "foolish, ordinary people."

By contrast, the *Sutra* admonishes the *bodhisattva* against taking either-or logic as the *modus operandi* for making judgements or understanding reality. Rather, it recommends taking the logical stance of "neither-nor" propositional form. Linguistically, it advocates neither affirming nor negating a "*dharma* or a no-*dharma*," or ontologically, it maintains neither being nor non-being. One of the important points that deserves special attention, here, is that the neither-nor propositional form offers a *holistic* perspective to the *bodhisattva* because this attitude does not admit a dichotomisation as a way of organising reality, as does the either-or attitude. In this recommendation, we have a glimpse of the *bodhisattva*'s departing from the egological stance to a non-egological stance, from dualism to non-dualism, although this transition is only implicit at this stage of our inquiry. What is established at this point is that the *Sutra* rejects either-or logic in favour of neither-nor logic, and in so doing adopts the process of reasoning that aims at freeing "the foolish, ordinary people" from their dualistic, either-or egological constitution that is structurally imposed by the everyday standpoint of the "foolish, ordinary people," although this freedom, when understood conceptually, is simply intellectual in nature. In order to actually embody freedom, a perspectival shift must be effected, as we shall see, through an existential transformation through meditation to the non-dualistic, non-egological stance. ...

With this brief articulation of the conceptual structure which the *Sutra* gives to the *bodhisattva*, we are now ready to analyse the meaning of the "logic of not" that is formulated as: "A is not A, therefore it is A." ...The *Sutra* intends the statement to be universally applicable to any (linguistic) sign used in subject–predicate structure and this is textually suggested by the use of the term *dharma*, the most comprehensive term in Buddhism. When this is translated into ordinary language, it means that A can be a (linguistic) sign for anything that *is* of and in this world. Accordingly, this means that A is linguistically a sign for a noun, a noun-phrase, or a noun-clause in the subject–predicate structure of a language, where the language may designate a logical, artificial or natural system of signs. Given this observation, then, we are led to think that A stands for anything whatsoever of this world as well as that which occurs in this world, where the world refers to a domain in which thing–events, including objects of the mind, are thematised through language and experience. The above specification of A is the most inclusive and comprehensive, and hence universal in the widest sense of the term, for it purports to exclude nothing of the world, including the idea of nothing, so long as it functions as a nominative in the subject-predicate structure of a given language, so long as we can thematise it in a discourse. ...

IV. Affirmation of A

What, then, does it mean to affirm A? Here I will examine the logical structure of affirming and recognising A as A. There are two logical senses on which I will focus with regard to the idea of A when it is seen in light of either-or logic: in affirming A, A is taken to be (1) self-same such that "A is the same as A," and (2) A is taken in relation to not-A without postulating a strict self-sameness where "strict" means that there is no gap or fissure in identifying A as A. The former takes the position that it is meaningful to make an identity statement by taking A to be self-same, while the latter does not take this position, because it believes that A can be understood only in relational terms, i.e. only in relation to not-A. Here I will examine only the first sense of A, so as to better clarify the second, relational sense of A later.

That A is a sign means that it can become a subject of a sentence, wherein an act of thematisation gives rise to A. Generally speaking, the act of thematisation is an operation of the ego-consciousness that is propelled by or invested in ego-interest and desire. For this reason, it is a homocentric way of understanding A. Moreover, although A is originally a fluid thing–event in the world, the thematisation, once it is realised as a subject of a sentence, suggests that A is "frozen" or "fixed" so that any speaker of a language can engage it, to borrow Wittgenstein's terminology, in a "language game." Once it is frozen in this manner, it enters into, and is situated in, a conceptual space that a speaker creates for the use of language. This suggests that it departs from experience and that it is oblivious to the original fact that A is an experience; a phenomenon of thing–event in the world. In other words, A functions in the mode of "as if" by disregarding the temporalisation of time. It becomes "frozen" as a sign in the language, and conforms to the syntax of a given language. That is to say, A appears to gain an *atemporal* status, for whenever a speaker uses (but not just mentions) A in any given domain of discourse, all other users can appeal to its "same" meaning.

When the self-sameness is asserted in respect of A, then, we tend to forget the factors mentioned above, as if A can stand on its own. By forgetting these factors, however, the idea of A *qua* A arises disregarding the fact that A is an artificial sign, where "artificial" means that it is divorced and abstracted from a flux of the changing world. This is so because the idea of A in the sense of the self-sameness is a linguistic and conceptual reification; it is linguistic because A is realised as A in the language, and it is conceptual because it is *thought* of as being atemporal or enduring through time. It occurs in the mind of a person who thinks of A. It needs to be pointed out, however, that experience subsumes the use of a language.

As we have seen in the previous section, the idea of self-sameness presupposes the grasping–grasped relationship, which Buddhism rejects as delusory, because it is a product of the discriminatory mind. Moreover, the self-sameness arises as a consequence of substantialising A. Once it is substantialised, it gives rise to an ontology in various formulations, ranging from a naturalistic to a metaphysical understanding of being. Substantialisation and ontologisation psychologically derive from the stance of attachment, and focus on a meaning that is intra-linguistically defined. Here we need not reiterate the argument concerning the grasping and grasped relationship. What needs to be noted, however, is the logical implication of the act of affirmation.

Chapter Four
Essential Sutras and Chan Teachings—Exploring the Heart of Buddhist Wisdom

The idea of self-sameness is predicated on a one-sidedness or on a prioritisation that accompanies the *modus operandi* of either-or logic. The act of affirmation presupposes this scheme. …

…the idea of self-sameness is predicated on the acceptance of either-or logic as the standard for thinking, as the *modus operandi* for making judgements. Either-or logic prioritises a thematic concern which is realised as A. In this respect, the act of affirmation and the act of negation presuppose each other, as long as they are framed within the structure of either-or logic. Here, there is a mutual dependency and relativity between them. From this analysis, it is clear that the idea of a self is an idea of a self if and only if both the affirmation and the negation of it are together in operation. Although the one is explicit, the other is implicit. When explicitly affirming A, its negation is implicit. Since the implicit does not surface in the affirmative judgement, the negative judgement recedes into the background. On the other hand, when explicitly negating A, the affirmation is implicit, and recedes into the background. …

When A is taken to be self-same, i.e. "A is the same as A," there must be a logical moment of self-reflexivity between the first occurrence of A and the second occurrence of A in the mind which makes this identification, such that they coincide with each other without jeopardizing the unity of each occurrence, and without creating a gap between them. That is, they must be conceptually juxtaposed with each other, wherein there must be a conceptual "distance" between the first occurrence of A and the second occurrence of A, whether the self-sameness is taken numerically or qualitatively. The establishment of the self-sameness in this regard is a bridging act of identification between these two occurrences. One must function as a subject and the other must function as an object in the subject–predicate relationship, and the former must be used as a standard to measure the latter to determine if they are the same with each other. In this case, the act of identification stands outside of the domain in which the self-sameness is to be asserted. That is, it is *as if* the act of identification is extrinsic to the idea of self-sameness. As long as there occurs a distinction between the subject and the object in the establishment of the sameness, a question arises if it is logically possible for the subject to identify or to judge the first occurrence of A and the second occurrence of A as being the same as itself. In order for the first occurrence as a subject to determine the second occurrence of A as A, there must be a *difference* between them. Otherwise, it is impossible to identify or judge that the first occurrence of A and the second occurrence of A are the same as itself. If this is the case, the idea of self-sameness presupposes a difference and only through this difference is it logically possible to identify A as the same as itself. In other words, the self-sameness is the self-sameness *qua* difference. There is no idea of self-sameness pure and simple. Here we can witness an operation of the prioritisation as well as interdependency intrinsic to either-or logic, when A is taken to be same as itself.

When ontology is envisioned by relying on the dualistic, either-or egological stance, while disregarding the above point, A stands for whatever is perceived and/or conceived to *be*. …

As long as the grasping–grasped relationship is operative in the theoretical construction of ontology, it does not object to them, for any ontology constructed in this way is that which the *Sutra* negates as delusory. However, it does provisionally recognise the ontological status of A, however A may be ontologised, either naturalistically or rationalistically. The *Sutra* grants a provisional sense of reality to A. The granting of the sense of reality to A is correlative with the nature of the ontologising activity of the cognitive subject. Yet, it is performed, we must note, by our everyday, commonsensical understanding of the world in which A can be singled out as a subject of discourse or as an object of experience. This leads us to the next section where I shall delve into the meaning of the negation of A as the *Sutra* conceives of it.

V. A is not A

In the preceding section, we have examined the idea of A as being self-same, wherein I pointed out that the idea of self-sameness presupposes the idea of difference in order for the idea of self-sameness to be intelligible. Along with this I also pointed out that prioritisation and interdependency are concurrent in establishing the idea of self-sameness. In this section we are concerned first with specifying the meaning of the negation of A, and secondly with specifying the meaning of negating A that includes "neither-nor" propositional form which implies a third perspective, i.e. one that cannot be accommodated by either-or logic.

Now, a question arises: "Can A in the sense of the self-sameness which the 'foolish, ordinary people' accept 'stand on its own' without reference to other things?" "Can A just be A outside of a domain of discourse where both A and not A are logically constituted together as the essential components?" The answer is no; one without the other is unintelligible in making either an affirmative or a negative statement. If we are to understand "standing on its own" in the sense, for example, of having an essence in light of this logical foundation, the "standing on its own" must be relative in its being and meaning, because without other things, i.e. not A, there is no A. That means that A is dependent for its being and for its meaning on other things. For this reason, the "standing on its own" cannot be taken as absolute or essential in meaning. It cannot fully or completely "stand on its own," because it is relative to, and dependent on, other things. The fact that A can be singled out as A (i.e. that it can be thematised as A in a given discourse by taking the subject–predicate sentence structure), already discloses this dependency and partiality, for it presupposes both its context and its relationship with other things. That is, without the context in which A is singled out as A, there can be no not-A either. This context is the ground out of which and upon which either the act of affirmation or negation can be made. This implies that when we attribute a self-sameness to A in its own right, we must understand it to be partial and relative in respect to its ground as well as to that which is not self-same. In other words, a self-same A cannot be conceived as the "foolish, ordinary people" want to have it. It entails, therefore, that A

Chapter Four
Essential Sutras and Chan Teachings—Exploring the Heart of Buddhist Wisdom

is absolutely neither self-sufficient nor self-contained. To believe, then, that A is absolutely self-same and that it can stand on its own is a linguistic fiction or illusion.

This linguistic fiction or illusion surfaces in the use of language when the speaker substantialises A in the conceptual space created by language, which entails the appearance of atemporality. ...

Recognising that this incompleteness is structurally embedded in either the act of affirmation or negation, the *Sutra* advocates the stance of non-attachment. ... the act of negation must be expanded to operate not only on the object but also on the act of negation itself. ...

We must note that the stance of non-attachment is not merely the consequence of logically negating the stance of attachment, although the *Sutra* does linguistically state it first in terms of the logical negation, as we illustrated above. That is, psychologically speaking, "foolish, ordinary people" may negate their attachment with a view to yielding non-attachment, but there arises in them an attachment to non-attachment. In other words, there arises an affirmation of what is negated. Since there is this affirmation, they need to further negate the affirmative attitude that is entailed by the initial act of negation. It is, however, impossible to logically achieve the stance of non-attachment by means of this logical or linguistic process, because it involves an infinite regress. That is, as soon as one negates the stance of attachment that arises out of an initial negation, there occurs an affirmation of this negation and then one must negate this affirmation, and so on *ad infinitum*. As long as the "foolish, ordinary people" remain on the logical plane of negating the stance of attachment, or as long as they approach the task as an intellectual issue, it is impossible to free themselves from repeatedly referring back to the previous stance of affirmation. At best, this process can yield a nihilistic stance, as we have just seen in the preceding paragraph. It can not yield the stance of non-attachment.

What causes the above-mentioned infinite regress is the fact that in addition to the content (i.e. the attitude of attachment) that needs to be negated, there remains in this process the *act* of negation that also needs to be negated in order for the negation to be complete, i.e. in order to embody the stance of non-attachment. However, there is no logical end to negating the act of negation, either. This path also involves an infinite regress, as long as the "foolish, ordinary people" remain in the egological and intellectual place, for it yields only a nominal sense of non-attachment. This arises because the issue of negating the attitude of attachment is conceptually framed within the standpoint of dualistic either-or egological structure. To embody an existential stance of non-attachment, the "foolish, ordinary people" must depart from the dualistic egological standpoint. This was stated in the *Sutra* that a *bodhisattva* must depart from all "objects of thought." The issue is not logical or intellectual in nature; it is deeply connected to the unconscious and the somaticity of the "foolish, ordinary people" which, for this reason, is more fundamental than the intellectual or logical approach to the issue of non-attachment, because the unconscious and the body support the activity of ego-consciousness without its knowledge. It demands an existential transformation of the negating subject. This is the very reason that the *Sutra* adopts the third perspective of the neither-nor propositional form, which advances neither attachment nor non-attachment. …

VI. Perspectival Shift

…I propose to interpret to mean a transformation existential in nature such that it effects a perspectival shift from the dualistic, egological stance to the non-dualistic, non-egological stance. I use the term "existential" here because the transformation must be effected by changing the unconscious–somatic dimension of the "foolish, ordinary people." That is, this transformation cannot be effected simply by intellection, i.e. by thinking or imagining it. "Not seeing" is a failure of seeing, because this seeing is constituted dualistically and egologically. It fails to "see" non-dualistically and non-egologically. Instead, the seer must see in the mode of nothing, wherein the seer's mind is rendered no-mind. When the seer is rendered nothing, no cognitive activity associated with the ego-consciousness is in operation. … Alternatively, it is a seeing without a seer, wherein there is only the activity of seeing without the ego-consciousness positing the self as a structuring and organising principle of experience. This activity of seeing is the activity of superconsciousness. As long as the "foolish, ordinary people" assume the dualistic, either-or egological stance, "seeing" in the sense indicated here cannot take place. …

But what about the statement that "*dharma* cannot be talked about"? How should we interpret it? It cannot be "talked about", for "this *dharma*" is extralinguistic; "this *dharma*" is that which appears in a meditation experience which ordinary language is not prepared to adequately express. Here, we need to examine what "extralinguistic" means in order to understand the statement that the "*dharma* cannot be talked about". I propose it to mean that it is outside conventional, ordinary language which employs subject–predicate structure, while accepting either-or logic as the standard for its *modus operandi*. In the subject–predicate structure of language, all that happens, including the experience of *dharma*, is gathered together into the subject, when in fact the experience itself must be expressed phenomenologically by the predicate. In this case it is the subject that is subsumed by the predicate, but not vice versa. …If, however, the predicate is subsumed under the subject, and if an experiencer is posited as the referential framework for the experience, it reveals that the experience of *dharma* is grasped dualistically and egologically. For the experience of *dharma* to be had and embodied, it must be had non-dualistically and non-egologically. That is to say, it can not be either subject or predicate in which the experience occurs, for it occurs in the stillness of meditation, i.e. in the state experientially and logically prior to the bifurcation between the subject and the object. It is "pure experience" admitting of no bifurcation between the experiencer and the experienced. Or put differently, when the "foolish, ordinary people" remain under the sway of either-or logic embedded in ordinary language, the prioritisation intrinsic to either-or logic occurs for the subject, because it believes that it operates under the subject–predicate structure. Consequently, a judgement made from this standpoint fails to achieve a balanced discernment, because it does not know the whole. It is made from within a partial or one-sided perspective. It is a human judgement that privileges the interests of ego-desire. For this reason, the *Sutra* has no choice except to say of "this *dharma*" that "it is neither a *dharma* nor a no-*dharma*" to indicate an (experiential) transcendence beyond and transdescendence into, the dualistic, either-or egological framework. This transcendence is actualisable only when it is accompanied practically by the trans-descendence into the human psyche by means of meditational practice. Meditational practice opens up both the transcendence and the trans-descendence, for meditation is a way of probing into the ground of being that is extra-linguistically nothing. ...

VII. Therefore it is A

In order to understand the last component in the "logic of not," i.e. "therefore it is A," it is necessary to examine briefly meditational experience, for it gives us an experiential background that informs us of the *Sutra*'s formulation....for the state of "neither image nor non-image" is a meditative stage recognised in the Pali Buddhist texts, in which the *experience* of emptiness (*sunyata*) initially obtains. Prior to this meditative state, Pali Buddhism recognises the hierarchical order of such meditative states as "awareness of [empty] sky with no boundary" and "awareness of no boundary," and "no-thing existing." Briefly, the meditative state of "awareness of [empty] sky of no boundary" is a state in which attachment is broken through, for there is nothing that one can attach oneself to once the meditator experiences the "[empty] sky of no-boundary." Here, however, an image of the empty sky still remains. That is, the noetic act is still operative, however subtle it may be. Next, the meditative "awareness of no boundary" is a state in which "names and forms" cease, and the mind becomes freed from its discriminatory function, because the name and form arise through the discriminatory function of the mind. Such a mind does not posit any object (noematic content), and because of this, its act is non-positional in nature, i.e. it does not take any attitude toward any object, it neither affirms nor negates it. The meditative state of "no-thing existing" is a further development of the meditative state of "awareness of no boundary," but significantly differs from the latter in that the mind becomes free from the self-projective image-experience. Here, there is the realisation that there is nothing one can claim to possess or to own. In addition, one gains insight into how the discriminatory activity of the mind operates, because the noetic act of the mind diminishes — the act of the ego-consciousness.

The achievement of these meditative states is followed by the meditative state of "neither image nor no-image." Such a state provides the experiential ground for the *Sutra* to advance its third perspective, i.e. "the middle perspective, where 'the middle' means that the being of the meditator is 'here' as well as 'there' but at the same time, it is neither 'here' nor 'there'." In the preceding quote, we see two moments: the first is an affirmation of the specific spatial determinations "here" and "there," which sensory perception can determine. In the meditative state of "neither image nor no-image," however, there occurs an interchangeability between "here" and "there." The second moment is thus a negation of the spatial determinations that are represented by "here" and "there." The negation of ordinary spatial determinations suggests that the mind in this state of no-mind is no longer bound by the spatial determination to which a particular thing is physically subject in the everyday standpoint. In no-mind, the discriminatory activity of the mind associated with the previous states of meditation is rendered inoperative and it suggests that the mind's non-discriminatory functions are activated. No-mind is no-place. That no-mind is no-place means that it can be any place without being subject to spatial determinations that are imposed on objects of perception by virtue of one's everyday epistemological stance. Hence, there is an interchangeability of "here" and "there." As such, it is an extraordinary experience when assessed from the everyday standpoint. Yet, their spatiality can be determinable as to their specific spatial location of "here" and "there," because their spatial determinations are not "fixed" or *a priori*, for they are an empty determination. The no-mind can move from "here" to "there." This is suggested by the statement that "it is neither here nor there," a perspective that allows an interchangeability between "here" and "there," because it transcends the stance from which "here" and "there" are viewed. In other words, the relationship between "here" and "there" and "neither here nor there" is an instance of determination *qua* indetermination and indetermination *qua* determination — a freedom from ordinary spatial determination. What is significant to note in this regard is that "here" and "there" in the state of no-mind (or no-place) are not simply determined in reference to the physicality or materiality of objects that are either "here" or "there," for "here" and "there" are images that appear in the meditative state of "neither image nor non-image." This is a rough construal of what it means for an object to be non-dualistically, non-egologically "constituted" where I enclose the word "constituted" in quotation marks to avoid the implication that there is some-thing that is doing the constitution, for here there is no such a "thing" *per se*. ...

VIII. Concluding Remarks

The preceding inquiry has enabled us to conclude that the *Sutra* provisionally relies on either-or logic to advance its philosophical position, and because of this reliance, its philosophical position is stated in a contradictory or paradoxical form. Its provisional use is based on the *Sutra*'s concern for the "foolish, ordinary people" because their either-or logic is a method of discourse most readily understandable and familiar to them in their use of ordinary language. In so doing, however, the *Sutra* was not successful, because it usually mystifies the "foolish, ordinary people," or if not that, it simply leads them to dismiss the linguistic formulation of its philosophical position as nonsensical. I have attempted to demonstrate that it is not nonsensical by articulating the epistemological standpoint of the "foolish, ordinary people," while disclosing the logical limitations that either-or logic intrinsically contains in its *modus operandi*. In point of fact, the *Sutra*'s philosophical position cannot be accommodated by either-or logic, which simply offers an either-or alternative, i.e. either affirmation or negation when translated into a linguistic formulation. The *Sutra*'s own position is a third perspective that cannot be accommodated by relying on either-or logic, and for this reason it chooses to express its philosophical position by relying on a "neither-nor" propositional form. In adapting this way of expressing its philosophical position, it rejects either-or logic as a proper way of discerning thing–events of the world and their linguistic articulation. …

C. Looking at Lineage: A Fresh Perspective on Chan Buddhism[①]
审视法脉：理解禅宗的新视角

John R. McRae
马克瑞

How should we begin this discussion of Chan Buddhism? One device would be to begin with a story, some striking anecdote to arouse the reader's curiosity. There are certainly many good possibilities within the annals of Chan. …The stock of legendary accounts that might be used, each with slightly different import, is endless. And there are other possible beginnings, as well. Many authors have their own favored ways of characterizing the most essential features of Chan, presenting some short list of features to sum up the entire tradition. Or we could avoid such bland generalization and simply celebrate the incredible creativity of the Chan tradition over the centuries, its vibrancy as a religious phenomenon.

The approach adopted here — already taken by posing these very deliberations — is to begin by asking questions, to arouse in the reader not merely a raw curiosity but the faculties of critical interrogation as well. Specifically, let us begin by directly considering the question of how we should look at Chan Buddhism: What approaches should we adopt, and which should we avoid? What forms of analysis will be fruitful, and which would merely repeat commonly accepted stereotypes?

…I have been a scholar and practitioner, student and teacher, lover and hermit, and what I

---

① Excerpted from John R. McRae, *Seeing Through Zen: Encounter, Transformation, and Genealogy in Chinese Chan Buddhism*, University of California Press, 2003.

am about to present here I have learned through a series of extended educational encounters in America and Japan. This text is intended for use by listeners and readers not only in China, but in Europe, the United States, and Japan as well — so how could I possibly presume to argue that there should be *one* way to look at Chan Buddhism? A multiplicity of perspectives and a certain fluidity of analytical typologies are givens in this postmodern world.

Deconstructing the Chan Lineage Diagram

(Figure 4: Lineage diagram of Chinese Chan Buddhism)

Chapter Four
Essential Sutras and Chan Teachings—Exploring the Heart of Buddhist Wisdom

For convenience, let me begin by defining a perspective on Chan that I wish to deconstruct and thereby avoid. I should confess that I mean only to caricature this perspective, so that we can use the observations made now to form a lever with which to push ourselves into a certain type of understanding (to paraphrase the positivist philosopher John Dewey and his student Hu Shih, who spoke of studying the past to create a lever with which to push China into a certain sort of future). The perspective to which I refer is the traditionalist approach depicted graphically in the lineage diagram presented in figure 4. ...here we can observe that the lineage diagram provides the basic model for how Chan appreciates its own historical background. That is, Chan does not define itself as being one among a number of Buddhist schools based on a particular scripture (such as the Tiantai [Tendai] school with its emphasis on the *Lotus Sutra,* for example). Instead, Chan texts present the school as Buddhism itself, or as *the* central teaching of Buddhism, which has been transmitted from the seven Buddhas of the past to the twenty-eight Indian patriarchs, the six Chinese patriarchs, and all the generations of Chinese and Japanese Chan and Zen masters that follow. ...

One of the advantages of beginning by considering this lineage diagram, to be sure, is that it introduces the most important players in our story. The seven Buddhas of the past are legendary figures to whom we need pay only scant attention. ...Nor must we pay much attention to the twenty-eight Indian patriarchs... On the other hand, the six Chinese patriarchs from Bodhidharma onward, along with Huineng and Shenxiu in the sixth generation and their several generations of disciples, will appear more often than any of the other players in this drama. (The reader will note at once that no disciples of Shenxiu's are listed in our lineage diagram, which is a telling omission in itself. ...The figures remembered as icons of the Linji (Rinzai) and Caodong (Soto) schools, whose names adorn the balance of the diagram, are among the most important in the history of the tradition.

We can draw some important basic inferences from this transmission diagram. First, a note on historical origins: the Chan lineage scheme is a combined product of Indian and Chinese culture. Often authors describe Chan as the "most Chinese" of all the Chinese Buddhist schools, and part of what they are referring to is the Chan genealogical model. (I am particularly allergic to this rhetoric, since such expressions are generally little more than unexplicated tautologies generated through a sense of cultural chauvinism rather than real analytical insight. And the fact that D. T. Suzuki and others say virtually the same thing with regard to Japanese Zen, that it represents somehow the essence of *Japanese* culture, should alert us to both the essential vacuity and the strategic intentions of such sentiments.) ...There are a number of parallels between the Chan transmission scheme and Chinese family genealogies of the eighth century and later, but we should remember that Indian Buddhists had parents and teachers, family genealogies and initiation lineages, just as the Chinese did. As an amalgamation of Indian and Chinese elements, though, the Chinese Chan transmission schema developed within the Chinese Buddhist context and was particularly well adapted to that milieu. Just as Deng Xiaoping talked about "socialism with Chinese characteristics," we could refer to the Chinese Chan transmission model as a "Buddhist genealogical theory with Chinese characteristics."

Second, by using the lineage diagram to define Chan as a "separate transmission outside the teachings," the advocates of Chan were declaring their school to be profoundly different from, and fundamentally better than, all other Buddhist schools: where the other schools represented only interpretations of Buddhism, Chan constitutes the real thing, Buddhism itself. This is a polemical move, meant to establish the superiority of Chan over all other schools. …Whether we view medieval Chinese Buddhists as concerned solely with the highest forms of wisdom or as working to obtain imperial patronage and other this-worldly benefits, or engaged in both endeavors simultaneously, at the very least they were competing with their contemporaries for intellectual and cultural hegemony. We should thus not overlook the polemical quality of the lineage theory. …

Third, what counts in the Chan transmission scheme are not the "facts" of what happened in the lives of Sakyamuni, Bodhidharma, Huineng, and others, but rather how these figures were perceived in terms of Chan mythology. …Whether or not any anecdote actually represents the words spoken and events that occurred "accurately" is only a historical accident…What is of far greater consequence is the process by which that anecdote was generated and circulated, edited and improved, and thus transmitted throughout an entire population of Chan practitioners and devotees, until it became part of the fluid body of legendary lore by which Chan masters came to be identified throughout Chinese culture. This is McRae's first law of Zen studies: "It's not true, and therefore it's more important." This is to say that fiction — actually, a different sort of truth — is more important than the simplistic criterion of the question "Did it really happen?"

Fourth, based on the rhetoric of *sunyata,* or emptiness, nothing is actually transmitted in this transmission scheme. What occurs between each teacher and his successor is merely an approval or authorization *(yinke; inka)* of the successor's attainment of complete enlightenment. This is first of all a doctrinal principle of Chan Buddhism itself, but we should recognize that the most important parts of the diagram are not the separate names of individual patriarchs, but the spaces between them, the lines that join them. That is, what is being represented is not only a series of human figures but the encounters between each figure and his immediate predecessor and successor. As is frequently stressed in the texts of Chan, there is no "thing" — such as enlightenment, the Buddha-mind, or whatever — that is actually passed from one patriarch to the next. The existence of such an entity would violate a fundamental Buddhist doctrinal theme, the

Chapter Four
Essential Sutras and Chan Teachings—Exploring the Heart of Buddhist Wisdom

denial of unchanging, substantive, and individual identity to the things and beings of this world. With regard to persons, this doctrinal theme is called "no-self" *(anatman)*; with regard to all the various component elements of existence, including persons, this is called "emptiness" *(sunyata)*. This is not a merely philosophical consideration, but rather an existential posture with profound genealogical impact: the focus is not on "what" is being transmitted, but on the relationship of encounter between the Buddhas and Patriarchs. The act of transmission thus involves not the bestowing of some "thing" from one master to the next, but the recognition of shared spiritual maturity. It is a cosmic dance involving a special set of partners, a relationship of encounter, a meeting at the deepest spiritual level.

Fifth, since the enlightenment of each Buddha and Patriarch is complete, there is no differentiation between the religious status of the Indian Buddhas and Patriarchs and their Chinese counterparts. This was perhaps the most important reason why this lineage-based exposition was attractive to medieval Chinese Buddhists, since it raised the authority of native Chinese figures to equal those of their Indian predecessors. This is very important in terms of the sinification of Buddhism, that is, the adaptation of Buddhism within Chinese culture, a subject that is vitally relevant to a wide range of subjects in Chinese religions and Chinese studies in general. At the moment, though, what I want to emphasize is the most striking and most frequently overlooked characteristic of this diagram: the homologizing impact of its very simple lines of succession.

By representing Chan Buddhism in terms of a straight-line succession from the seven Buddhas of the past through the six Chinese Patriarchs, diagrams such as this are used to simplify fantastically complicated sets of cultural and religious phenomena. Every time a straight-line relationship between two masters is posited in a lineage diagram, an entire world of complexity, an intricate universe of human relationships and experiences, is effectively eliminated from view. Could any religious figure's identity possibly be adequately summarized by selecting only one out of a whole lifetime of relationships? Even a quick look at the biographies of Chinese Chan masters shows the extent of the distortion involved: where the sources are adequate, we sometimes see multiple awakening experiences catalyzed by different teachers and events, yet in the lineage diagrams these are all reduced to single lines of transmission. The use of lineage diagrams to represent the Chan tradition, then — and their use is as old as the tradition itself, since it was by explicating genealogical specifics that Chan generated its own identity as a specific religious movement — is a hegemonic trope, the willful extension of one way of perceiving the world to the exclusion of all other viewpoints…

Sixth, the "genealogical model" is important not only for the historical self-understanding of the Chan school in its transmission from Sakyamuni Buddha through Bodhidharma and onward, but also for the manner in which it defines how Chan spiritual practice itself is carried out. That is, in contrast to a basically Indian conception of meditation practice as an individual yogic endeavor of self-purification and progressive advancement toward buddhahood, the Chan genealogical model implies that the most important aspect of spiritual cultivation takes place in the *encounter between teacher and student*. Chan trainees still spent long hours in the meditation hall — we can be sure of that, even though the texts often do not bother confirming the fact — but the focus of Chan rhetoric and literature is on the dialogues and exchanges between each master and his students, or between each student destined to be a master and his various teachers. It is thus not only the Chan school's self-understanding of its own religious history, but the religious practice of Chan itself that is fundamentally genealogical. By saying that Chan practice is fundamentally *genealogical,* I mean that it is derived from a genealogically understood encounter experience that is *relational* (involving interaction between individuals rather than being based solely on individual effort), *generational* (in that it is organized according to parent-child, or rather teacher-student, generations), and *reiterative* (i.e., intended for emulation and repetition in the lives of present and future teachers and students). No matter what the comparison or relationship between Chinese Chan and earlier forms of Indian Buddhist meditation practice, this particular complex of qualities is not found in other schools or forms of Buddhist training.

In the most basic historical terms, though, we should recognize that the homologizing impact of the Chan lineage diagram represents a profound distortion of the subject matter. This is McRae's second rule of Zen studies: "Lineage assertions are as wrong as they are strong." In more formal language, this means that lineage assertions are problematic in direct proportion to their significance. That is, every time we read that the masters of such-and-such a group are related to each other in a lineal succession, the statement is probably inaccurate in some sense, and the more important it is to the religious identity of the individuals involved, the less accurate it will be. If nothing much is made of the relationship, the lineage assertion is more likely to be correct than if a great deal rides on it. Almost always, of course, the figure at the end of the list, or even that individual's students, has the most at stake in making such assertions. And if his religious identity must be defined on the basis of a lineal succession, if his historical status depends on being the recipient of the cumulative charisma of one particular set of predecessors, then it always seems that some significant distortion of the facts has taken place. Of course, my use of the word *facts* should remind you of the first rule, which remains relevant here: The presentation of reality in lineage schema represents a certain type of myth-making, and what is not "true" *per se* is inevitably more important!

Seventh, I referred above to "each teacher and *his* successor" and the gender-specific terminology is appropriate. The Chan tradition is overwhelmingly male-dominated, and the strong implications of the term *patriarchal* in English (referring both to Chan figureheads and a

Chapter Four
Essential Sutras and Chan Teachings—Exploring the Heart of Buddhist Wisdom

male-centered ideology) is entirely suitable here. ...

Avoiding the "String of Pearls" Fallacy

...To represent Chan Buddhism in terms that are congruent with the lineage paradigm is to run the risk of mere repetition, without saying anything fundamentally insightful. ...Here it is useful to make a clear insider/outsider distinction: What is both expected and natural for a religious practitioner operating *within* the Chan episteme, what is necessary in order to achieve membership within the patriarchal lineage, becomes intellectually debilitating for those standing, even if only temporarily, *outside* the realm of Chan as its observers and analysts. ...

Seen from this perspective, the issue is really quite simple: Whenever we pretend to explain Chan in terms of lineal successions from one great master to another, we run the risk of committing the "string of pearls" fallacy, in which the evolution of Chan Buddhism is described in terms of a sequence of individual masters like pearls on a string. This is a variant of the "great man" fallacy of historical writing, in which one explains the inevitably messy details of past realities in terms of the willful endeavors of a limited number of heroic men. ...To be more logically precise, it is also an example of the fallacy of archetypes, which "consists in conceptualizing change in terms of the re-enactment of primordial archetypes which exist outside of time."...

I am not suggesting that we never include descriptions of lineage successions in our writing on Chan — far from it — but only that, when we do so, we should be conscious of the reasons for their use and remain aware of the risks involved. Not only would it be impossible to talk about Chan without ever using concepts related to lineage — to the extent it can be described as a continuous set of processes, Chan is at its most profound level a *genealogical* set of phenomena — but we will gain the greatest benefit from shifting our focus and perspective repeatedly as we move through the evidence. To commit the "string of pearls" fallacy is to remain fixed and unaware in a single posture. Rather than simply move to a different static position, however, we should work to illuminate our subject from a number of angles, to encounter it with different aspects of our interpretive capacities.

A Provisional Device: The Phases of Chan

PROTO-CHAN ca. 500–600	Bodhidharma (d. ca. 530) Huike (ca. 485 to ca. 555 or after 574) *Treatise on the Two Entrances and Four Practices* SUMMARY: Multiple locations in north China; practice based on Buddha-nature; no known lineage theory. Known through traditional texts and a few Dunhuang documents.

EARLY CHAN ca. 600–900	Hongren (601–74) Shenxiu (606?–706), Huineng (638–713) Shenhui (684–758) Northern, Southern, Oxhead factions *Platform Sñtra of the Sixth Patriarch* SUMMARY: Various loosely defined factions/groups, with different approaches to "contemplation of the mind"; relationship between this and proto-Chan unclear; lineage theories appear from 689 on as a unifying ideology; known through numerous Dunhuang documents and traditional sources.
MIDDLE CHAN ca. 750–1000	Mazu (709–88), Shitou (710–90) Linji (d. 867), Xuefeng Yicun (822–908) Hongzhou and Hubei factions, antecedents of the Five Houses *Anthology of the Patriarchal Hall* SUMMARY: Emergence of "encounter dialogue" as primary mode of practice and discourse, recorded in colloquial form and massive quantity in 952, and implying a genealogical model of religious cultivation; not present in Dunhuang documents but known through Song Dynasty texts and idealized as a golden age during Song.
SONG-DYNASTY CHAN ca. 950–1300	Dahui (1089–1163), Hongzhi (1091–1157) Five Houses, Linji and Caodong schools *Blue Cliff Record* SUMMARY: Greatest flourishing of Chan, which as an administrative ideology dominated the Chinese monastic establishment; the image of Tang Dynasty masters operating in enlightened spontaneity was inscribed in highly ritualized Song Dynasty settings; snippets of encounter dialogue were collected, edited to serve as precedents of enlightened activity, and used as topics of meditative inquiry.

(Figure 5: Simplified chart of the phases of Chinese Chan)[①]

Figure 5 is a simple chart describing Chan in a manner quite different from that of the lineage diagram (Figure 4) discussed above. Where the traditional Chan diagram lists names of individual human beings, this chart lists named phases or trends in the evolution of Chan. The names of these phases or trends are not universally accepted in writings about Chan, and the boundaries between them are subject to debate. I preserve these ambiguities by not adopting this terminology and periodization without question throughout these chapters; on the contrary, we should pay close attention to the intrinsic fuzziness of the borders between the phases named

---

[①] In order to cover Chan from the end of the Song Dynasty up to the present, this chart should include at least a postclassical phase or perhaps multiple later phases. However, since the developments of these later periods are not treated in this book, I will not attempt a periodization here.

Chapter Four
Essential Sutras and Chan Teachings—Exploring the Heart of Buddhist Wisdom

so uniquely and unambiguously here. It is in large part through considering the failure of any margins to tightly capture these arbitrary entities that we will be able to see the utility of this periodization.

Each of the named phases refers not to a specific set of individuals *per se* (although some of the most representative figures are listed), but to a style or configuration of religious activity that is known through a variety of sources…each phase of Chan can be described in terms of multiple dimensions: its exemplary human representatives, the geography and timing of their activities, the texts that describe their activities and convey their teachings, and so forth. Figure 2 provides information of this sort briefly in the summary for each phase.

Hence, the basic difference between the lineage diagram and the chart in figure 2 is that, where the diagram tends to homologize all the individuals represented as identically enlightened representatives of a single confraternity — to enable (and simultaneously limit) the understanding of them according to a meaningful yet unitary religious mode — the chart seeks to distinguish qualitative differences along a chronological axis, to facilitate multiple perspectives and modes of understanding. The goal of the chart is the generation of meaningful distinctions, not the assertion of an unbroken continuity of patriarchal authority.

…It has long been recognized that Huineng and Shenxiu, the figureheads of the so-called Southern and Northern schools, function within traditional Chan ideology not as two isolated individuals, but as an inextricably related pair simultaneously linked in collaborative and competitive relationship. Together they constitute a single literary and religious polarity expressed as a relationship between two human exemplars. Convenient shorthand for this complex bimodality is the French word *duel,* which carries the meanings of both "duel" and "dual" in English. Thus the doctrine of sudden enlightenment associated with the Southern school cannot be explained without reference to a gradualist doctrine attributed to the Northern school. (This simplistic explanation of sudden versus gradual is woefully inadequate in the face of historical reality, but it must have been very effective in disabusing trainees of their simplistic notions of meditative "achievement.") Note that these two schools, along with Oxhead Chan, are included together in the "early Chan" phase of the eighth century — and this is an intentional grouping, meant to indicate that these three factions were more alike than different, or at least that their religious identities were so intimately intertwined that they must be represented together. …

You might assume that the chart depicts a chain of historical causality, but it actually characterizes the retrospective identity of the various phases of Chan. The periodization of any set of past events represents an act of reconstruction — not the mere reorganization and ordering of information, but the total remaking of the past as the structured image of our imaginations. …

This retrospective quality pervades the Chan tradition. Time and again we find we are dealing, not with what happened at any given point, but with what people thought happened previously. We deal not so much in facts and events as in legends and reconstructions, not so much with accomplishments and contributions as with attributions and legacies. The legends and reconstructions, not the supposedly "actual" events, determined later religious and social praxis. This observation may have a broad application beyond Chinese Chan, in describing what it is that makes traditions traditions. But it is certainly applicable to Chan: not true, and therefore more important. …

Proto-Chan

The designation *proto-Chan* refers to the ill-defined activities of a set of practitioners surrounding Bodhidharma and Huike who were known for their dedication to ascetic practices and meditation. Beginning roughly around the year 500 and overlapping with the so-called early Chan phase in the seventh and perhaps even into the eighth century, this group operated in a variety of north China locations. The extent to which the individuals involved conceived of themselves as participating in a single group or movement is unclear…We know of a small number of figures who studied under Bodhidharma, and a somewhat larger number who were primarily associated with Huike, presumably after his master's death. There is a certain quantity of biographical information about the participants in proto-Chan, and although it attests to the variety of their backgrounds, it imparts only a shadowy image of any shared group esprit.

One important feature of proto-Chan — at the very least, a feature important for the subsequent evolution of the school — was its common focus on a text circulated under Bodhidharma's name, the *Treatise on the Two Entrances and Four Practices (Erru sixing lun)*. As this text circulated, practitioners who identified with Bodhidharma's message appended their own comments to it, making it an expanding anthology of the earliest Chan teachings. Thus, while we cannot describe the scope of proto-Chan activities with any accuracy, the *Treatise on the Two Entrances and Four Practices* provides insight into precisely those ideas that formed the doctrinal nucleus of subsequent Chan practice ideology. This text describes a fundamental attitude of emphasis on the existence of the Buddha-nature or potential for enlightenment within all sentient beings, as well as an attitude toward how this understanding of Buddhism may be carried out in daily life.

Early Chan

Early Chan designates the phase when the school, or what was to become a school eventually, first articulated its lineage-based ideology in clear and extensive form. Actually, the Dunhuang manuscripts and traditional Chan records include an amazing variety of different formulations from this phase, and it seems evident that a great deal of experimentation was taking place, involving a number of variations on commonly accepted themes, as the Chan movement matured and crystallized over time. Some of these formulations describe specific methods of contemplation practice, sometimes presented in a progressive series of steps. Others describe the role of the Buddha-nature, or "pure mind," within, as well as the behavior of the illusions — the false thoughts, or "impure mind" — that obscure the appreciation of our inner purity. Compared to later Chan texts, these formulations often seem odd but are not particularly enigmatic or difficult; the emphasis at this point was on clarity in expressing this new form of the Buddhist teaching, not on generating entirely different modes of expression.

In contrast to proto-Chan, the early Chan phase manifests a great stability of location: Daoxin and Hongren spent exactly a half-century, from 624 to 674, in the same monastic complex in Huangmei ("Yellow Plum," Hubei Province) and it is not unreasonable to include Shenxiu's quarter century, from 675 to 701, at the not-too-distant Jade Spring Temple (Yuquansi, in Jingzhou, which overlaps both Hubei and Hunan Provinces) in this phase as well. Matters become more complex with the explosion of Chan into the two imperial capitals of Chang'an and Luoyang during the eighth century. Therefore, whereas investigation of proto-Chan leaves one with the impression of an indefinable will-o'-the-wisp, analyzing the sources for early Chan imparts a sense of continuous community development and a growth pattern that moves from geometric increase throughout much of the seventh century to explosive expansion in the eighth. Also, where proto-Chan refers to a single, albeit incohesive and ill-defined, style of religiosity, early Chan may be understood as a collection of different communities, groups, and factions.

In the most straightforward sense, the label *East Mountain teaching* refers to both the community and doctrines of Daoxin and Hongren, but there is an important sense in which these matters are known solely through information transmitted by their successors. Those successors identified themselves not as purveyors of their own doctrinal innovations, but as transmitters of the East Mountain teaching. We need to recognize that the ideas associated with the names Daoxin and Hongren were primarily those of their followers' later reconstruction; this recognition does not sever the connection between those ideas and the East Mountain teaching figureheads themselves, but it does lend an important retrospective quality to the process. That those successors, who were active in Chang'an and Luoyang in the early decades of the eighth century, came to be known by the label *Northern school* is a curious historical detail. The *Southern school* derives from the mid-eighth-century activities of Shenhui (684–758), although later this label came to be adopted for the Chan school as a whole. The *Oxhead school* is a somewhat later development, a faction or lineage that played an important historical role through its apparent involvement in the composition of the *Platform Sutra,* the hallmark and culminating text of early Chan. …

Middle Chan

An event of overwhelming significance takes place in the "middle Chan" phase: the emergence of "encounter dialogue," the idiosyncratic manner in which Chan masters are depicted in dialogue with their students. Associated initially with such celebrated figures as Mazu Daoyi (709–788) and his successors Baizhang Huaihai (749–814), Nanquan Puyuan (748–834), and Linji Yixuan (d. 867), as well as Shitou Xiqian and his successors Dongshan Liangjie (807–869) and Caoshan Benji (840–901), this is when Chan appears to have become really Chan, when Chan masters seem to have really behaved like Chan masters. The anecdotes of middle Chan encounter dialogue represent the stories repeated most often in popular books on Chan/Zen as examples of paradoxical but enlightened behavior. Here the locus of religious practice was firmly removed from individual effort in the meditation hall and replaced by a demanding genre of interrogation that sought to destabilize all habitual, logical patterns. Spontaneity was the rule, iconoclastic behavior the norm.

Or so it seems. For here we will have to consider, not only the momentous import of encounter dialogue as the dominant model of religious undertaking, but also the difficult questions of *when* all this spontaneous interaction was actually being practiced and *what* precisely was going on. We will see that there is a substantial gap between when the most famous stories of Chan lore are supposed to have happened, and when we first see them in written form. We will also see that these stories have complex origins, bearing features of both oral and written literature. ...

Song Dynasty Chan

The contours assumed by Chan Buddhism during the Song Dynasty represent the mature pattern which defines the tradition up until the modern period. Using an ecological metaphor, I refer to this pattern as a "climax paradigm," which describes the dynamic equilibrium achieved by a mature forest or ecological system. Earlier writers (both scholarly and apologist) have tended to ignore this period, partly out of the wish to explore the more "creative" masters of the Tang, or to jump across the waters to emphasize the emerging Zen school of Japan. The Song has also been denigrated in general textbooks as the beginning of the decline of Chinese Buddhism, its ossification into institutional formalism. This attitude is changing, as Song Dynasty religion has become perhaps the primary focus of the study of pre-modern Chinese religion, by Euro-American scholars at least. And with this change our impression of Song Dynasty Chan has been transformed as well. It is now increasingly recognized that the Song Dynasty witnessed the emergence of a basic configuration of Chan that was disseminated throughout East Asia, and now the world. This is apparent most dramatically in the life and teachings of Dahui Zonggao (1089–1163), the innovator and greatest exponent of "viewing the critical phrase" or *ko'an*

Chapter Four
Essential Sutras and Chan Teachings—Exploring the Heart of Buddhist Wisdom

practice in the history of Chinese Chan. But the picture of Song Dynasty Chan is not complete without looking closely at the style of meditative introspection advocated by Hongzhi Zhengjue (1091–1157) and other members of the Caodong lineage, evaluating their recommendations on their own terms and not simply in light of the polemical characterization by Dahui as mere "silent illumination." Ultimately, we will see that the Linji and Caodong approaches present an inseparable pair that mimics the sudden/gradual debate of the eighth century, and which resonates with the "two entrances" of the treatise attributed to Bodhidharma.

Exercises

I. Vocabulary Practice

Define the following terms taken from the Buddhist texts and use each term in a sentence that reflects its philosophical meaning:

1. emptiness (空)
2. self (我)
3. bodhisattva (菩萨)
4. enlightenment (觉)
5. prajna (般若)

II. Comprehension

A. Read *The Heart Sutra* and answer the following questions:

6. What is the significance of the statement "emptiness is not separate from form, form is not separate from emptiness; whatever is form is emptiness, whatever is emptiness is form. 色不异空，空不异色，色即是空，空即是色" in the whole sutra?
7. What are the differences between prajna and wisdom?
8. Explain the meaning of emptiness.

B. Analyze the teachings in *The Diamond Sutra* and answer the following questions:

9. How should we understand "When the illusory nature of form is perceived, the Tathagata is recognized. 若见诸相非相，即见如来"?
10. What is the nominalistic premise in the statement "the Buddha teaches that that which is no-body is known as a large body. 佛说非身是名大身" in the last sentence of the selection?

C. Reflect on the theme of the Buddha Nature 佛性 in *Sutra Spoken by the Sixth Patriarch* and answer the following questions:

11. How does the story of Hui-Neng illustrate the idea of "people may differ in appearance, but not in Buddha Nature"?
12. Explain why Buddha Nature is non-dualistic.

D. Analyze the literary settings of the sutras.

13. Poems often function as a sign of enlightenment in Chan literature. What are the different achievements reflected in the two "mirror" poems written by Hui-Neng and Shin-shau in *Sutra Spoken by the Sixth Patriarch*?
14. In what ways of narrative *Spoken by the Sixth Patriarch* differ from *The Diamond Sutra*?

E. *Sutra Spoken by the Sixth Patriarch* marks a turning point in the history of the signification of Indian Buddhism. Read the sutra and figure out:

15. The Chinese ethical ideologies in the sutra.
16. The different pedagogies applied by the "teachers" — Buddha in *The Diamond Sutra* on one side, and the Patriarch in *Sutra Spoken by the Sixth Patriarch* on the other.

F. Read these three major Mahayana sutras and:

17. Find out the common doctrines illustrated in all the three sutras.
18. Take one doctrine as a sample to compare their different paradigms of argument.
19. Point out the limitations of language in attaining Buddhist enlightenment.
20. Summarize the steps of conquering dualism and nihilism on the way to achieve enlightenment.

III. Application and Interpretation

A. Translate the underlined sections from the "Looking at Lineage: A Fresh Perspective on Chan Buddhism" and discuss the writer's opinion on "Often authors describe Chan as the 'most Chinese' of all the Chinese Buddhist schools, and part of what they are referring to is the Chan genealogical model. (I am particularly allergic to this rhetoric, since such expressions are generally little more than unexplicated tautologies generated through a sense of cultural chauvinism rather than real analytical insight. And the fact that D. T. Suzuki and others say virtually the same thing with regard to Japanese Zen, that it represents somehow the essence of *Japanese* culture, should alert us to both the essential vacuity and the strategic intentions of such sentiments.)" Write a responsive essay to give your opinion to that matter.

B. Do some extra research and write an essay on how Indian Buddhism came to China along the Silk Road.

C. Summarize the steps of logical reasoning of "A is not A, therefore it is A" in Shigenori Nagatomo's "The Logic of the *Diamond Sutra*: A is not A, therefore it is A".

Chapter Five

The Diverse Intellectual Landscapes of Ancient China—Beyond the Mainstream

导读

本章课文节选了《墨经》《韩非子》《公孙龙子》《孙子兵法》的部分章节。四篇拓展性阅读材料从以下篇目而来：A篇为普林斯顿大学东亚系奠基人牟复礼所撰《中国认识论的内涵》；B篇选自《中国人的精神》，由中国第一个用英、德两种语言将《论语》《中庸》翻译到西方的辜鸿铭所著；C篇为英国当代汉学家苏立文所写《中国艺术遗产》节选；D篇《中国园林艺术的完善》选自18世纪英国作家奥利弗·哥德史密斯的《世界公民》。

Introduction

In the vast expanse of Chinese intellectual history, the currents of Confucianism, Buddhism, and Daoism have often dominated the narrative, yet this chapter ventures beyond the mainstream to explore the rich and varied tributaries that have contributed to the complex tapestry of Chinese thought. We delve into the lesser-known but equally profound philosophies that have shaped the Chinese worldview through the ages.

1. Unearthing the Foundations: The Bedrock of Chinese Intellectual Diversity

The Basic Readings section serves as an archaeological delve into the rich strata of Chinese philosophy, unearthing seminal texts that have been instrumental in shaping the cultural ethos of China. Here, we encounter a constellation of ideas that extend beyond the familiar triad of Confucianism, Taoism, and Buddhism, revealing a multifaceted intellectual landscape.

***The Mohist Canons*: Universal Love and Utilitarian Ethics**

The *Mohist Canons* introduces us to Mohist philosophy, with its advocacy for "universal love" (jian ai) and its rejection of nepotism and favoritism. It underscores the importance of meritocracy and the utilitarian approach to governance, where actions are judged by their utility and moral righteousness. The text challenges us to consider the ethics of impartiality and the collective good over individual interests, offering a unique perspective on social harmony and statecraft.

Han Fei Tzu: Legalism and the Way of Rule

Han Fei Tzu, a cornerstone of Legalist thought, presents a pragmatic and authoritarian approach to governance. It emphasizes the necessity of strict laws, a strong centralized state, and the infallible application of rewards and punishments to ensure social order and state control. The text provides insight into the Legalist belief in the power of law and the role of the ruler as the ultimate legislator and executor of justice, casting light on the strategic aspects of ruling an empire.

The Kung-sun Lung Tzu: The Paradoxes of Logic and Nature of Language

The Kung-sun Lung Tzu, with its famous "White Horse Dialogue," opens the door to the intricate world of Chinese logic and ontology. It challenges conventional thinking with paradoxes that question the nature of identity and classification, such as the famous argument that a "white horse is not a horse." This text invites us to ponder the complexities of categorization and the essence of language, offering a philosophical exploration that is both profound and playful.

The Art of War: Strategic Insight and Military Wisdom

Sun Tzu's *The Art of War* is not merely a military treatise but also a guide to strategic thinking in all aspects of life. It offers timeless principles such as the importance of knowing oneself and one's enemy, the art of deception, and the utilization of terrain and situations to one's advantage. The text encapsulates the essence of strategic planning and adaptive leadership, demonstrating the profound influence of military strategy on Chinese thought.

These foundational texts collectively represent a cross-section of Chinese philosophy that is as strategic as it is ethical, as logical as it is practical. They provide us with a deeper understanding of the philosophical underpinnings that have guided Chinese thought, influencing not only the governance and military strategy but also the ethical and logical dimensions of everyday life. Through these readings, we gain a more nuanced appreciation of the intellectual diversity that has contributed to the enduring legacy of Chinese civilization.

2. Modern Interpretations: Unfolding the Unique Tapestry of Chinese Culture

The tapestry of Chinese culture is woven with threads of profound uniqueness, reflecting a philosophical spectrum that is both broad and deep. From the practical orientation of its thought to the moral force that underpins its society, modern scholars present a distinctive profile that sets it apart from other civilizations.

Chapter Five
The Diverse Intellectual Landscapes of Ancient China—Beyond the Mainstream

The Distinctive Epistemological Path

In "Implications of Chinese Epistemology" by Frederick W. Mote, we encounter a philosophical exploration that is quintessentially Chinese, characterized by a pragmatic approach to knowledge and a divergence from the speculative nature of Western philosophy. This epistemological stance is not merely a matter of intellectual debate but a reflection of a deeper cultural ethos that values the application of wisdom in the practical affairs of life. The concept of a "cosmological gulf" suggests a fundamental difference in the way Chinese thought perceives and interacts with the world, one that is less about abstract theorizing and more about the harmony and order of existence.

The Moral Compass and Social Harmony

Gu Hongming's *The Spirit of the Chinese People* articulates the cultural distinctiveness of China, offering a spirited defense of its moral framework. In contrast to the moral dilemmas that plague Western societies, Gu highlights the role of moral force and good citizenship as timeless solutions to social unrest and militarism. This emphasis on ethical conduct and social responsibility is not just a philosophical ideal but a lived reality that has shaped the Chinese spirit and its pursuit of a harmonious society.

The Confluence of Art and Philosophy

The transition from philosophy to the arts in Michael Sullivan's "The Heritage of Chinese Art" reveals the seamless integration of aesthetic expression with philosophical thought. Chinese painting and calligraphy are not mere artistic endeavors but are deeply intertwined with the understanding of the universe and the human condition. The pursuit of harmony and the embodiment of life movement in these art forms are a testament to the Chinese conception of the cosmos, where every brush stroke carries the weight of philosophical reflection and spiritual resonance.

The Garden as a Moral Allegory

Oliver Goldsmith's "The Perfection of the Chinese in the Art of Gardening" takes us through the intricate relationship between aesthetics and morality in Chinese garden design. These gardens are not just places of beauty and repose but are imbued with moral and philosophical lessons that guide the soul toward virtue. The cultivation of nature in Chinese gardens is an art form that reflects the profound understanding of the interplay between humanity and the natural world, where the landscape itself becomes a teacher of wisdom and virtue.

Together, these readings paint a picture of a culture that is deeply rooted in its unique philosophical, ethical, and aesthetic principles. Chinese culture is not just a collection of ideas but a living tradition that has shaped and continues to shape the lives of its people, offering a vision of a world where wisdom, morality, and beauty are inextricably linked. The uniqueness of Chinese culture lies in this holistic approach to life, where every aspect of existence—from thought to art to the cultivation of nature—is infused with a profound sense of meaning and purpose.

《墨经》选篇[1] Selections from the *Mohist Canons*[2]

止，彼以此其然也，说是其然也；我以此其不然也，疑是其然也。此然是必然，则俱。

谓：四足兽，与生鸟与，物尽与，大小也。

为麋同名。俱斗，不俱二，二与斗也。包、肝、肺、子，爱也。楙茅，食与招也。白马多白，视马不多视，白与视也。为丽不必丽，不必丽与暴也。为非以是不为非，若为夫勇不为夫，为屦以买不为屦，夫与屦也。

二与一亡，不与一在，偏去之。

有之实也，而后谓之；无文实也，则无谓也。若敷与美，谓是，则是固美也，谓他，则是非美，无谓则疑也。

Analogism: If A is B and B is C, then it is an inevitable result that A is C; but if A is B but B is not C, then it is not an inevitable insult that A is C. An inevitable result comes from a matching analogy.

The set of "four-legged animal" is larger than "ox" or "horse" and smaller than "animal." Everything belongs to different sets, which can be larger or smaller.

Both the mare and the deer belong to the same large category (the four legged animal). When the mare and the deer are fighting, there may be more than two four-legged animals in the fight. There is difference between "two animals are fighting" and "two small categories of four-legged animals are fighting." The embryo, the liver and the lung are all parts of a mother's body, yet "the love for one's child" is different from "the love of one's body." Both the orange and the cogon may serve as food, yet the former is food for man and the latter is sacrifice to god. The white horse is almost white; you can "examine a horse" but you cannot "almost examine" it. Beauty may not expose itself, so "the beautiful" may not always be "the extravagant." A man with weak points may not be weak; a man in husbandry may not be a husband; the straw to make sandals is not a sandal.

When a whole is divided into two parts, it exists no longer as a whole but as the two parts generated thereof.

If the name and the substance coincide, the object is called rightfully by that name; if the name and the substance do not coincide, the object cannot be rightfully called by that name. Let's

---

[1] 选自汪榕培、王宏译：《英译〈墨经〉：汉英对照》，上海：上海外语教育出版社，2010 年。

[2] Excerpted from Wang Rongpei and Wang Hong trans., *The Mohist Canons*, Shanghai Foreign Language Education Publishing House, 2010.

Chapter Five
The Diverse Intellectual Landscapes of Ancient China—Beyond the Mainstream

take "flower" and "beautiful" as an example. Something that is called a flower is beautiful; something else that is called by some other name is not beautiful.

Without proper names, there comes uncertainty. In terms of the features of an object, what can be seen and what cannot be seen are not separable from each other. For example, width and length coexist in the same plane; hardness and whiteness coexist in the same stone.

见不见不离，一二相盈，广修，坚白。

He who can lift a weight but does not pick up a needle is not to be blamed, if it is not the duty of a strong man. Guessing at whether a handful of items is in the odd number or in the even number is not the duty of a mathematician. The ears can hear but cannot see while the eyes can see but cannot hear.

举不重，不与箴，非力之任也。为握者之觭倍，非智之任也。若耳目异。

Which is longer, a plank of wood or a night? Which do you possess more, wisdom or grains? Which is more valuable, rank or parents or virtue or price? Which is taller, the height of a deer or the flight of a crane? Which is more sorrowful, the chirrup of a cicada or the music of a zither?

木与夜孰长，智与粟孰多，爵、亲、行、贾，四者孰贵？麋与霍孰高？蚓与瑟孰瑟？

The total volume of the removed part plus the remaining part is the same as the whole.

偏，俱一无变。

Loan-name: A loan-name is certainly a name loaned to name something else; otherwise, it would not have been called a loan-name. A dog with the loan-name of "crane" is not a crane.

假必非也而后假。狗假霍也，犹氏霍也。

……

……

It is admissible to call something by the loan-name of "crane." As something with the loan-name of "crane" is not a crane, to say that something with the loan-name of "crane" is a crane is not admissible. The name I give to an object must agree with the name another person gives to the object. If the loan-name I use in naming an object agrees with what he uses, my loan-name will do. If what I use to name an object does not agree with what he uses to name the object, what I use to name the object will not do.

惟，谓是霍可，而犹之非夫霍也，谓彼是是也。不可谓者，毋惟乎其谓。彼犹惟乎其谓，则吾谓不行。彼若不惟其谓，则不行也。

If the south has a limit, the number of people is exhaustible; if the south does not have a limit, the number of people is inexhaustible. If whether or not the south has a limit is unknown,

无，南者有穷则可尽，无穷则不可尽。有穷无穷未可智，则可尽不可尽未可智。

— 219 —

人之盈之否未可智，而人之可尽不可尽亦未可智。而必人之可尽爱也，悖。人若不盈无穷，则人有穷也。尽有穷无难。盈无穷，则无穷尽也，尽无穷无难。

不，不智其数，恶智爱民之尽之也？或者遗乎其问也？尽问人则尽爱其所问，若不智其数而智爱之尽之也，无难。

仁，仁爱也。义，利也。爱利，此也。所爱所利，彼也。爱利不相为内外，所爱利亦不相为外内。其为仁内也，义外也，举爱与所利也，是狂举也。若左目出右目入。

学，以为不知学之无益也，故告之也，是。使智学之无益也，是教也，以学为无益也教，悖。

论诽，诽之可不可，以

we will not know whether the number of people is exhaustible or not. If we do not know whether the people have filled the universe or not, we do not know whether the number of people is exhaustible or not. Then, is it mistaken to hold the view that we can love all the people in the universe? If the people cannot fill the limitless universe, the number of people will be exhaustible. Therefore, we can love an exhaustible number of people and the view of universal love is not mistaken. If the people can fill the limitless universe, the number of people will be inexhaustible. Therefore, we can love an inexhaustible number of people and the view of universal love is not mistaken.

How can we love the people all over the universe without knowing their number? What if we miss some of the people in our count? If we count all people we know, we love all the people we know. This is universal love. Therefore, there is no doubt about the view that we can love all the people although we do not know their number.

Benevolence: To be benevolent is to love others and to be righteous is to others. I bestow love and benefit upon others while others receive my love and benefit. As both the love and the benefit I bestow upon others are from within, we cannot say that the love is from within and the benefit is from without. As both the love and the benefit others receive are from without, we cannot say the love is from within and the benefit is from without. In view of "benevolence from within and righteousness from without," love is cited as an example of being within and benefit is cited as an example of being without. These examples are partial. In the same way, the statement "you exhale with your left nostril and inhale with your right nostril" is a self-contradiction.

Learning: Thinking that people do not know "It is useless to learn," those who are against learning tell them about this. But to make people know about this is actually to teach them to learn about this. Those are in the wrong that take learning as useless on the one hand and teach people to learn on the other.

Criticism: Here is a comment on whether something is to

be criticized or not. If something ought to be criticized as a result of logical reasoning, the criticism is correct no matter how much criticism is given; if something ought not to be criticized as a result of logical reasoning, the criticism is wrong no matter how little criticism is given. When someone says that there should not be too much criticism, he seems to be comparing something long with something short.

If you attack other people's criticism, you are making criticism yourself and your own criticism should be attacked too. If you accept other people's criticism, your mistake can be exposed to criticism. Being open to criticism helps you to consolidate your arguments.

……

Selections from *Han Fei Tzu* [1]

There are four things that enable the enlightened ruler to achieve accomplishments and establish fame; namely, timeliness of the seasons, the hearts of the people, skill and talents, and position of power. Without the timeliness of the seasons, even the Yaos cannot grow a single ear of grain in the winter. Acting against the sentiment of the people, even Meng Pen and Xia Yv (famous men of great strength) could not make them exhaust their efforts. Therefore with timeliness of the seasons, the grains will grow of themselves. If the ruler has won the hearts of the people, they will exhort themselves without being pressed. If skill and talents are utilized, results will be quickly achieved without any haste. If one occupies a position of power, his fame will be achieved without pushing forward. Like water flowing and like a boat floating, the ruler follows the course of Nature and enforces an infinite number of commands. Therefore he is called an enlightened ruler.

……

理之可诽，虽多诽，其诽是也；其理不可非，虽少诽，非也。今也谓多诽者不可，是犹以长论短。

非诽，非己之诽也。不非诽，非可非也。不可非也，是不非诽也。

……

《韩非子》选段 [2]

明君之所以立功成名者四：一曰天时，二曰人心，三曰技能，四曰势位。非天时，虽十尧不能冬生一穗；逆人心，虽贲、育不能尽人力。故得天时，则不务而自生；得人心，则不趣而自劝；因技能，则不急而自疾；得势位，则不推进而名成。若水之流，若船之浮。守自然之道，行毋穷之令，故曰明主。

……

---

① Excerpted from Wing-Tsit Chan ed., *A Source Book in Chinese Philosophy*. Princeton: Princeton University Press, 1969.

② 选自《韩非子》，高华平、王齐洲、张三夕译注，北京：中华书局，2010 年。

问者曰："申不害、公孙鞅，此二家之言孰急于国？"

应之曰："是不可程也。人不食，十日则死；大寒之隆，不衣亦死。谓之衣食孰急于人，则是不可一无也，皆养生之具也。今申不害言术而公孙鞅为法。术者，因任而授官，循名而责实，操杀生之柄，课群臣之能者也。此人主之所执也。法者，宪令著于官府，刑罚必于民心，赏存乎慎法，而罚加乎奸令者也。此臣之所师也。君无术则弊于上，臣无法则乱于下，此不可一无，皆帝主之具也。"

……

明主之所导制其臣者，二柄而已矣。二柄者，刑德也。何谓刑德？曰：杀戮之谓刑，庆赏之谓德。为人臣者畏诛罚而利庆赏，故人主自用其刑德，则群臣畏其威而归其利矣，故世之奸臣则不然，所恶，则能得之其主而罪之；所爱，则能得之其主而赏之。今人主非使赏罚之威利出于己也，听其臣而行其赏罚，则一国之人皆畏其臣而易其君，归其臣而去其君矣。此人主失刑德之患也。夫虎之所以能服狗者，爪牙也，使虎释其爪牙而使狗用之，则虎反服于狗矣。人主者，以

The questioner asks, "Of the doctrines of the two schools of Shen Buhai and Shang Yang, which is of more urgent need to the state?"

I reply: "They cannot be evaluated. A man will die if he does not eat for ten days. He will also die if he wears no clothing during the height of a severe cold spell. If it is asked whether clothing or food is more urgently needed by a man, the reply is that he cannot live without either, for they are both means to preserve life. Shen Buhai advocated statecraft and Shang Yang advocated law. Statecraft involves appointing officials according to their abilities and demanding that actualities correspond to names. It holds the power of life and death and inquires into the ability of all ministers. These are powers held by the ruler. By law is meant statutes and orders formulated by the government, with punishments which will surely impress the hearts of the people. Rewards are there for those who obey the law and punishments are to be imposed on those who violate orders. These are things the ministers must follow. On the higher level, if the ruler has no statecraft, he will be ruined. On the lower level, if ministers are without laws, they will become rebellious. Neither of these can be dispensed with. They both are means of emperors and kings."

……

The means by which the enlightened ruler controls his ministers are none other than the two handles. The two handles are punishment and kindness. What do we mean by punishment and kindness? To execute is called punishment and to offer congratulations or rewards is called kindness. Ministers are afraid of execution and punishment but look upon congratulations and rewards as advantages. Therefore, if a ruler himself applies punishment and kindness, all ministers will fear his power and turn to the advantages. As to treacherous ministers, they are different. They would get [the handle of punishment] from the ruler [through flattery and so forth] and punish those whom they hate and get [the handle of kindness] from the ruler and reward those, whom they love. If the ruler does not see to it that the power of reward and punishment proceeds from himself but instead leaves it to his ministers to apply reward and punishment, then everyone in the state will fear the ministers and slight the ruler, turn to them and get away from the ruler. This is the trouble of the ruler who loses the handles of punishment and kindness.

For the tiger is able to subdue the dog because of its claws and fangs. If the tiger abandons its claws and fangs and lets the dog use them, it will be subdued by the dog. Similarly, the ruler controls his ministers through punishment and kindness. If the ruler abandons his punishment and kindness and lets his ministers use them, he will be controlled by the ministers.

When a ruler wants to suppress treachery, he must examine the correspondence between actuality and names. Actuality and names refer to the ministers' words and deeds. When a minister presents his words, the ruler assigns him a task in accordance with his words and demands accomplishments specifically from that work. If the results correspond to the task and the task to the words, he should be rewarded. If the accomplishments do not correspond to the task or the task not to the words, he will be punished. If the minister's words are big but his accomplishment is small, he will be punished. The punishment is not for the small accomplishment but for the fact that the accomplishment does not correspond to the words. If the minister's words are small and his accomplishments are big, he will also be punished. It is not that the ruler is not pleased with the big accomplishments but he considers the failure of the big accomplishments to correspond to the words worse than the big accomplishments themselves. Therefore he is to be punished.

刑德制臣者也。今君人者释其刑德而使臣用之，则君反制于臣矣。故田常上请爵禄而行之群臣，下大斗斛而施于百姓，此简公失德而田常用之也，故简公见弑。子罕谓宋君曰："夫庆赏赐予者，民之所喜也，君自行之；杀戮刑罚者，民之所恶也，臣请当之。"于是宋君失刑百子罕用之。故宋君见劫。田常徒用德而简公弑，子罕徒用刑而宋君劫。故今世为人臣者兼刑德而用之，则是世主之危甚于简公、宋君也。①故劫杀拥蔽之主，兼失刑德而使臣用之，而不危亡者，则未尝有也。

人主将欲禁奸，则审合刑名；刑名者，言与事也。为人臣者陈而言，君以其言授之事，专以其言责其功。功当其事，事当其言，则赏；功不当其事，事不当其言，则罚。故群臣其言大而功小者则罚，非罚小功也，罚功不当名也；群臣其言小而功大者亦罚，非不说于大功也，以为不当名也害甚于有大功，故罚。

Selections from *The Kung-sun Lung Tzu* ②

On the White Horse

A: Is it correct to say that a white horse is not a horse?

《公孙龙子》选篇③

白马论

[曰:] "白马非马"，可乎？

---

① 此处有部分文字并未在英文中译出。为确保中英文基本对应，故此处未译出文字用斜体表示。
② Excerpted from Wing-Tsit Chan, *A Source Book in Chinese Philosophy*, Princeton University Press, 1969.
③ 选自黄克剑译注：《公孙龙子（外三种）》，北京：中华书局，2012年。

曰：可。

曰：何哉？

曰：马者，所以命形也；白者，所以命色也。命色形非命形也。故曰：白马非马。

曰：有白马，不可谓无马也。不可谓无马者，非马也？有白马为有马，白之非马何也？

曰：求马，黄、黑马皆可致；求白马，黄、黑马不可致。使白马乃马也，是所求一也。所求一者，白者不异马也。[使]所求不异，如黄、黑马有可有不可，何也？可与不可，其相非明。故黄、黑马一也，而可以应有马，不可以应有白马，是白马之非马，审矣。

曰：以马之有色为非马，天下非有无色之马也！天下无马，可乎？

曰：马固有色，故有白马。使马无色，有马如已耳，安取白马？故白马非马也。白马者，马与白也。马与白，马也？故曰：白马非马也。

曰：马未与白为马，白未与马为白；合马与白，复名"白马"。是相与以不相与为名，未可。故曰："白马非马"未可。

曰：以有白马为有马，

B: It is.

A: Why?

B: Because "horse" denotes the form and "white'" denotes the color. What denotes the color does not denote the form. Therefore we say that a white horse is not a horse.

A: There being a horse, one cannot say that there is no horse. If one cannot say that there is no horse, then isn't [it] a horse? Since there being a white horse means that there is a horse, why does being white make it not a horse?

B: Ask for a horse, and either a yellow or a black one may answer. Ask for a white horse, and neither the yellow horse nor the black one may answer. If a white horse were a horse, then what is asked in both cases would be the same. If what is asked is the same, then a white horse would be no different from a horse. If what is asked is no different, then why is it that yellow and black horses may yet answer in the one case but not in the other? Clearly the two cases are incompatible. Now the yellow horse and the black horse remain the same. And yet they answer to a horse but not to a white horse. Obviously a white horse is not a horse.

A: You consider a horse with color as not a horse. Since there is no horse in the world without color, is it all right [to say] that there is no horse in the world?

B: Horses of course have color. Therefore there are white horses. If horses had no color, there would be simply horses. Where do white horses come in? Therefore whiteness is different from horse. A white horse means a horse combined with whiteness. [Thus in one case it is] horse and [in the other it is] a white horse. Therefore we say that a white horse is not a horse.

A: [Since you say that] before the horse is combined with whiteness, it is simply a horse, before whiteness is combined with a horse it is simply whiteness, and when the horse and whiteness are combined they are collectively called a white horse, you are calling a combination by what is not a combination. This is incorrect. Therefore it is incorrect to say that a white horse is not a horse.

B: If you regard a white horse as a horse, is it correct to say that a white horse is a yellow horse?

A: No.

B: If you regard a white horse as different from a yellow horse, you are differentiating a yellow horse from a horse. To differentiate a yellow horse from a horse is to regard the yellow horse as not a horse. Now to regard a yellow horse as not a horse and yet to regard a white horse as a horse is like a bird flying into a pool or like the inner and outer coffins being in different places. This would be the most contradictory argument and the wildest talk.

A: [When we say that] a white horse cannot be said to be not a horse, we are separating the whiteness from the horse. If [the whiteness] is not separated from [the horse], then there would be a white horse and we should not say that there is [just] a horse. Therefore when we say that there is a horse, we do so singly because it is a horse and not because it is a white horse. When we say that there is a horse, we do not mean that there are a horse [as such] and another horse [as the white horse].

B: It is all right to ignore the whiteness that is not fixed on any object. But in speaking of the white horse, we are talking about the whiteness that is fixed on the object. The object on which whiteness is fixed is not whiteness [itself]. The term "horse" does not involve any choice of color and therefore either a yellow horse or a black one may answer. But the term "white horse" does involve a choice of color. Both the yellow horse and the black one are excluded because of their color. Only a white horse may answer. What does not exclude [color] is not the same as what excludes [color]. Therefore we say that a white horse is not a horse.

Selections from *The Art of War*[1]

I. Laying Plans

Sun Tzu said: The art of war is of vital importance to the

谓有马为有黄马，可乎?

曰：未可。

曰：以有马为异有黄马，是异黄马于马也；异黄于马，是以黄为非马。以黄马为非马，而以白马为有马，此飞者入池而棺椁异处，此天下之悖言乱辞也。

曰："有白马不可谓无马"者，离白之谓也；不离者，有白马不可谓有马也。故所以为有马者，独以马为有马耳，非有白马为有马。故其为有马也，不可以谓"马马"也。

曰："白者不定所白"，忘之而可也。白马者，言白定所白也。定所白者，非白也。马者，无去取于色，故黄、黑皆所以应；白马者，有去取于色，黄、黑马皆以所色去，故唯白马独可以应耳。无去［取］者非有去［取］也，故曰："白马非马。"

《孙子兵法》选篇[2]

计篇第一

孙子曰：兵者，国之大事，

---

[1] Excerpted from Lionel Giles trans., *The Art of War*, Pax Librorum Publishing House, 2009.
[2] 选自骈宇骞、王建宇、牟虹、郝小刚译注：《孙子兵法·孙膑兵法》，北京：中华书局，2007年。

死生之地，存亡之道，不可不察也。

故经之以五事，校之以计，而索其情。一曰道，二曰天，三曰地，四曰将，五曰法。道者，令民与上同意也，故可以与之死，可以与之生，而不畏危也。天者，阴阳、寒暑、时制也。地者，远近、险易、广狭、死生也。将者，智、信、仁、勇、严也。法者，曲制、官道、主用也。凡此五者，将莫不闻，知之者胜，不知之者不胜。

势篇第五

……势如彍弩，节如发机。

纷纷纭纭，斗乱而不可乱也；浑浑沌沌，形圆而不可败也。乱生于治，怯生于勇，弱生于强。治乱，数也；勇怯，势也；强弱，形也。故善动敌者，形之，敌必从之；予之，敌必取之。以利动之，以卒待之。

State. It is a matter of life and death, a road either to safety or to ruin. Hence it is a subject of inquiry which can on no account be neglected.

The art of war, then, is governed by five constant factors, to be taken into account in one's deliberations, when seeking to determine the conditions obtaining in the field. These are: (1) the Moral Law; (2) Heaven; (3) Earth; (4) the Commander; (5) method and discipline.

The Moral Law causes the people to be in complete accord with their ruler, so that they will follow him regardless of their lives, undismayed by any danger.

Heaven signifies night and day, cold and heat, times and seasons.

Earth comprises distances, great and small; danger and security; open ground and narrow passes; the chances of life and death.

The Commander stands for the virtues of wisdom, sincerity, benevolence, courage and strictness.

By method and discipline are to be understood the marshaling of the army in its proper subdivisions, the graduations of rank among the officers, the maintenance of roads by which supplies may reach the army, and the control of military expenditure.

These five heads should be familiar to every general: he who knows them will be victorious; he who knows them not will fail.

V. Energy

...Energy may be likened to the bending of a crossbow; decision, to the releasing of a trigger.

Amid the turmoil and tumult of battle, there may be seeming disorder and yet no real disorder at all; amid confusion and chaos, your array may be without head or tail, yet it will be proof against defeat.

Simulated disorder postulates perfect discipline; simulated fear postulates courage; simulated weakness postulates strength.

Hiding order beneath the cloak of disorder is simply a question of subdivision; concealing courage under a show of timidity presupposes a fund of latent energy; masking strength with weakness is to be effected by tactical dispositions.

Thus one who is skillful at keeping the enemy on the move maintains deceitful appearances, according to which the enemy will act. He sacrifices something, that the enemy may snatch at it.

By holding out baits, he keeps him on the march; then with a body of picked men he lies in wait for him.

The clever combatant looks to the effect of combined energy, and does not require too much from individuals. Hence his ability to pick out the right men and to utilise combined energy. When he utilises combined energy, his fighting men become as it were like unto rolling logs or stones. For it is the nature of a log or stone to remain motionless on level ground, and to move when on a slope; if four-cornered, to come to a standstill, but if round-shaped, to go rolling down.

故善战者，求之于势，不责于人，故能择人而任势。任势者，其战人也如转木石。木石之性，安则静，危则动，方则止，圆则行。故善战人之势，如转圆石于千仞之山者，势也。

Thus the energy developed by good fighting men is as the momentum of a round stone rolled down a mountain thousands of feet in height. So much on the subject of energy.

Extensive Readings

A. Implications of Chinese Epistemology[①]
中国认识论的内涵

Frederick W. Mote
牟复礼

Were we to review all the other known philosophies of the Golden Age, we would find in most of them practical concern for the problem of order in society, efforts to establish theories of human nature, and philosophic justifications for particular patterns of living. We would find but little speculation just for speculation's sake. China had a distinct dearth of "pure philosophers" who spun out theories about abstract philosophical issues. But as the foregoing discussions of Mohism and the logicians show, some ancient Chinese thinkers did consider the formal problems of logic and had the ability to deal with epistemological issues in a fairly advanced and sophisticated manner. The lack of further development in China, therefore, reflects a choice.

---

① Excerpted from Frederick W. Mote. *Intellectual Foundations of China*. Alfred A. Knopf, 1971.

Yet Chinese thought had its characteristic mode, one that was quite different from the modes of classical Greek, ancient Indian, and other notable early philosophic traditions. What caused China's distinctiveness? Is the "cosmological gulf" between China and the rest of the world, if it can be considered fully established, sufficient explanation of all these further points of distinctiveness? Or is the cosmological gulf itself merely part of a cultural set, the whole of which demands more fundamental explanation of its distinctiveness, or of its Chineseness?

Coupled with the characteristic mode of Chinese thought, as illustrated in its handling of the problem of knowledge, are several other distinctive features of Chinese intellectual history. Many scholars have noted these, and some have attempted to formulate explanations based on comparisons with Western intellectual history. Joseph Needham has observed certain cases in the history of Chinese mathematical and astronomical sciences where the ancient Chinese adopted solutions conceptually quite different from, but not necessarily scientifically inferior to, those adopted in the West. Chinese mathematics was from its beginnings more algebraic, whereas Greek mathematics was more geometric in character. Again, Chinese astronomy was polar and equatorial in conception and method, whereas Western astronomy was ecliptic. Wolfram Eberhard quotes Needham: "If, like all Chinese science, Chinese astronomy was fundamentally empirical and observational, it was spared the excesses and aberrations, as well as the triumphs, of Occidental theorizing." [1]

We may also observe that the development of epistemological and metaphysical theory in classical Greek thought came after a prior interest in and development of mathematics. Pythagoras antedated Socrates by a century and a half. In China, the great interest in and development of mathematics occurred in the Han Dynasty, some centuries after the Golden philosophy had more or less fixed the characteristic mode in thought. So the sequence of these developments was reversed. But does this observation explain anything?

The Polish historian of Chinese thought, Januz Chmielewski, notes a preoccupation with the concept and significance of nonidentity in early Chinese logic: this contrasts in his mind with Greek logicians' functionally analogous but qualitatively different focus on the concept of identity, as in the syllogism.

Throughout this book we have stressed the perceptiveness of psychological observation and the unifying preoccupation with the psychological element in almost all early Chinese schools of thought. All these generalized observations display the distinctiveness of Chinese thought. What, however, do they contribute to explaining that distinctiveness? Moreover, do they bear in any way on the generally noted Chinese preference for the practical, the applied aspects as opposed to

---

[1] Quoted in Wolfram Eberhard's review of Needham's work, *Journal of Asian Studies*, 19 (November 1959), p. 65.

the more theoretical approach of Western philosophy?

While it by no means offers a comprehensive or wholly satisfactory explanation of what makes Chinese thought distinctive, the fact that all schools of Chinese thought have looked with great suspicion upon the concern with any purely speculative theory of knowledge disputatiously maintained (was the association of theory and dispute necessary?) must have acted as a major deterrent to the development of such fields of inquiry, and that constriction must be judged to have affected the profile of Chine thought markedly. At the same time this, unwillingness to argue about theory displays further the characteristic mind-set of the early Chinese intellectual world; it is in the pattern. We have noted that Confucius's doctrine of the rectification of names had only ethical, not theoretical or epistemological intent.

Similarly, among later thinkers, any concern which did not prove useful in immediate application tended to be rejected. Zhuang Zi said: "If we look at Hui Shi's ability from the standpoint of Heaven and Earth, it was only like the restless activity of a mosquito or gadfly; of what service was it to anything?" Xun Zi, who went further than any other Confucian in sharpening the tools of thinking, nonetheless noted that Hui Shi's teachings "could not serve as the basis for government" and that he "worked much but accomplished little." He concluded that Hui Shi was "blinded by phrases and didn't know realities." The historian Sima Tan, of the second century B.C., although somewhat sympathetic toward Taoism and therefore not so relentlessly practical-minded as the typical orthodox Confucians, complained that Hui Shi "lost sight of human feelings." In the second century A.D., the great Confucian scholar and historian, Ban Gu, though acknowledging that "correct names" are important and that in fact the search for them had been started by Confucius, nevertheless added that, when the search becomes disputatious, it creates only division and disorder. With him, as characteristically with all later Confucians, order and practical social good were more important in any philosophy than a search for abstract truth.

B. Selections from *The Spirit of the Chinese People*[①]
中国人的精神

Gu Hongming

辜鸿铭

In the first early and rude stage of society, mankind had to use physical force to subdue

---

① Excerpted from Gu Hongming, *The Spirit of the Chinese People*, City Press, 2008.

and subjugate human passions. Thus hordes of savages had to be subjugated by sheer physical force. But as civilization advances, mankind discovers a force more potent and more effective for subduing and controlling human passions than physical force and this force is called moral force. The moral force which in the past has been effective in subduing and controlling the human passions in the population of Europe, is Christianity. But now this war with the armament preceding it, seems to show that Christianity has become ineffective as a moral force. Without an effective moral force to control and restrain human passions, the people of Europe have had again to employ physical force to keep civil order. As Carlyle truly says, "Europe is Anarchy plus a constable." The use of physical force to maintain civil order leads to militarism. In fact militarism is necessary in Europe today because of the want of an effective moral force. But militarism leads to war and war means destruction and waste. Thus the people of Europe are on the horns of a dilemma. If they do away with militarism, anarchy will destroy their civilization, but if they keep up militarism, their civilization will collapse through the waste and destruction of war. But Englishmen say that they are determined to put down Prussian militarism and Lord Kitchner believes that he will be able to stamp out Prussian militarism with three million drilled and armed Englishmen. But then it seems to me when Prussian militarism is thus stamped out, there will then arise another militarism, —the British militarism which again will have to be stamped out. Thus there seems to be no way of escape out of this vicious circle.

But is there really no way of escape? Yes, I believe there is. The American Emerson long ago said, "I can easily see the bankruptcy of the vulgar musket worship, —though great men be musket worshippers; and 'tis certain, as God liveth, the gun that does need another gun, the law of love and justice alone can effect a clean revolution." Now if the people of Europe really want to put down militarism, there is only one way of doing it and that is, to use what Emerson calls the gun that does not need another gun, the law of love and justice, —in fact, moral force. With an effective moral force, militarism will become unnecessary and disappear of itself. But now that Christianity has become ineffective as a moral force, the problem is where are the people of Europe to find this new effective moral force which will make militarism unnecessary?

I believe the people of Europe will find this new moral force in China, —in the Chinese civilization. The moral force in the Chinese civilization which can make militarism unnecessary is the Religion of good citizenship. But people will say to me, "There have also been wars in China." It is true there have been wars in China; but, since the time of Confucius 2500 years ago, we Chinese have had no militarism such as that we see in Europe today. In China war is an accident, whereas in Europe war has become a necessity. We Chinese are liable to have wars, but we do not live in constant expectation of war. In fact the one thing intolerable in the state of Europe, it seems to me, is not so much war as the fact that everybody is constantly afraid that his

Chapter Five
The Diverse Intellectual Landscapes of Ancient China—Beyond the Mainstream

neighbor as soon as he gets strong enough to be able to do it, will come to rob and murder him and he has therefore to arm himself or pay for an armed policeman to protect him. Thus what weighs upon the people of Europe is not so much the accident of War, but the constant necessity to arm themselves, the absolute necessity to use physical force to protect themselves.

Now in China because we Chinese have the Religion of good citizenship a man does not feel the need of using physical force to protect himself; he has seldom the need even to call in and use the physical force of the policeman, of the State to protect him. A man in China is protected by the sense of justice of his neighbor; he is protected by the readiness of his fellow men to obey the sense of moral obligation. In fact, a man in China does not feel the need of using physical force to protect himself because he is sure that right and justice is recognized by everybody as a force higher than physical force and moral obligation is recognized by everybody as something which must be obeyed. Now if you can get all mankind to agree to recognize right and justice, as a force higher than physical force, and moral obligation as something which must be obeyed, then the use of physical force will become unnecessary; then there will be no militarism in the world. But of course there will be in every country a few people, criminals, and in the world, a few savages who will not or are not able to recognize right and justice as a force higher than physical force and moral obligation as something which must be obeyed. Thus against criminals and savages a certain amount of physical or police force and militarism will always be necessary in every country and in the world.

......

In fact, what I want to say here, is that the wonderful peculiarity of the Chinese people is not that they live a life of the heart. All primitive people also live a life of the heart. The Christian people of medieval Europe, as we know, also lived a life of the heart. Matthew Arnold says: "the poetry of medieval Christianity lived by the heart and imagination." But the wonderful peculiarity of the Chinese people, I want to say here, is that, while living a life of the heart, the life of a child, they yet have a power of mind and rationality which you do not find in the Christian people of medieval Europe or in any other primitive people. <u>In other words, the wonderful peculiarity of the Chinese is that for a people, who have lived so long as a grown-up nation, as a nation of adult reason, they are yet able to this day to live the life of a child—a life of the heart.</u>

Instead, therefore, of saying that the Chinese are a people of arrested development, one ought rather to say that the Chinese are a people who never grow old. In short the wonderful peculiarity of the Chinese people as a race, is that they possess the secret of perpetual youth.

Now we can answer the question which we asked in the beginning: —What is the real Chinaman? The real Chinaman, we see now, is a man who lives the life of a man of adult reason with the heart of a child. In short, the real Chinaman is a person with the head of a grown-up man and the heart of a child. The Chinese spirit, therefore, is a spirit of perpetual youth, the spirit of national immortality. Now what is the secret of this national immortality in the Chinese people? You will remember that in the beginning of this discussion I said that what gives to the Chinese type of humanity—to the real Chinaman—his inexpressible gentleness is the possession of what I called sympathetic or true human intelligence. This true human intelligence, I said, is the product of a combination of two things, sympathy and intelligence. It is a working together in harmony of the heart and head. In short it is a happy union of soul with intellect. Now if the spirit of the Chinese people is a spirit of perpetual youth, the spirit of national immortality, the secret of this immortality is this happy union of soul with intellect.

You will now ask me where and how did the Chinese people get this secret of national immortality—this happy union of soul with intellect, which has enabled them as a race and nation to live a life of perpetual youth? The answer, of course, is that they got it from their civilization. Now you will not expect me to give you a lecture on Chinese civilization within the time at my disposal. But I will try to tell you something of the Chinese civilization which has a bearing on our present subject of discussion.

Let me first of all tell you that there is, it seems to me, one great fundamental difference between the Chinese civilization and the civilization of modern Europe. Here let me quote an admirable saying of a famous living art critic, Mr. Bernard Berenson. Comparing European with Oriental art, Mr. Berenson says: "Our European art has the fatal tendency to become science and we hardly possess a masterpiece which does not bear the marks of having been a battlefield for divided interests." Now what I want to say of the European civilization is that it is, as Mr. Berenson says of European art, a battlefield for divided interests; a continuous warfare for the divided interests of science and art on the one hand, and of religion and philosophy on the other; in fact a terrible battlefield where the head and the heart—the soul and the intellect—come into constant conflict. In the Chinese civilization, at least for the last 2400 years, there is no such conflict. That, I say, is the one great fundamental difference between the Chinese civilization and that of modern Europe.

In other words, what I want to say, is that in modern Europe, the people have a religion which satisfies their heart, but not their head, and a philosophy which satisfies their head but not their heart. Now let us look at China. Some people say that the Chinese have no religion. It is certainly true that in China even the mass of the people do not take seriously to religion. I mean religion in the European sense of the word. The temples, rites and ceremonies of Taoism and Buddhism in China are more objects of recreation than of edification; they touch the aesthetic sense, so to speak, of the Chinese people rather than their moral or religious sense; in fact, they appeal more to their imagination than to their heart or soul. But instead of saying that the Chinese have no religion, it is perhaps more correct to say that the Chinese do not want—do not feel the need of religion.

Now what is the explanation of this extraordinary fact that the Chinese people, even the mass of the population in China, do not feel the need of religion? It is thus given by an Englishman. Sir Robert K. Douglas, Professor of Chinese in the London University, in his study of Confucianism, says: "Upwards of forty generations of Chinamen have been absolutely subjected to the dicta of one man. Being a Chinaman of Chinamen the teachings of Confucius were specially suited to the nature of those he taught. The Mongolian mind being eminently phlegmatic and unspeculative, naturally rebels against the idea of investigating matters beyond its experiences. With the idea of a future life still unawakened, a plain, matter-of-fact system of morality, such as that enunciated by Confucius, was sufficient for all the wants of the Chinese."

That learned English professor is right, when he says that the Chinese people do not feel the need of religion, because they have the teachings of Confucius, but he is altogether wrong, when he asserts that the Chinese people do not feel the need of religion because the Mongolian mind is phlegmatic and unspeculative. In the first place religion is not a matter of speculation. Religion is a matter of feeling, of emotion; it is something which has to do with the human soul. The wild, savage man of Africa even, as soon as he emerges from a mere animal life and what is called the soul in him, is awakened, —feels the need of religion. Therefore although the Mongolian mind may be phlegmatic and unspeculative, the Mongolian Chinaman, who, I think it must be admitted, is a higher type of man than the wild man of Africa, also has a soul, and, having a soul, must feel the need of religion unless he has something which can take for him the place of religion.

C. Chinese Painting and Calligraphy[①]
中国的绘画与书法

Michael Sullivan
苏立文

In China, painting, and more especially landscape-painting, is mistress of the arts. That this should be so seems not unnatural when we consider that one of the aims of Chinese philosophy and religion has always been to discover the workings of the universe and to attune man's actions to them. A Chinese painting, therefore, not only embodies the visible forms and forces of

---

① Excerpted from Michael Sullivan, "The Heritage of Chinese Art," from *The Legacy of China*, ed. Raymond Dawson. Clarendon Press, 2009, pp.193-200.

nature, but also displays the painter's understanding of their operation. His purpose is to present the subtle and complex forces of nature as harmoniously interacting, to show man in his true relationship to her, and to convey the life that is in all things by means of the springing vitality of his brushwork. In a sense, therefore, every picture, however slight, is a generalized philosophical, or rather metaphysical statement, even though it may be inspired by a particular place or memory. For the painter is not concerned with individual events, or with the accidents of time and place.

This generalization, this apparent detachment, so different from the passionate attachment to visible objects that we find in Rembrandt, Chardin, or Van Gogh—makes it difficult for the Western viewer to appreciate Chinese painting at first encounter. He finds it remote, tranquil, or merely decorative, and he is sometimes wearied in the long run by what he takes to be a sameness in style and content. The English critic Eric Newton, for example, finds Chinese painting, for all its charm, ultimately cold and unsatisfying; In its tendency to generalization he sees "an air of finality, that precludes any possibility of change, or development, or surprise."[①] There is some justification for this view. The restless "search for form," the experiments with style and technique which give such interest to the study of Western art, play little part in Chinese painting. Like the concert pianist, the Chinese painter must be fully master of his technique and repertoire before he can consider presenting his work to others. He will not hesitate to make use of the vocabulary of "type-forms" and brush-strokes evolved by his predecessors; and often it is only a highly trained eye that can detect the differences between two painters in the same tradition; between, say, figure studies by Qiu Ying and Tang Yin[②], or a landscape by Wen Zhengming and his nephew Wen Boren[③]. And yet, in another sense, the Chinese painter's statement is anything but final; for only a clear statement about something specific can be final—Chardin's bottles, for example, or a Rembrandt self-portrait. On the contrary, he is acutely aware that he is only hinting at the truth; whether he presents a swiftly sketched spray of bamboo, or a vast panorama of mountains and valleys, he is giving us no more than a glimpse of a totality that lies beyond expression.

The apparent lack of perspective in Chinese painting is bound up with this desire to avoid a complete or finite statement. If by perspective we mean the delineation of forms on a flat surface as they would appear to a viewer standing at a fixed point, then Chinese painting indeed has no perspective. The eleventh-century critic Shen Kuo[④] took the landscapist Li Cheng[⑤] to task for his skill in what he called "painting his eaves from below." "This is absurd," he wrote.

---

① Eric Newton, *European Painting and Sculpture*, Harmondsworth, 1941, p. 30.
② （明）仇英和唐寅。
③ （明）文徵明和文伯仁。
④ （北宋）沈括。
⑤ 北宋三大家之一，李成。

Chapter Five
The Diverse Intellectual Landscapes of Ancient China—Beyond the Mainstream

"All landscapes have to be viewed from the angle of totality to behold the part. ...If we apply his method to the painting of mountains, we are unable to see more than one layer of the mountain at one time. How could we then see the totality of its unending ranges?... Li Cheng surely does not understand the principle of viewing the part from the angle of totality. His measurement of height and distance is certainly a fine thing. But should one attach paramount importance to the angles and corners of buildings?" Shen Kuo objects to Li Cheng's application of the principle of one-point perspective because it sets arbitrary limits to the power of the artist to embrace the whole. There are indications that until the end of the Northern Song Dynasty at least, other painters beside Li Cheng were making experiments along these lines, a remarkable example being the long handscroll by Zhang Zeduan depicting preparations for the Qingming festival which has recently been discovered in China. But such experiments ceased after the end of Northern Song, when the aim of the scholar-painter was no longer to reveal nature but to express himself. Most characteristic of Chinese landscape-painting in all periods is what might be termed a continuous perspective, which shifts horizontally in the handscroll and vertically in the hanging scroll, so that the view of each successive area is correct to the eye directly opposite that point. By thus avoiding a fixed viewpoint, and by the subtle placing in his panorama of a winding mountain path, a ferry, perhaps a tea-house, and a few small figures, the painter not only creates the illusion of an actual landscape, but he also cunningly invites us to explore it.

The Chinese view of what constitutes suitable subject-matter for painting presents another striking contrast with that of Europe. The Chinese painter's aim is always to present a view of the world that is satisfying and spiritually refreshing; consequently only themes which carry this message would he consider worthy of his brush. He would regard with horror the rapes, executions, and massacres which, whether of religious inspiration or not, we are trained to contemplate as works of art; for to him art is indivisible, and our Western ability to admire color, form, and composition in a picture without being in any way affected by distasteful subject-matter implies, if not a corrupt view of the world, then at least a dangerously fragmented one.

The lofty calm and detachment from worldly things implicit in a Chinese painting suggests that the painter himself lived in a world apart. But this was only partly true. While some of China's greatest painters—Ni Zan[①], for example, or Shi Qi—have been eccentrics and hermits, many led an active public life, whether as cabinet ministers or district magistrates, which brought them face to face with the world and its problems. But when these men returned home at the end of a busy day to paint a landscape or compose verses, they deliberately left the "dusty world" behind them. The Ming scholar-painter Wen Zhengming, for example, was during the middle

---

① （元）倪瓒。

years of his life too busy with his historical work in the Hanlin Academy to spend his time wandering in the mountains, as he no doubt would have preferred. But he could still take up his brush to paint a landscape panorama that would bring refreshment to himself and pleasure to his friends. To say that such a painting was "escapist" might suggest that it was insincere. Yet it was in the highest sense escapist because it liberated the mind from material things. To achieve this, a painting had to be tranquil, harmonious, and meaningful. Mere originality counted for little or nothing.①

To fulfill its role, moreover, it was necessary that a painting conforms in its colors and shapes to those of nature, not because realism as such was desirable, but because not to paint things correctly would suggest that the artist did not understand them. Accuracy in depicting the procession of the seasons, for example, with the trees and plants in their appropriate colors and foliage was an outward sign of a deeper understanding. But accuracy alone was never enough. Too meticulous a conformity to nature would rob the painting of the quality essential above all—vitality; for it was through the springing movement of the artist's (and the calligrapher's) brush that he expressed his awareness of the life of nature. Finally, and increasingly as time went on, it was desirable that the painting should contain some reference, in composition or brushwork, or even merely in title, to the work of some great master of the past.

These fundamental requirements of a painting were, so far as we know, first set down in writing by the painter and critic Xie He (5th century) in the short preface to his classified list of still earlier masters. His celebrated "six principles" might be briefly translated as follows: spirit-consonance and life-movement; the "bone method" in the use of the brush; conformity to the shapes of objects in nature; conformity to their colors; care in placing and arranging the elements in the composition; transmission of the tradition by copying past models. Fidelity to nature and convincing scale relationships were particularly important during this formative period, when painters were still wrestling with elementary problems of proportion and distance; while the last principle enshrines an attitude to tradition which is unique to China, and is discussed further in the next section of this chapter. Later critics and theorists emphasized one aspect or another, but all were agreed upon the fundamental importance of the first. Xie He's Qi Yun② ("spirit-consonance"). Its precise meaning has been endlessly debated, and every Western historian of Chinese art has produced his own

---

① An excellent introduction to Chinese painting from the Chinese point of view is Chiang Yee, *The Chinese Eye* (London, 1935). In addition to the work of Osvald Sirén cited in note 1, p. 198, general surveys include William Cohn, *Chinese Painting* (London, 1957); Sherman E. Lee, *Chinese Landscape Painting* (revised edition, Cleveland, 1962); while James Cahill's *Chinese Painting* (Geneva, 1960) is notable for its fresh outlook and sympathetic treatment of the literary school; Sirén's *Chinese Painting* (7 vols., London, 1956 and 1958) is encyclopedic in its scope.

② 气韵。

Chapter Five
The Diverse Intellectual Landscapes of Ancient China—Beyond the Mainstream

rendering of the term. It may simply be said that it concerns the vital cosmic spirit or breath (Qi) to which the painter must attune himself (yun) if he is to be able to express the life and movement, or perhaps life-in-movement, that is manifest in nature. This vitality is conveyed by means of the second principle, the structural strength and tension of the brush-stroke, implied by the apt use of the "bone" image, that painting and calligraphy share in common.[①]

It was through the practice of calligraphy—whether the square, powerful li-shu[②] (clerk's hand) of the Han Dynasty, the elegant standard kai-shu[③], the cursive xing-shu[④], or the still more cursive cao-shu[⑤] (grass writing)—that the scholar-gentleman refined and developed his sense of balance, movement, and form[⑥]. Calligraphy has often been compared to modern Western abstract expressionism and "action painting," for both are the product of the controlled nervous energy of the hand that holds the brush. But the comparison is a misleading one. For the Western abstract painter, pure form, divorced from content, is all; form, in fact, is content. But even the most extreme of Chinese expressionists always sought a meaning beyond pure form. The passage of calligraphy would be less admirable if it were totally illegible or its content trivial. In painting, the most outrageous techniques of the modern abstract expressionists were anticipated by Chinese eccentrics in the eighth and ninth centuries: one master would flip his ink-soaked hair at the silk; another splash it with ink while he danced to music, facing in the opposite direction; a third would spread ink in pools on silk laid out on the floor, then drag an assistant round and round sitting on a sheet. But these bizarre methods were never ends in themselves. The records tell us—for unhappily not one of these remarkable pictures has survived—that having thus spilled their ink, the painters then proceeded, by the deft addition of scattered trees, waterfalls, and pavilions, to turn their smears and blotches into landscapes. The Zen ink painters of the twelfth and thirteenth centuries expressed their moment of illumination in brushwork hardly less explosive. Here at least we might expect to find pure abstraction. But Mu Xi[⑦] and Ying Yuqian conveyed their metaphysical excitement not in empty gestures with the brush, but in the shape of a monk tearing up the sutras, or a mountain village emerging out of the mist. For the painter, as for the calligrapher, mere form was never enough.

---

① Osvald Sirén's Chinese on *the Art of Painting* (Peking, 1936), of which a revised edition is in preparation, provides a useful introduction to Chinese critical and theoretical writings, some of which are translated and discussed in more detail in William R. B. Acker, *Some Tang and Pre-Tang Texts on Chinese Painting* (Leiden, 1954).

② 隶书。

③ 楷书。

④ 行书。

⑤ 草书。

⑥ Chiang Yee, *Chinese Calligraphy* (London, 1954), is a good general introduction to this subject.

⑦ （南宋）牧谿。

D. The Perfection of the Chinese in the Art of Gardening[①]
中国园林艺术的完善

Oliver Goldsmith
奥利弗·哥德史密斯

The English have not yet brought the art of gardening the same perfection with the Chinese, but have lately begun to imitate them; Nature is now followed with greater assiduity than formerly; the trees are suffered to shoot out the utmost luxuriance; the streams no longer forced from their native beds, are permitted to wind along the valleys; spontaneous flowers take place of the finished parterre, and the enameled meadow of the shaven green.

Yet still the English are far behind us in this charming art; their designers have not yet attained a power of uniting instruction with beauty. A European will scarcely conceive my meaning, when I say that there is scarce a garden in China which does not contain some fine moral, couched under the general design, where one is not taught wisdom as he walks, and feels the force of some noble truth or delicate precept resulting from the disposition of the groves, streams or grottoes. Permit me to illustrate what I mean by a description of my gardens at Quamsi. My heart still hovers round those scenes of former happiness with pleasure; and I find a satisfaction in enjoying them at this distance, though but in imagination.

You descended from the house between two groves of trees, planted in such a manner, that they were impenetrable to the eye; while on each hand the way was adorned with all that was beautiful in porcelain, statuary, and painting. This passage from the house opened into an area surrounded with rocks, flowers, trees, and shrubs, but all so disposed as if each was the spontaneous production of Nature. As you proceeded forward on this lawn, to your right and left hand were two gates, opposite each other, of very different architecture and design; and before you lay a temple built rather with minute elegance than ostentation.

The right hand gate was planned with the utmost simplicity, or rather rudeness; ivy clasped round the pillars, the baleful cypress hung over it; time seemed to have destroyed all the smoothness and regularity of the stone: two champions with lifted clubs appeared in the act of guarding its access; dragons and serpents were seen in the most hideous attitudes, to deter the spectator from approaching; and the perspective view that lay behind, seemed dark and gloomy to the last degree; the stranger was tempted to enter only from the motto: PERVIA VIRTUTI.

The opposite gate was formed in a very different manner; the architecture was light, elegant,

---

① Excerpted from Oliver Goldsmith, *The Citizen of the World*, J. M. Dent & Sons Ltd., 1934.

and inviting; flowers hung in wreaths round the pillars; all was finished in the most exact and masterly manner; the very stone of which it was built, still preserved its polish; nymphs, wrought by the hand of a master in the most alluring attitudes, beckoned the stranger to approach; while all that lay behind, as far as the eye could reach, seemed gay and capable of affording endless pleasure. The motto itself contributed to invite him; for over the gate written these words FACILIS DESCENSUS.

<u>By this time I fancy you begin to perceive that gloomy gate was designed to represent the road to Virtue; the opposite, the more agreeable passage to Vice.</u> It is but natural to suppose, that the spectator was always to tempted to enter by the gate, which offered him so many allurement; I always in these cases left him to his choice; but generally found that he took to the left, which promised most entertainment.

Immediately upon his entering the gate of Vice, the trees and flowers were disposed in such a manner as to make the most pleasing impression; but as he walked farther on, he insensibly found the garden assume the air of a wilderness, the landscapes began to darken, the paths grew more intricate, he appeared to go downwards, frightful rocks seemed to hang over his head, gloomy caverns, unexpected precipices, awful ruins, heaps of unburied bones, and terrifying sounds, caused by unseen waters began to take place of what at first appeared so lovely; it was in vain to attempt returning, the labyrinth was too much perplexed for any but myself to find the way back. In short when sufficiently impressed with the horrors of what he saw, and the imprudence of his choice, I brought him by a hidden door, a shorter way back into the area from whence at first he had strayed.

The gloomy gate now presented itself before the stranger; and though there seemed little in its appearance to tempt his curiosity, yet encouraged by the motto, he generally proceeded. The darkness of the entrance, the frightful figures that seemed to obstruct his way, the trees of a mournful green, conspired at first to disgust him: as he went forward, however all began to open and wear a more pleasing appearance, beautiful cascades, beds of flowers, trees loaded with fruit or blossoms, and unexpected brooks, improved the scene: he now found that he was ascending, and, as he proceeded, all Nature grew more beautiful, the prospect widened as he went higher, even the air itself, seemed to become more pure. Thus pleased and happy from unexpected beauties, I at last led him to an arbor, from whence he could view the garden, and the whole country around, and where he might own that the road to Virtue terminated in Happiness.

Though from this description you may imagine, that a vast tract of ground was necessary to exhibit such a pleasing variety in, yet be assured I have seen several gardens in England take up ten times the space which mine did, without half the beauty. A very small extent of ground is enough for an elegant taste; the greater room is required if magnificence is in view. <u>There is no</u>

spot, though ever so little, which a skillful designer might not thus improve, so as to convey a delicate allegory, and impress the mind with truths the most useful and necessary. Adieu.

Exercises

I. **Vocabulary Practice**

1. Define the term "universal love" (jian ai) as presented in the *Mohist Canons* and use it in a sentence to reflect its philosophical meaning.
2. Explain the concept of "Legalism" in the context of *Han Fei Tzu* and provide an example of how this might be applied in governance.
3. Use the term "meritocracy" in a sentence that illustrates its significance in the Mohist philosophy.
4. Explain the "white horse dialogue" from *The Kung-sun Lung Tzu*.
5. Explain the strategic concept of "knowing one's self and one's enemy" from *The Art of War* by Sun Tzu, and discuss its relevance in non-military contexts.

II. **Comprehension**

A. Read the excerpts from the Basic Readings and answer the following questions:

6. How does the *Mohist Canons* challenge conventional thinking regarding the ethics of favoritism and nepotism?
7. In *Han Fei Tzu*, what is the significance of the ruler's control over the power of punishment and kindness?
8. Explain the paradox presented in *The Kung-sun Lung Tzu* regarding the identity of a white horse in relation to the concept of a horse and its bearing on the nature of language.
9. What are the five constant factors of warfare mentioned in *The Art of War*, and why are they essential for a general to understand?

B. Analyze the modern interpretations in the extensive readings and answer the following questions:

10. How does Frederick W. Mote's "Implications of Chinese Epistemology" contrast Chinese thought with Western philosophy?
11. According to Gu Hongming in *The Spirit of the Chinese People*, what is the role of moral force in Chinese civilization, and how does it differ from the role of Christianity in Europe?
12. In Michael Sullivan's view, how does Chinese painting and calligraphy reflect the

understanding of the universe and human condition?

13. Explain the moral allegory present in the art of Chinese gardens as described by Oliver Goldsmith, and how it serves as a medium for imparting wisdom.

III. Application and Interpretation

A. Compare the Mohist concept of universal love with the Confucian idea of love, and explore how they might be applied to address modern societal issues such as inequality and discrimination.

B. Consider the broader impact of Chinese intellectual history and write essays on:

14. The influence of Chinese philosophical thought on contemporary environmental practices and the concept of living in harmony with nature.
15. The potential impact of adopting Chinese epistemological approaches on Western scientific methodologies and vice versa.
16. The relevance of ancient Chinese military strategy on modern geopolitical conflicts and the pursuit of peace.
17. A comparative analysis of Chinese and Western approaches to art and aesthetics, and their implications for global cultural exchange.

C. Reflect on personal development and societal roles:

18. How can the teachings of *The Art of War* inform personal strategies for self-improvement and conflict resolution in one's personal life?
19. How might the Chinese emphasis on moral force and good citizenship, as described by Gu Hongming, inspire or critique current models of civic education and social responsibility?